Analytical studies in transport economics

Analytical studies in transport economics

Edited by

Andrew F. Daughety

The University of Iowa

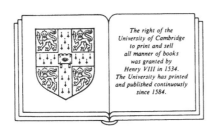

The right of the
University of Cambridge
to print and sell
all manner of books
was granted by
Henry VIII in 1534.
The University has printed
and published continuously
since 1584.

CAMBRIDGE UNIVERSITY PRESS

Cambridge

London   New York   New Rochelle

Melbourne   Sydney

CAMBRIDGE UNIVERSITY PRESS
Cambridge, New York, Melbourne, Madrid, Cape Town, Singapore, São Paulo

Cambridge University Press
The Edinburgh Building, Cambridge CB2 8RU, UK

Published in the United States of America by Cambridge University Press, New York

www.cambridge.org
Information on this title: www.cambridge.org/9780521268103

First published 1985
This digitally printed version 2008

A catalogue record for this publication is available from the British Library

Library of Congress Cataloguing in Publication data
Main entry under title:
Analytical studies in transport economics.
Includes index.
1. Transportation – Addresses, essays, lectures.
I. Daughety, Andrew F.
HE152.6.A53   1985   380.5′9   85–2615

ISBN 978-0-521-26810-3 hardback
ISBN 978-0-521-07087-4 paperback

Contents

Contributors   vii
Preface   ix

INTRODUCTION

1. **Analytical transport economics – structure and
   overview**   3
   Andrew F. Daughety

TECHNOLOGY AND DEMAND

2. **Augmentation effects and technical change in the
   regulated trucking industry, 1974–1979**   29
   Ann F. Friedlaender and Sharon Schur Bruce
3. **An econometric analysis of the cost and production
   structure of the trucking industry**   65
   Andrew F. Daughety, Forrest D. Nelson, and
   William R. Vigdor
4. **Network effects and the measurement of returns to
   scale and density for U.S. railroads**   97
   Douglas W. Caves, Laurits R. Christensen,
   Michael W. Tretheway, and Robert J. Windle
5. **Using indexed quadratic cost functions to model
   network technologies**   121
   Richard H. Spady
6. **Joint estimation of freight transportation decisions
   under nonrandom sampling**   137
   Daniel McFadden, Clifford Winston, and
   Axel Boersch-Supan

EQUILIBRIUM, PRICING, AND MARKET
BEHAVIOR

7. **Freight network equilibrium: a review of the state
   of the art.**   161
   Terry L. Friesz and Patrick T. Harker

8. Efficient pricing with rivalry between a railroad and a pipeline   207
Ronald R. Braeutigam

9. Airline deregulation, fares, and market behavior: some empirical evidence   221
Gregory D. Call and Theodore E. Keeler

Index   249

Contributors

Axel Boersch-Supan, J. F. Kennedy School of Government, Harvard University

Ronald R. Braeutigam, Department of Economics, Northwestern University

Sharon Schur Bruce, Tri County Regional Planning Commission, Lansing, Michigan

Gregory D. Call, Department of Economics, University of California, Berkeley

Douglas W. Caves, Department of Economics, University of Wisconsin-Madison and Christensen Associates

Laurits R. Christensen, Department of Economics, University of Wisconsin-Madison and Christensen Associates

Andrew F. Daughety, College of Business Administration, University of Iowa

Ann F. Friedlaender, Department of Economics, Massachusetts Institute of Technology

Terry L. Friesz, School of Engineering and Applied Science, University of Pennsylvania

Patrick T. Harker, The Wharton School, University of Pennsylvania

Theodore E. Keeler, Department of Economics, University of California, Berkeley

Daniel McFadden, Department of Economics, Massachusetts Institute of Technology

Forrest D. Nelson, College of Business Administration, University of Iowa

Richard H. Spady, Bell Communications Research, Morristown, New Jersey

Michael W. Tretheway, Faculty of Commerce and Business Administration, The University of British Columbia

William R. Vigdor, College of Business Administration, University of Iowa

Robert J. Windle, Department of Economics, University of Wisconsin-Madison and Christensen Associates

Clifford Winston, The Brookings Institution

Preface

This book is a collection of new research papers concerned with the application of modern economic theory and analytical techniques to current issues in transportation economics, especially for many of the systems that are undergoing, or have recently undergone, regulatory change. Two themes unite the chapters of this volume. First, characterization: How should we think about the agents and interactions we see? How should we model carrier technology, shipper demand, network structure, and market equilibrium? Second, policy formation and evaluation: How can we use analytical techniques to examine policies of the past, present, and future? How do we examine the effects of regulation on industry productivity or structure, or the effects of regulatory change on industry competitiveness? All the chapters of this book involve (to varying degrees) these two themes of characterization and policy formation and evaluation.

It is especially easy to thank the appropriate people for their help with this book; the reader need only look at the table of contents to see most of the names that deserve mention. Ronald Braeutigam, Douglas Caves, Ann Friedlaender, Theodore Keeler, Forrest Nelson, Richard Spady, Michael Tretheway, and Clifford Winston all did extra duty by helping in the refereeing/reviewing process for one or more of the chapters. I also especially wish to thank Ann Friedlaender for her early support and ready commitment on this project and Donald McCloskey for his helpful advice at the formative stages of its development. Nejat Anbarci provided very able assistance by almost single-handedly performing the onerous task of constructing the index. Colin Day, Margaret Willard, and Cynthia Benn of Cambridge University Press successfully conspired to make the process of developing and producing this book pleasant. The National Science Foundation provided support under the Regulation and Policy Analysis Program, grant SES-8218684.

Introduction

CHAPTER 1

Analytical transport economics – structure and overview

ANDREW F. DAUGHETY

> The nature of the subject has made it essential to the convenient and concise demonstration of the principles which are the objects of the research, to admit the introduction of mathematical formula throughout the investigation.
>
> Charles Ellet, Jr., *An Essay on the Laws of Trade* (1839)

Since Charles Ellet's insightful analysis of optimal tariffs for a waterway in a competitive environment, a rich and extensive literature has developed involving the application of microeconomic theory and analysis to issues and policies in the economics of transportation, via the use of mathematical and statistical techniques. This book contributes to this literature in three ways. First, all of the chapters are concerned with the analysis of current issues: questions of industry productivity, of economies of density and scale, of pricing and competition, of the structure of technology, and of the prediction of equilibrium. Second, each of these essays endeavors to extend and apply microeconomic theory to its particular issue. This often involves an extension of modeling and statistical techniques in the process. Furthermore, in pursuing this second aspect the authors of the essays have been able to present their research design and methodology in more detail than is usually possible in a journal article. Thus a third contribution is to lower the costs of entry for nonspecialists into this field.

The purpose of this chapter is to help place the volume in context.[1] A mathematical structure within which to cast the chapters in the current book and those in the recent literature will be provided. A model of a carrier, incorporating aspects of its network, will be developed, followed by a related

Support by National Science Foundation grant SES-8218684 is gratefully acknowledged. This chapter has benefited from comments by Clifford Winston.

[1] Standard sources for institutional aspects of the transportation industries are Locklin (1972) and Pegrum (1968). For an early comprehensive analysis of regulatory issues in transportation, see Friedlaender (1969). Winston (1984) discusses some of the issues covered here in a less formal manner.

3

model for a shipper.[2] This will allow comparison and integration of the five chapters of the second part of this book, which are concerned with technology and demand. The last three chapters in the volume consider problems of forecasting equilibria, formulating optimal price regulation, and analyzing evolving market structure under deregulation. These analyses implicitly or explicitly draw on variations of the carrier and shipper models.

The essays in this volume examine a broad range of issues in technology, demand, equilibrium, pricing, and market structure. Each is self-contained, but a number of linkages exist between the chapters.

1.   Agents

1.1.   Technology: the carriers

Producers of transport service are called "carriers." Carriers redistribute (spatially and temporally) physical quantities of goods. A carrier moves goods from one location to another, and such moves take time. The markets that a carrier serves consist of pairs of geographically separated points. For example, a railroad might provide service from New York (NY) to Chicago and then provide service from Chicago to Los Angeles (LA), and then turn around and make the Los Angeles to Chicago run, followed by return to New York. Thus, the railroad serves six markets: NY–Chicago, Chicago–LA, LA–Chicago, Chicago–NY, NY–LA via Chicago, and LA–NY via Chicago. We can imagine this as a simple three-node network as illustrated in Figure 1.1.

The arcs between the nodes (the solid lines) help to designate the markets. For convenience, let i and j be two nodes in a firm's network. If i and j are directly linked (and the link allows travel from i to j) then we can denote an "arc" as (i,j). A "path" between two nodes i and j is a sequence of arcs and nodes that are traversed in order to proceed from i to j, and is specified by a tuple that lists, in order, the nodes encountered on the path, starting at i and ending at j. Thus, for example, arcs are "one-step" paths.

As in the case of the railroad mentioned previously, the markets for a carrier are the paths of its network. This can be seen by examining Figure 1.1 again. If the firm could add the direct service from Los Angeles to New York (the dashed line) a new market would be added; this is a new path in the

---

2 In the next subsection two agents are considered: carriers and shippers. There is, of course, a third agent, namely, the state. Positive models of this agent pursuing objective functions other than social welfare maximization have been developed; see Stigler (1971) and Peltzman (1976). However, since the only chapter in this book explicitly examining problems of regulators (Braeutigam, Chapter 8), is normative and involves a social-welfare-maximizing regulator, the following exposition will be limited to this situation.

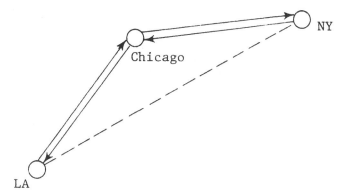

Figure 1.1. A simple network.

network, which is likely to entail different costs for the carrier from the LA–Chicago–NY path and may possibly serve different customers than the old path from LA to NY, since it is likely to incur shorter transit times than the old path.

To formalize this, let M be the set of origin–destination (OD) nodes served by a carrier (for convenience, there are m such nodes). Thus, OD pairs are drawn from $M \times M$. Further, let M' be the set of nodes that *augment* M by being locations of pure transshipment (for example, consolidation and break-bulk facilities for less-than-truckload (LTL) motor carriers).[3] Thus, the set of nodes for the firm's network is $M \cup M'$. Finally, let A be the set of arcs linking elements of $M \cup M'$. For a railroad this is line haul track; for a regulated motor carrier this is its operating rights and route authority; for a water carrier it is the river system.

In the terminology of graph theory (see Harary, 1969) the nodes and arcs describe a graph (or network) $\mathbf{G} = (M \cup M', A)$. Note that $\mathbf{G}$ represents a spatial arrangement of nodes and their interconnections, and not the actual facilities, markets, plants, roads, track, and so on. These items are part of capital inputs (to the degree that the firm must provide them).

Let $\mathcal{P}$ be the set of all paths from elements of $M \cup M'$ to $M \cup M'$. As an example, consider Figure 1.2, which shows a path p from node i_0 to node i_5 in a network. The dark lines represent the path (note that it is not the only way to get from i_0 to i_5), and the dashed lines represent the rest of the network. We can subdivide the set $\mathcal{P}$ into two parts, market paths and nonmarket paths. If i_0 (the path origin) and i_5 (the path destination) each belong to M, we will say

---

[3] For a railroad, M' contains the end points of stretches of a competitor's network over which the firm under study has trackage rights.

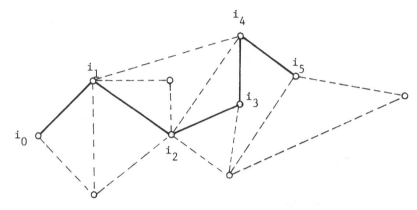

Figure 1.2. The path $(i_0, i_1, i_2, i_3, i_4, i_5)$.

that p is a "market" path; the set of such paths is denoted $\mathcal{P}^M$. All other paths will be denoted $\mathcal{P}^{\bar{M}}$, the nonmarket paths.

The set $\mathcal{P}^M$ is the set of "products" (outputs) of the carrier. Changes in this set of paths (additions, deletions) represent changes in the firm's mix of product lines. Changes in $\mathcal{P}^{\bar{M}}$ are taken to reflect purely operational effects. Thus, if a facility location is added to M' and paths change in $\mathcal{P}^{\bar{M}}$ but not in $\mathcal{P}^M$, then that change in facility location has had no effect on the firm's product mix (it may, however, affect the cost of providing service – that is, of producing the products). Elements of $\mathcal{P}^{\bar{M}}$ involve paths from M to M', from M' to M and from M' to M'. Note that concatenations of some of these paths yield paths in $\mathcal{P}^M$. Finally note that the foregoing setup is not as restrictive as might first appear. The definitions of M and M' depend upon the firm (or the analyst) and thus can be as coarse or as fine as necessary.

Associated with a path $p \in \mathcal{P}$ is a vector of quantities of goods moved and a vector of service characteristics provided. Let z_{pk} be the quantity of commodity k shipped on path p, and let $\mathbf{z} \in R^{PK}$ be the vector of such flows, where P is the number of paths and K the number of commodities. Activity on a path is also characterized by various service characteristics. Examples of service characteristics are speed; schedule reliability (some notion of variability of departure or arrival times); physical reliability (record of loss and damage, for example); availability or frequency of service and accessibility (by means of a rail spur to a plant, for instance). Let $\mathbf{s}_{pk}$ be the vector of service characteristics associated with the movement of commodity k on path p; thus $\mathbf{s}_{pk} \in R^S$, where S is the number of service characteristics. The vector $\mathbf{s} \in R^{SPK}$ provides levels of service characteristics on all paths for all commodities.

To summarize, the output of the firm is its market paths $\mathcal{P}^M$ and associated characteristics $(\mathbf{z}, \mathbf{s})^M$, where the superscript M denotes the portion of the vector $(\mathbf{z}, \mathbf{s})$ associated with the market paths. The nonmarket paths $\mathcal{P}^{\overline{M}}$ and associated characteristics $(\mathbf{z}, \mathbf{s})^{\overline{M}}$ should be thought of as intermediate products of the firm, that is, activity necessary in the production of final product.

Now let $\mathbf{x} \in R^n$ ($\mathbf{x} \geq 0$) be a vector of inputs (capital, labor, fuel, and so forth) and let $\mathbf{q} \in R^n$ ($\mathbf{q} > 0$) be the prices at which the firm can purchase $\mathbf{x}$. Finally, let T represent technology, which is an implicit transformation function relating the graph $\mathbf{G}$ and output characteristics $\mathbf{z}$ and $\mathbf{s}$ to input factor levels $\mathbf{x}$, given that $\mathbf{G}$ is specified as previously:

$$T(\cdot, \cdot, \cdot|\mathbf{G}): \quad R^{PK} \times R^{SPK} \times R^n \to R.$$

Feasible production of $(\mathbf{z}, \mathbf{s})$ occurs if there is a vector $\mathbf{x}$ such that $T(\mathbf{z},\mathbf{s},\mathbf{x}|\mathbf{G}) \leq 0$. Thus, the technology that takes inputs $\mathbf{x}$ and transforms them to path characteristics $(\mathbf{z}, \mathbf{s})$ is dependent on the graph $\mathbf{G}$; changes in $\mathbf{G}$ are thought of as shifts over a family of T functions (see McFadden, 1978 for the role of shift parameters in technology characterizations).

Dual to this technology is the firm's cost function (see McFadden, 1978 or Shephard, 1970), which is defined to be a function of $(\mathbf{z}, \mathbf{s})^M$, the input prices $\mathbf{q}$, and the graph $\mathbf{G}$.

$$C((\mathbf{z}, \mathbf{s})^M, \mathbf{q}|\mathbf{G}) = \min\{\mathbf{q}'\mathbf{x}| \ T(\mathbf{z}, \mathbf{s}, \mathbf{x}|\mathbf{G}) \leq 0\}.$$

Note that (besides $\mathbf{q}$ and $\mathbf{G}$) only output characteristics on market paths are held fixed; output characteristics on $\mathcal{P}^{\overline{M}}$ are varied optimally by the firm to achieve minimum cost.

The dimension of $(\mathbf{z}, \mathbf{s})^M$ is at least $K(1 + S)(m^2 - m)$, where m is the number of nodes in M. This is because there are K commodities, S service characteristics [and thus $K(1 + S)$ elements per path in $\mathcal{P}^M$] and at least $m^2 - m$ paths in $\mathcal{P}^M$ (assuming nodes do not ship to themselves). Even for small values of K, S, and m this dimension is large. Because of this problem, analyses have often proceeded by introducing some sort of aggregate-flow variable, the typical one being ton-miles. Let $d(p)$ be the length of path p and let $z_p = \sum_k z_{pk}$. If z_{pk} are measured in tons and path length in miles, then the standard ton-mile aggregate, y, is simply

$$y = \sum_{p \in \mathcal{P}^M} z_p \cdot d(p),$$

thereby yielding the aggregate-flow cost model $C(y, (\mathbf{s})^M, \mathbf{q}|\mathbf{G})$. Further simplification has often been achieved by ignoring service characteristics and suppressing $\mathbf{G}$, yielding the model $C(y,\mathbf{q})$. Finally, as will be seen subsequently, some railroad studies have allowed for aggregate freight and passenger variables, y_F and y_P. If "commodity" K is passengers, then this approach may be viewed as the aggregation

$$y_F = \sum_{p \in \mathcal{P}^M} \sum_{k=1}^{K-1} z_{pk} d(p),$$

$$y_p = \sum_{p \in \mathcal{P}^M} z_{pK} d(p),$$

and the corresponding cost model is $C(y_F, y_P, \mathbf{q})$.

Notions of scale and scope economies (see Baumol, Panzar, and Willig, 1982) can be precisely applied by controlling elements of $\mathbf{z}$, $\mathbf{s}$, and $\mathbf{G}$. Following Keeler (1974) and Harris (1977), economies (diseconomies) of density occur if, holding the size of a transport system fixed, increases in throughput are associated with decreases (increases) in average costs, while economies (diseconomies) of size occur if increases in throughput are associated with decreases (increases) in average costs (allowing the size of the firm to vary). A number of considerations are implicit in the foregoing definitions. First, service characteristics on $\mathcal{P}^M$, denoted $(\mathbf{s})^M$, are held constant. Second, density economies involve holding $\mathbf{G}$ constant, whereas size economies involve varying $\mathbf{G}$ in some way such as varying M as by mergers or route expansions (note that end-to-end mergers involve changes in $\mathcal{P}^M$, whereas purely parallel mergers might affect $\mathcal{P}^{\overline{M}}$ only). Third, reference to "average costs" reflects the use of an aggregate measure of throughput, such as ton-miles (y). When cast in the more current terminology, density economies are measured as ray (or product-specific) scale economies for fixed $\mathbf{G}$, whereas "size" economies actually depend on product-specific economies, scope economies, and cost subadditivity (since changes in the product set $\mathcal{P}^M$ are involved). The issue of "declining" cost in terms of size economies is more properly posed, then, as the question of whether (varying $\mathbf{G}$) the technology generates a subadditive cost structure. Of course, if the cost model in question uses an aggregate measure of throughput such as ton-miles, the ability to examine scope economies is lost, although size economies are measured allowing $\mathbf{G}$ to vary. Aspects of this issue are discussed in three chapters of this book: Friedlaender and Bruce (Chapter 2), Daughety, Nelson, and Vigdor (Chapter 3), and, especially, Caves, Christensen, Tretheway, and Windle (Chapter 4).

Table 1.1 uses the foregoing model specification to classify a section of carrier cost models for railroads (RR) and motor carriers (MC). It is important to note that this table is not meant to be comprehensive. Rather, the purpose is to list studies that reflect significant differences and important commonalities in cost function models and approaches. Note also that studies involving production-function approaches have been left out because the table concentrates on cost models.[4] Moreover, nonoptimizing approaches, as is common in expenditure models based on accounting costs or engineering relationships, have also been excluded.

The vast majority of studies have been cross-section analyses of a sample of firms, usually using data from the Interstate Commerce Commission (or, in the case of motor carriers, from Trincs, which uses ICC data). The Jara-Diaz and Winston (1981), Braeutigam, Daughety, and Turnquist (1982, 1984), and Daughety, Turnquist, and Griesbach (1983) studies of railroads provide firm-level analyses and use proprietary data, which allow explicit network representations or measurement of service characteristics. Wang Chiang and Friedlaender (1984) provide a cross-section study of motor carriers in which subaggregates of throughput (LTL traffic for various mileage blocks) and measures of network characteristics are used in the cost function (for a recent review of some cost models, see Jara-Diaz, 1982). Attempts to control for the mix of commodity types through incorporation of per ton-mile insurance cost are used by some of the more recent motor carrier studies (including both the Friedlaender and Bruce and the Daughety, Nelson, and Vigdor chapters in this book).

1.2.   Demand: the shipper

Shippers and receivers (as well as travelers) are the consumers of transport service. Given the coverage of this book, this discussion will focus on shippers and receivers, although many of the ideas apply to travelers as well. Shippers and receivers engage in productive activity that is spatially distributed and requires transport service to bring raw materials to plants, ship intermediate products between fabrication and assembly points, move final product to national, regional, or local warehouses, and distribute goods from warehouse inventories to stores or directly to customers. They may also need to ship natural gas or crude oil or petroleum products from fields to refineries or from refineries to stocking points, power plants, or gas stations, or they may ship coal or grain or live or processed animals nationally or internationally. The shipping firm can be characterized as a network wherein arcs and paths are a mix of firm-operated transport (firm-owned fleets, for example), purchased transport (from carriers), and publicly provided transport (say, to move workers to and from plants and other facilities).

The model of a shipper that will be developed is similar to the carrier model in the previous section. In particular a shipper will be viewed as operating a firm that consists of spatially separated nodes, and using carriers to provide

[4] See, for example, Borts (1952), Klein (1953), and Hasenkamp (1976).

Table 1.1. *Recent cost studies for railroad and motor carriers*

Studies	z	s	q	G	Model	Data used (source, time frame, number, type of series)
Railroads						
Grilliches (1972)	Ton-miles	—	—	Miles of road	L	ICC, 1957–61: 97 selected firms (CS)
Keeler (1974)	Ton-miles, passenger-miles	—	Track-miles[a]	—	NL	ICC, 1967–70: 51 selected firms (CS)
Harris (1977)	Revenue, ton-miles, revenue tons	—	—	Miles of road, urban/ nonurban	L	ICC, 1972–73: 55 selected firms (CS)
Harmatuck (1978)	Ton-miles	—	Way and structures, yard, train, equipment	Miles of road, region	TL	ICC, 1968–70: 40 selected firms (CS) –subset of Keeler
Caves, Christensen, and Swanson (1980, 1981)	Ton-miles, length of haul, passenger-miles, length of trip	—	Labor, fuel, capital, and materials	—	TL	ICC, 1955, 63, 74: 58, 56, 40 selected firms (CS/TS)
Friedlaender and Spady (1981)	Revenue-ton-miles, passenger-miles	—	General labor, yard labor, crews, fuel and material, equipment, way, and structures capital[a]	Low-density route-miles, length of haul, traffic mix	TL, FOAC	ICC, 1968–70: 58 selected firms (CS/TS)
Jara-Diaz and Winston (1981)	Origin–destination specific tons	—	Fuel	Explicit representation of three-node railroad (class III)	Q	Firm data 1975–80: (monthly) 2 firms (TS)
Braeutigam, Daughety, and Turnquist (1982, 1984)	Ton-miles	Speed through system	Fuel, labor, equipment, miles of track[a]	—	TL, FOAC	(1982): firm data 1969–78: (monthly) class II railroad (TS)

10

Study	Output		Inputs	Other variables	Functional form	Data
						(1984): firm data 1976–78: (monthly) class I railroad (TS)
Daughety, Turquist, and Griesbach (1983)	Short-, medium-, and long-haul carloads constructed from network model and path marginal costs	—	Fuel, labor, equipment, miles of track[a]	Explicit network model	TL	1976–79 (monthly): class I railroad (TS)
Caves, Christensen, Tretheway, and Windle (Chapter 4)	Ton-miles, length of haul, passenger-miles, length of trip	—	Labor, fuel, materials, and capital	Route-miles, firm-specific effects	TL	ICC, 1951–75: panel data on 43 selected firms (CS/TS)
Motor carriers						
Koenker (1977)	Ton-miles, length of haul, load	—	—	—	CD with lags	Trincs, 1948–72: 25 selected firms (CS/TS) (CS/TS)
Spady and Friedlaender (1978)	Hedonic output: ψ (ton-miles, length of haul, size, load, insurance, % LTL)	—	Labor, fuel, capital, purchased transportation	—	TL–TL: partial quartic	Trincs, 1972: 168 selected firms for Central, Mid-Atlantic and New England ICC regions (CS)
Friedlaender and Spady (1981), Friedlaender, Spady, and Wang Chiang (1981)	Ton-miles	—	Labor, fuel, capital, purchased transportation	Length of haul, load, size, % LTL, insurance, ton-miles/terminal (for interregional carriers)	TL	Trincs, 1972: 362 specialized commodity carriers by region (official South-West); 362 general freight carriers by region and type (CS) (official, South-West, interregional)

(continued)

Table 1.1. (Continued)

Studies	z	s	q	G	Model	Data used (source, time frame, number, type of series)
Harmatuck (1981)	Number and weight of truckload shipments, number and weight of LTL shipments, length of haul	—	Line-haul, pickup/delivery, billing, handling	—	TL	Trincs, 1976: 100 selected general freight carriers (CS)
Wang Chiang and Friedlaender (1984)	Hedonic output: ψ (ton-miles by type of LTL shipment ≤250, 250–500, ≥500 miles), TL ton-miles, corridor-specific operating characteristics		Labor, fuel, equipment, general capital, purchased transportation	Network measures: connectivity, density, indirect routing, terminal density	TL, CD function for ψ	ICC Continuing Traffic Survey, 1976: 105 selected firms (CS)
Friedlaender and Bruce (Chapter 2)	Ton-miles, insurance cost per ton-mile, % LTL traffic	—	Labor, fuel, equipment, general capital, purchased transportation	Length of haul, load, size	TL with time augmentation	ICC Annual Report Tapes, 1974–79: 85 selected firms (CS/TS)
Daughety, Nelson, and Vigdor (Chapter 3)	Ton-miles, insurance cost per ton-mile	—	Labor, fuel, capital, purchased transportation	Length of haul, load, size	TL–TL: partial quartic	Trincs, 1953–58: 3,085 observations on general-commodity carriers (CS/TS)

Abbreviations: CD, Cobb–Douglas; CS, cross section; FOAC, first-order autocorrelation error structure; L, linear; NL, nonlinear; Q, quadratic; TL, translog; TS, time series.

Note: Dash means variable type not used.

[a]Fixed factor. In the case of Keeler (1974) and Brauetigam, Daughety, and Turnquist (1984), this variable was used to provide envelope cost functions.

12

the arcs between the nodes. The nodes will be of three types: (1) the set of origins, denoted $\mathcal{O}$; (2) the set of destinations $\mathcal{D}$; these would typically be points of sale of goods (markets, stores, or customers); (3) the set intermediate points $\mathcal{I}$; these would typically be warehouses or other points of transshipment. Thus the set of nodes for the shipper is $N = \mathcal{O} \cup \mathcal{D} \cup \mathcal{I}$. In such a setup, the resulting graphs will have paths with arcs going from $\mathcal{O}$ to $\mathcal{D}$ via $\mathcal{I}$, but not the reverse.

Pieces of market paths from carrier networks therefore provide paths that link up elements of N for the shipper. Of course it may be necessary to concatenate a few pieces of paths from different carriers to provide a path in the shipper's network; in this practice, called "interlining," a sequence of carriers is used to ship a good from one point in N to another. Moreover, because more than one carrier (and possibly more than one transport technology) may provide paths between the same two points in N, the shipper faces a choice among modes and carriers.

Let z_{ijkp} be the quantity of commodity k ($k = 1, \ldots, K$) to be shipped from origin i ($i \in \mathcal{O}$) to destination j ($j \in \mathcal{D}$) following path p (which starts at i and ends at j) and let $\mathbf{z}$ be the vector of such flows. Here a path will not only reflect a sequence of nodes in N but also the carriers (and modes) used in sequence along the path. Thus two paths could follow the same sequence of nodes in N but be different (and have different values of the index p) because different carriers were used to accomplish the job.

To formalize this, let $\mathcal{A}(N, \mathcal{C}, K)$ be the set of arc sets A such that every node in N appears as the end point in at least one arc in A, and where $\mathcal{C}$ is the arc-specific list of carriers and modes. Thus picking an arc set A from $\mathcal{A}(N, \mathcal{C}, K)$ produces a graph $\mathbf{G} = (N,A)$ wherein elements of N are linked up by the arcs. Further, we have fully specified which carriers or modes are linking which points and which commodities are on which arcs. For example, if $N = \{A,B\}$, $k = 1$, and $\mathcal{A} = \{\{A \text{ to } B \text{ by rail}\}, \{A \text{ to } B \text{ by truck}\}\}$, then one possible A is $A = \{A \text{ to } B \text{ by truck}\}$.

A choice of an arc set A means that associated with the path p (in $\mathbf{G} = (N,A)$) is the vector of service characteristics $\mathbf{s}_{pk} \in R^S$. Let the vector of characteristics for a specific arc set A be $\mathbf{s}_A$. This vector of characteristics of the carriers or modes to be used to move the various commodities from $\mathcal{O}$ to $\mathcal{D}$ is an *input* to the overall production process of the shipper, which involves the acquisition of raw materials and the production and distribution of products.

Let $\mathbf{x}^1$ be the vector of nontransport inputs to the firm such as labor and capital, and let $\mathbf{q}^1$ be the vector of prices. Let $\mathbf{x}^2$ be the vector of transport inputs where a representative element of $\mathbf{x}^2$ is x^2_{ijkp}; that is, each element of $\mathbf{x}^2$ is a flow on an arc (i,j) that belongs to a path p, over which commodity k is being sent. The associated vector of transport rates is $\mathbf{q}^2$. Moreover, let $\mathbf{x}^2$ be of maximum dimension – that is, of length sufficient for an arc set that would create a *complete* graph **G** (arcs between every two nodes in N). Thus, for any particular A, many of the elements of $\mathbf{x}^2$ are zero, while others add up to the flows in **z**. Finally, let $\mathbf{x} \equiv (\mathbf{x}^{1'}, \mathbf{x}^{2'})'$; **x** is the column vector concatenation of $\mathbf{x}^1$ and $\mathbf{x}^2$, and $\mathbf{q} \equiv (\mathbf{q}^{1'}, \mathbf{q}^{2'})'$ is the associated price vector.[5] Thus, total expenditure for the firm is $\mathbf{q}'\mathbf{x}$.

Let technology be represented as $T(\mathbf{z}, \mathbf{x}, \mathbf{s}_A|(N,A))$, with feasibility when $T(\mathbf{z}, \mathbf{x}, \mathbf{s}_A|(N,A)) \leq 0$. Then the cost function for the shipper is the following:

$$C(\mathbf{z},\mathbf{q}|N) = \{\min_{\mathbf{x}, s_A, A \in \mathscr{A}} \mathbf{q}'\mathbf{x} \quad |T(\mathbf{z},\mathbf{x},\mathbf{s}_A|(N,A)) \leq 0\}.$$

Thus, for given **z**, **q**, and N, arc sets $A \in \mathscr{A}(N,\mathscr{C},K)$ are varied, as is the associated characteristics vector $\mathbf{s}_A$ and the total input vector **x,** until minimum expenditure is achieved.

Let z_{ijk} be the aggregate flows of commodity k from $i \in \mathcal{O}$ to $j \in \mathscr{D}$. Revenue will be denoted as $R(\tilde{\mathbf{P}},\mathbf{z}|N)$ where $\tilde{\mathbf{P}}$ is the vector of prices $\tilde{P}_{jk}$ for a unit of commodity k at destination j. Thus,

$$R(\tilde{\mathbf{P}},\mathbf{z}|N) = \sum_{k=1}^{K} \sum_{j\in\mathscr{D}} \sum_{i\in\mathcal{O}} \tilde{P}_{jk} z_{ijk}.$$

This leads to the profit function $\pi(\tilde{\mathbf{P}},\mathbf{q}|N)$ for the firm:

$$\pi(\tilde{\mathbf{P}},\mathbf{q}|N) = \max_{\mathbf{z}} R(\tilde{\mathbf{P}},\mathbf{z}|N) - C(\mathbf{z},\mathbf{q}|N),$$

which has the usual properties of a profit function (see McFadden, 1978). Note that the preceding description assumes all variables (especially **x** and $\mathbf{s}_A$, as well as **z** in the profit function) are continuously variable. It may be, however, that $\mathbf{s}_A$ is not adjustable. In this case, the cost function, C, and therefore π would contain the service variables, rather than their being eliminated by optimization. This is especially likely to occur for shippers using regulated carriers.

This point becomes particularly important when the preceding model is used to generate demand for freight transport models. Two types of demand functions are immediately possible. First, one could use $C(\mathbf{z},\mathbf{q}|N)$ (or $C(\mathbf{z},\mathbf{q},\mathbf{s}|N)$) to provide *conditional* transport demand functions (conditional on **z**):

$$\mathbf{x}^{2*}(\mathbf{z},\mathbf{q}|N) = \nabla_{\mathbf{q}^2} C(\mathbf{z},\mathbf{q}|N) \; (\mathbf{x}^{2*}(\mathbf{z},\mathbf{q},\mathbf{s}|N) = \nabla_{\mathbf{q}^2} C(\mathbf{z},\mathbf{q},\mathbf{s}|N)),$$

---

5 If transport rates involve a fixed portion (f_i) and a variable portion (q_i) then we could expand $\mathbf{x}^2$ to be twice its present size, with the latter half of the new vector a zero/one vector (use/don't use) and expand $\mathbf{q}^2$ so that the latter half has the fixed costs in it.

or one can use $\pi(\bar{\mathbf{P}},\mathbf{q}|N)$ (or $\pi(\bar{\mathbf{P}},\mathbf{q},\mathbf{s}|N)$) to compute *unconditional* transport demand functions:

$$\mathbf{x}^{2*}(\bar{\mathbf{P}},\mathbf{q}|N) = -\nabla_{\mathbf{q}^2}\,\pi(\bar{\mathbf{P}},\mathbf{q}|N) \text{ or } (\mathbf{x}^{2*}(\bar{\mathbf{P}},\mathbf{q},\mathbf{s}|N) = -\nabla_{\mathbf{q}^2}\,\pi(\bar{\mathbf{P}},\mathbf{q},\mathbf{s}|N)),$$

where each of the parenthetical cases is for the situation where $\mathbf{s}$ was not adjustable. For convenience, we shall proceed with that case ($\mathbf{s}$ unadjustable) because that has been the main case of interest to researchers examining regulated systems. It is important to note that, with deregulation we might see such inflexibility vanish.

Table 1.2 provides a list of some recent demand analyses[6]; only those leading to an estimated model are provided. Theoretical models include Baumol and Vinod (1970), Das (1974), Allen (1977), and Daughety (1979). The structural scheme I have described is employed to categorize the models discussed. A few qualifications are in order, since the papers reflect somewhat more variety than the "model type" column may suggest. Boyer's paper is not based on a theoretical model, though it is roughly consistent with a firm minimizing costs. Levin's and Winston's papers are random utility formulations of the mode choice problem. Most of the papers incorporate some notion of inventory costs, often using the value of the good multiplied by transit time; when this was done, the paper was viewed as not using the profit function π, even though $\bar{\mathbf{P}}$ was in the analysis. Thus, only the analyses by Daughety and Inaba, Winston, and McFadden, Winston, and Boersch-Supan are based on profit-maximization models. These three studies and the paper by Townsend employ individual (disaggregate) shipment data; the other choice models use aggregate data. The Oum model and the Friedlaender and Spady model treat the shipper as minimizing total production costs and use Shephard's lemma to generate demand functions; Oum assumes homotheticity and works with the unit cost function, thereby deleting $\mathbf{z}$, whereas Friedlaender and Spady use the value of shipments (assumed proportional to aggregate output) as an aggregate output variable. Friedlaender and Spady's is the only study to include nontransport inputs. They include a labor price and fixed-factor levels for materials and capital stock (the cost function for the shipper is a short-run variable-cost function). Finally, Oum provides link-specific analysis for some of his models.

A number of concerns have been raised about the use of quantal choice models. Daughety and Inaba (1978) and Daughety (1979) use a portfolio model to show that firms need not choose to ship by only one mode (a standard assumption of discrete-choice studies), but optimally choose to mix modes and destinations in a decision; proper use of a discrete-choice model is

---

[6] Winston (1983) provides a review of a number of demand studies.

Table 1.2. *Selected demand studies*

Studies	P̄	z	s	q	G	Model type	Data used	Comments
Townsend (1969)	—	Tons by commodity type	Transit time, carrying cost based on value of good	Transport rate	—	$x^2(\mathbf{z},\mathbf{q},\mathbf{s}|\mathbf{G})$	Census, 1963: 400 selected plants, 100 to 200 bills of lading per plant	Rail/truck/air; early probit-type choice model (based on Baumol–Vinod, 1970)
Boyer (1977)	—	Tons, dummies for commodity class	Carrying cost based on value of good	Relative transport rates or difference of rates	Miles	$x^2(\mathbf{z},\mathbf{q},\mathbf{s}|\mathbf{G})$	Various sources, 1967: 18 commodity groups	Rail/truck; logit model; model used to provide welfare estimates
Daughety and Inaba (1978, 1981)	Value/bushel at market	Bushels of corn shipped by mode/market	Expected carrying cost due to equipment availability	Transport rates	Type of market	$x^2(\bar{\mathbf{P}},\mathbf{q},\mathbf{s}|\mathbf{G})$	Survey of country grain elevators in Iowa, Illinois, and Indiana, 1975: 122 elevators	Rail/truck; logit model; movement of corn (domestic and to export). 1981 version used in equilibrium analysis
Levin (1978)	—	Market shares by alternative mode used, by commodity, mileage and weight class	Transit time, carrying cost, variability of transit time	Difference in transport rates	—	$x^2(\mathbf{z},\mathbf{q},\mathbf{s}|\mathbf{G})$	Census, ICC–DOT Carload Waybill Sample, 1972: 698–308 (depending upon model)	Rail/truck/piggyback; logit model; model used to compute welfare estimates

Oum (1979)	—	—	(Per ton-mile unit cost function used)	Variety of models employing mode specific aggregator of rate, speed, reliability, and distance	Link-specific, region-based for some models	$x^2(\mathbf{z},\mathbf{q},\mathbf{s}\mid G)$	Canadian Freight Transportation Model Data Base, 1970: 8 commodity groups for 69 regions	Rail/truck; translog, system of equations–cost function and factor share equation
Friedlaender and Spady (1980)	—	Value of shipments, commodity dummies	Inventory cost equation based on average load, haul, density, and commodity value	Labor price, materials (fixed factor), capital stock (fixed factor), transport rate	Regional dummies	$x^2(\mathbf{z},\mathbf{q},\mathbf{s}\mid G)$	1972: 96 selected 3-digit industries	Rail/truck; translog, system of equations–cost, factor share, inventory cost equations
Winston (1981b)	Value/lb	Aggregate sales, amounts shipped	Transit time, schedule reliability	Freight charges	Miles from rail (also used to indicate loss and damage aspect)	$x^2(\bar{\mathbf{P}},\mathbf{q},\mathbf{s}\mid G)$	1975–77: choice-based sample for 12 commodity groups ≈ 2,400 observations	Rail/regulated truck/unregulated truck; dependent probit model
McFadden, Winston, and Boersch-Supan (Chapter 6)	Value/lb	Amount shipped (agricultural products)	Mean transit time	Freight charges (fixed and variable charges)	—	$x^2(\bar{\mathbf{P}},\mathbf{q},\mathbf{s}\mid G)$	U.S. DOT, 1977: Produce Study	Rail/truck (exempt); probit model: mode-choice and shipment-size equations

Note: Dash means variable type not used.

commodity specific, since some commodities do move in an all-or-nothing manner. Oum (1979) and Braeutigam and Noll (1984) examine the restriction associated with logit models that total transport demand is inelastic. McFadden, Winston, and Boersch-Supan (Chapter 6) deal with this problem by incorporating shipment size and frequency decisions in their model.

2.   Agent interactions

Carriers and shippers interact in markets. To examine behavior in various types of markets, two types of equilibrium models have been developed: those primarily developed by economists and those primarily developed by engineers. Economists have used demand and supply (or cost) models to compute equilibria and to examine potential regulatory policies and their effects on prices, quantities, and welfare. Recent examples of equilibrium analyses of regulated surface transport markets include Levin (1981), Friedlaender and Spady (1981), and Daughety and Inaba (1981); all three analyses involve rail–truck competition, the first two at the national level; the third was concerned with a specific commodity (corn). Models of deregulated markets (in particular, airline markets) include Trapani and Olson (1982), Graham, Kaplan, and Sibley (1983), and Call and Keeler (Chapter 9). The major concerns in these studies have been the issues of the level of prices and services and the degree of competitiveness of recently deregulated airline markets. Call and Keeler also provide an extensive review of some of the oligopoly models that potentially characterize deregulated airline markets. (For an analysis of regulated airline markets, see Keeler, 1972 and Douglas and Miller, 1974.) In general, characterization of the networks that firms use has been ignored or simplified so as to incorporate details of regulation and market structure. It has often, though not always, also been true that such studies ignored service characteristics, or took these as given and fixed.

Engineers, on the other hand, have focused on network aspects (and to some degree the provision of service characteristics), usually simplifying or ignoring other economic aspects (such as optimal firm behavior or strategic interaction in markets). Friesz and Harker (Chapter 7) and Harker (1985) provide an extensive review of this literature, which will not be repeated here (see also Friesz, Tobin, and Harker, 1983). A clear implication of this book is that these two groups are starting to learn from each other.

Market interactions may be under conditions of full, partial, or no regulation. The literature on optimal regulation and pricing has concerned economists for over a century (see Ellet, 1839, Dupuit, 1844, and Hotelling, 1938, among others). This literature produced the notion of "first-best" pricing: Price at marginal cost and (if necessary) subsidize any losses. More recently, Baumol and Bradford (1970), drawing on Ramsey (1927), have provided socially optimal pricing schemes for multiproduct firms subject to a break-even constraint for the firm. The resulting prices, called Ramsey prices, provide for "second-best" regulation. This scheme is second best since if the firm runs a loss under marginal-cost pricing (somehow subsidized by the public), the level of welfare achieved is potentially higher than under Ramsey pricing, because of the break-even constraint. Cautionary use is made of the word "potentially," because, as Baumol and Bradford point out, the subsidy is likely to be obtained through some sort of distortionary policy affecting other parts of the economy.

Braeutigam (1979) used the notion of Ramsey prices to examine welfare implications for total and partial regulation of intermodal competition. His essay in this book (Chapter 8) considers this problem when both carriers enjoy scale economies. Braeutigam (1980) has also employed Ramsey prices to examine standard cost-allocation procedures used by regulators. Ramsey prices have also been used (again, in rail–truck competition cases) to compute welfare loss estimates (see Levin, 1981, and Winston, 1981a).

3.   A brief overview of the essays in this book

The eight essays that form the rest of this book follow the general categorization I have just outlined: technology, demand, equilibrium, pricing, and market behavior.

Ann Friedlaender and Sharon Schur Bruce (Chapter 2) analyze the sources of productivity growth and technical change in the regulated trucking industry using data from the mid to late 1970s on eighty-five selected firms. They employ a third-order flexible functional-form (translog) cost model with time augmentation of input prices, output, and operating characteristics (specifically, average length of haul, average load, percentage of freight in LTL lots, average shipment size, and unit insurance cost). This allows them to calculate augmentation rates for each input price, for output, and for each operating characteristic, and to separate and test potential sources of technical change.

Two principal findings emerge. Friedlaender and Bruce find that the main avenue for technical change to enter the cost function is through the operating characteristics, as opposed to the input prices or output. Unfortunately, they also find that predicting the overall effect of technical change is not possible, because of the nonhomothetic structure of the underlying technology; most of the industry experienced cost reductions over time, but further general characterizations of the precise nature of these adjustments is not possible.

In Chapter 3, Forrest Nelson, William Vigdor, and I also examine the technology of the trucking industry, estimating a distribution of cost functions by taking a flexible-form (translog) cost model involving output and factor prices, and expanding the parameters of the cost to be functions of spatial and environmental attributes of each firm (specifically, average length of haul, average load, and average size of shipment); output is taken to be throughput in ton-miles and per ton-mile cargo loss and damage insurance expenses. The data used are 3,085 yearly observations on firms operating as general commodity carriers between 1953 and 1958; this period was picked to control for both technical and regulatory change.

There are two results of the analysis. First, the spatial environment of the firm is a crucial determinant of the technology employed. In particular, the role of the attributes reflecting the spatial context of the firm is in the selection of input mix and input level, and is only incidentally related to the nature and mix of outputs. Second, differences in costs of firms are almost wholly attributable to technological heterogeneity, and this appears as relatively mild shifts in substitution and demand elasticities.

An interesting parallel exists between Chapters 2 and 3. The attributes used in the model in Chapter 3 comprise most of the operating characteristics used in the model in Chapter 2. Juxtaposing the analyses suggests that these variables play a crucial role in characterizing the way inputs become outputs, in terms of the technologies employed and the technical change those technologies undergo.

In Chapter 4, Douglas Caves, Laurits Christensen, Michael Tretheway, and Robert Windle examine a generalized translog cost model for U.S. railroads, using a panel data set on forty-three firms in the 1951–75 time frame, to obtain unbiased estimates of returns to scale (size) and density. Although previous studies have generally found constant returns to scale, conflicting results on the degree of density economies have been produced. In particular, it is shown that the variety of findings on returns to density reflect the use of a biased estimator, since unobservable firm-specific effects (such as network or management differences) were not controlled for. To correct this, a model allowing for observed (route-miles) and unobserved firm-specific effects is used to provide unbiased estimates of scale and density economies.

The two principal results are that (1) the industry does face constant returns to scale and increasing returns to density (as found by some of the earlier studies) and (2) the degree of density economies is significantly greater than estimated in previous cross-section analyses. Moreover, when the model is estimated omitting the correction for unobserved network effects, the degree of density economies falls into the range suggested by the previous studies.

A common problem in all of these studies is how to represent the network that firms use. There are two reasons for this problem. First, many data sources provide limited (or no) information on firm network attributes. Finding such information for even a small sample of firms is a time-consuming process. The second reason, however, is more fundamental. Even if such data were readily available, incorporating it into a cost model to fully represent the firm's network by a collection of variables is likely to lead to a parameter explosion. This is especially true in the context of flexible-form cost-function models, where the number of parameters is at least quadratic in the number of primary variables.

This problem is addressed by Richard Spady in Chapter 5. Spady proposes a second-order function called a "restricted indexed quadratic" (RIQ) function. The RIQ function (which is a quadratic in output and technology shift variables) has the property of providing an exact representation of an aggregate technology that depends only on the *number* of output and characteristics variables and the means and variances of the outputs and characteristics. In other words, using the notation given earlier, the representation depends on the number of market paths, on the mean of $(\mathbf{z},\mathbf{s})^M$ and on the covariance matrix for $(\mathbf{z},\mathbf{s})^M$. This makes estimation of network–firm cost functions a reasonable option. Spady also shows that although an RIQ cost model is more restrictive than standard flexible functional forms with respect to the input price variables, it is every bit as flexible in the output variables.

Daniel McFadden, Clifford Winston, and Axel Boersch-Supan (Chapter 6) provide an exploratory analysis of a complex problem in freight demand modeling, the analysis of joint mode and shipment-size decisions and the estimation of such a choice model in the face of choice-based sample data. After proposing an inventory model that unites size, frequency, and mode decisions, optimality conditions for choice of shipment size (a continuous variable) and mode (a discrete variable) are used to construct the likelihood function for a probit model. The analysis proceeds to compare a number of choice-based sample estimation techniques and apply them to data on rail and truck shipments of produce. The estimated full-information concentrated likelihood model is then used to compute choice-probability elasticities, allowing comparison of modal rate and service attributes.

Chapter 7, by Terry Friesz and Patrick Harker, shifts the focus of the volume from separate models of the agents to integrating such models to examine interactions of the agents via network equilibrium modeling, an area that has received considerable attention over the past few decades from engineers. Economists are just starting to become aware of this area, and thus this chapter is especially timely. The power of these models is their ability to provide reasonable firm-level detail (such as network structure) and simultaneously explicitly aggregate individual decisions up to a market (and even economy) level. Friesz and Harker provide three "products." First, they provide a review of a number of the existing network equilibrium models, comparing and contrasting them on the basis of a number of criteria. Next, they provide a detailed discussion of a network equilibrium model that allows for multiple carrier and shipper firms, making simultaneous supply and demand decisions. Service characteristics are allowed (delay), and price-taking behavior by all participants is assumed. Finally, the chapter briefly reviews some tests of the application of two of these models to problems of rail–water competition and to the prediction of coal movements in the United States.

Ronald Braeutigam (Chapter 8) also addresses the question of intermodal competition, but in the context of a normative economic analysis of the regulation of competing firms where all firms operate with economies of scale. In particular, he examines the problem of characterizing economically efficient industry structure and pricing when a railroad (providing a number of different outputs) faces competition in one of its markets from a pipeline, the clear example being coal slurry pipelines. After a discussion of the technology of such systems and a review of some of the history of such competition, Braeutigam proceeds to characterize the Ramsey optimum (maximum welfare subject to break-even constraints for both the railroad and the pipeline) for the problem. He shows that when both types of firms transport coal, tariffs will exceed marginal costs and the markup of price over marginal cost will be greater in markets served by rival firms than in markets monopolized by one of the technologies. Moreover, Braeutigam also shows that it can be socially optimal for one of the firms to earn extranormal profits.

Finally, in Chapter 9 Gregory Call and Theodore Keeler examine data from deregulated airline markets to test the applicability of the contestable markets model of market structure and price behavior. After reviewing a number of oligopoly models as possible explanations of pricing behavior in deregulated air travel markets, Call and Keeler use data from 1980 on the eighty-nine highest density routes to test for a relationship between concentration and level of fares charged, and especially to examine how airline fares are affected by entry of a trunk airline into a new market. They find a significant positive relationship between market concentration (as measured by the Herfindahl index) and air fares, and they also find that entry of a trunk carrier reduces fares. Both of these results suggest that the market behavior in question does not correspond to the contestability hypothesis. Furthermore, although their results seem to reject the contestable markets hypothesis, they appear to support the "fat-cat" incumbent model, which involves a large incumbent enjoying a large market share (that reflects product differentiation), not matching fares of entrants who cater to somewhat different customers (see Schmalensee, 1983, and Fudenberg and Triole, 1984). Finally, Call and Keeler discuss the implications of the analysis for long-term trends, in particular, the trend of the system toward a competitive structure in the long run.

References

Allen, W. B. (1977). "The Demand for Freight Transportation: A Micro Approach." *Transportation Research,* 11, no. 1: 9–14.
Baumol, W. J., and D. F. Bradford (1970). "Optimal Departures from Marginal Cost Pricing." *American Economic Review,* 60, no. 3, June: 265–83.

Baumol, W. J., and H. D. Vinod (1970). "An Inventory Theoretic Model of Freight Transport Demand." *Management Science,* 16, March: 413–22.

Baumol, W. J., J. C. Panzar and R. D. Willig (1982). *Contestable Markets and the Theory of Industry Structure.* New York: Harcourt Brace Jovanovich.

Borts, G. (1952). "Production Relations in the Railway Industry." *Econometrica,* 20: 71–79.

Boyer, K. D. (1977). "Minimum Rate Regulation, Model Split Sensitivities, and the Railroad Problem." *Journal of Political Economy,* 85, no. 3, June: 493–512.

Braeutigam, R. R. (1979). "Optimal Pricing with Intermodal Competition." *American Economic Review,* 69, no. 1, March: 38–49.

   (1980). "An Analysis of Fully Distributed Cost Pricing in Regulated Industries." *The Bell Journal of Economics,* 11, no. 1, Spring: 182–96.

Braeutigam, R. R., and R. G. Noll (1984). "The Regulation of Surface Freight Transportation: The Welfare Effects Revisited." *The Review of Economics and Statistics,* 66, no. 1, February: 80–87.

Braeutigam, R. R., A. F. Daughety, and M. A. Turnquist (1982). "The Estimation of a Hybrid Cost Function for a Railroad Firm." *The Review of Economics and Statistics,* 64, no. 3, August: 394–404.

   (1984). "A Firm Specific Analysis of Economies of Density in the U.S. Railroad Industry." *Journal of Industrial Economics,* 33, no. 1, September: 3–20.

Caves, D., L. Christensen, and J. Swanson (1980). "Productivity in U.S. Railroads." *The Bell Journal of Economics,* 11, no. 1, Spring: 166–81.

   (1981). "Productivity Growth, Scale Economies, and Capacity Utilization in U.S. Railroads, 1955–74." *American Economic Review,* 71, no. 5, December: 994–1002.

Das, C. (1974). "Choice of Transport Service: An Inventory Theoretic Approach." *Logistics and Transportation Review,* 10, no. 2; 181–87.

Daughety, A. F. (1979). "Freight Transport Demand Revisited: A Microeconomic View of Multimodal, Multicharacteristic Service Uncertainty and the Demand for Freight Transport." *Transportation Research,* 13B, no. 4: 281–88.

Daughety, A. F., and F. S. Inaba (1978). "Estimation of Service-Differentiated Transport Demand Functions." *Transportation Research Record,* 688: 23–30.

   (1981). "An Analysis of Regulatory Change in the Transportation Industry." *The Review of Economics and Statistics,* 63, no. 2, May: 246–55.

Daughety, A. F., M. A. Turnquist, and S. L. Griesbach (1983). "Estimating Origin–Destination Specific Railroad Marginal Operating Cost Functions." *Transportation Research,* 17A, no. 6, November: 451–62.

Douglas, G., and J. Miller (1974). *Economic Regulation of Domestic Air Transport.* Washington, D.C.: The Brookings Institution.

Dupuit, J. (1952). "On the Measurement of the Utility of Public Works." (Translated by R. H. Barback from "de la Mesure de l'Utilité des Travaux Publics," *Annales des Ponts et Chaussées,* 2ne Series, vol. 8, 1944.) *International Economics Papers,* 2: 83–110.

Ellet, C., Jr. (1966). *An Essay on the Laws of Trade in Reference to the Work of Internal Improvement in the United States.* (Originally published 1839.) New York: Augustus M. Kelley.

Friedlaender, A. F. (1969). *The Dilemma of Freight Transport Regulation.* Washington, D.C.: The Brookings Institution.

Friedlaender, A. F., and R. H. Spady (1980). "A Derived Demand Function for Freight Transportation." *The Review of Economics and Statistics,* 62, no. 3, August: 432–41.

   (1980). *Freight Transport Regulation: Equity, Efficiency and Competition in the Rail and Trucking Industries.* Cambridge, Mass.: MIT Press.

Friedlaender, A. F., R. H. Spady, and S. J. Wang Chiang (1981). "Regulation and the Structure of Technology in the Trucking Industry." In T. G. Cowing and R. E. Stevenson, eds., *Productivity Measurement in Regulated Industries.* New York: Academic Press.

Friesz, T. L., R. L. Tobin, and P. T. Harker (1983). "Predictive Freight Network Models: The State of the Art." *Transportation Research,* 17A, 6: 407–17.

Fudenberg, D., and J. Triole (1984). "The Fat-Cat Effect, The Puppy-Dog Ploy, and the Lean and Hungry Look." *American Economic Review,* 74, no. 2, May: 361–366.

Graham, D. R., D. P. Kaplan, and D. S. Sibley (1983). "Efficiency and Competition in the Airline Industry." *The Bell Journal of Economics,* 14, no. 1, Spring: 118–38.

Grilliches, Z. (1972). "Cost Allocation in Railroad Regulation." *The Bell Journal of Economics and Management Science,* 3, no. 1, Spring: 26–41.

Harary, F. (1969). *Graph Theory.* Reading, Mass.: Addison-Wesley.

Harker, P. T. (1985). "The State of the Art in the Predictive Analysis of Freight Transportation Systems." *Transportation Reviews.*

Harmatuck, D. J. (1978). "A Policy-Sensitive Railway Cost Function." *The Logistics and Transportation Review,* 15, no. 2; 255–76.

——— (1981). "A Motor Carrier Joint Cost Function: A Flexible Functional Form with Activity Prices." *Journal of Transport Economics and Policy,* 15, no. 1, May: 135–53.

Harris, R. G. (1977). "Economies of Traffic Density in the Rail Freight Industry." *The Bell Journal of Economics,* 8, no. 2, Autumn: 556–64.

Hasenkamp, G. (1976). *Specification and Estimation of Multiple-Output Production Functions,* New York: Springer-Verlag.

Hotelling, H. (1938). "The General Welfare in Relation to Problems of Taxation and of Railway and Utility Rates." *Econometrica,* 6: 242–269.

Jara-Diaz, S. R. (1982). "The Estimation of Transport Cost Functions: A Methodological Review." *Transport Review,* 2, no. 3: 257–78.

Jara-Diaz, S., and C. Winston (1981). "Multiproduct Transportation Cost Functions: Scale and Scope in Railway Operations." In Nicklaus Blatther et al., eds., *Eighth European Association for Research in Industrial Economics,* vol. 1. Basel: University of Basel.

Keeler, T. E. (1972). "Airline Regulation and Market Performance." *The Bell Journal of Economics and Management Science,* 3, no. 2, Autumn: 399–424.

——— (1974). "Railroad Costs, Returns to Scale, and Excess Capacity." *The Review of Economics and Statistics,* 56, no. 2, May: 201–8.

Klein, L. (1953). *A Textbook of Econometrics.* Evanston, Ill.: Row Peterson.

Koenker, R. (1977). "Optimal Scale and the Size Distribution of American Trucking Firms." *Journal of Transport Economics and Policy,* 11, no. 1, January: 54–67.

Levin, R. C. (1978). "Allocation in Surface Freight Transportation: Does Rate Regulation Matter?" *The Bell Journal of Economics,* 9, no. 1, Spring: 18–46.

——— (1981). "Railroad Rates, Profitability, and Welfare under Deregulation." *The Bell Journal of Economics,* 12, no. 1, Spring: 1–26.

Locklin, D. P. (1972). *Economics of Transportation,* 7th ed. Homewood, Ill.: Richard D. Irwin.

McFadden, D. F. (1978). "Cost, Revenue and Profit Functions." In M. Fuss and D. McFadden, eds., *Production Economics: A Dual Approach to Theory and Applications.* Amsterdam: North Holland.

Pegrum, D. F. (1968). *Transportation: Economics and Public Policy.* Homewood, Ill.: Richard D. Irwin.

Peltzman, S. (1976). "Toward a More General Theory of Regulation." *Journal of Law and Economics,* 19, no. 2, August: 211–40.

Oum, T. H. (1979). "A Warning on the Use of Linear Logit Models in Transportation Mode Choice Studies." *The Bell Journal of Economics,* 10, no. 1, Spring: 374–90.

——— (1979). "A Cross Sectional Study of Freight Transport Demand and Rail–Truck Competition in Canada." *The Bell Journal of Economics,* 10, no. 2, Autumn: 453–82.

Ramsey, F. (1927). "A Contribution to the Theory of Taxation." *Economic Journal,* March: 47–61.

Schmalensee, R. (1983). "Advertising and Entry Deterrence: An Exploratory Model." *Journal of Political Economy*, 90, August: 636–53.

Shephard, R. W. (1970). *Theory of Cost and Production Functions*. Princeton, N. J.: Princeton University Press.

Spady, R. H., and A. F. Friedlaender (1978). "Hedonic Cost Functions for the Regulated Trucking Industry." *The Bell Journal of Economics*, 9, no. 1, Spring: 159–79.

Stigler, G. (1971). "The Economic Theory of Regulation." *The Bell Journal of Economics and Management Science*, 2, no. 1, Spring: 3–21.

Townsend, H. (1969). "Two Models of Freight Modal Choice." *Studies in the Demand for Freight Transportation*, 3. Princeton, N.J.: Mathematica.

Trapani, J. M. and C. V. Olson (1982). "An Analysis of the Impact of Open Entry on Price and the Quality of Service in the Airline Industry." *The Review of Economics and Statistics*, 64, no. 1, February: 67–76.

Wang Chiang, S. J., and A. F. Friedlaender (1984). "Output Aggregation, Network Effects, and the Measurement of Trucking Technology." *The Review of Economics and Statistics*, 66, no. 2, May: 267–76.

Winston, C. (1981a). "The Welfare Effects of ICC Rate Regulation Revisited." *The Bell Journal of Economics*, 12, no. 1, Spring: 232–44.

(1981b). "A Disaggregate Model of the Demand for Intercity Freight Transportation." *Econometrica*, 49, July: 981–1006.

(1983). "The Demand for Freight Transportation: Models and Applications." *Transportation Research*, 17A, no. 6, November: 419–27.

(1984). "Conceptual Developments in the Economics of Transportation: An Interpretive Survey." *Journal of Economic Literature*, 23, no. 1, March: 57–94.

Technology and demand

Augmentation effects and technical change in the regulated trucking industry, 1974–1979

ANN F. FRIEDLAENDER AND
SHARON SCHUR BRUCE

In recent years there has been considerable analysis of the structure of costs and technology of the regulated trucking industry.[1] These studies have generally focused upon the question of economies of scale and the extent to which the industry could be expected to operate competitively in a deregulated environment. Thus, they have primarily concentrated on the questions of industry structure and conduct and performance, with particular attention to rates and service levels.

An equally important aspect of industry performance, however, is productivity. Although this has been largely ignored in analyses of the trucking industry, the implications of regulation for dynamic efficiency and productivity may be just as important as its implications for static efficiency and pricing policies. Indeed, preliminary work in this area by Friedlaender and Wang Chiang (1983) indicates that substantial productivity gains arise through operating characteristics, such as length of haul, that can be affected by regulatory policies dealing with route and operating authorities.

Although previous work has been suggestive, data limitations have prevented a definitive analysis of the sources and nature of technological change in the trucking industry. Without this information, however, it is difficult to determine whether technical change and productivity growth primarily arise from input effects, operating characteristic effects, or output effects, and hence whether regulation can be said to have had a major impact upon productivity growth. If, for example, it can be shown that operating characteristics have a major impact on the nature and extent of productivity growth, and that these operating characteristics are affected by regulation (length of haul, load, and so forth), then one can probably infer that changes in regulatory policy may have substantial effects upon productivity growth and technical change.

Support from the National Science Foundation is gratefully acknowledged. We wish to thank Clifford Winston and Ernst Berndt for helpful comments and suggestions.
[1] See for example, Harmatuck (1981), Koenker (1977), and Wang Chiang and Friedlaender (1984).

29

But if the sources of productivity growth and technical change primarily arise from input or output effects, the role of regulation in productivity growth is much less clear.

In this essay we attempt to provide an answer to these questions by analyzing the nature and sources of productivity growth and technical change in the regulated trucking industry by using a time-series, cross-section analysis of eighty-five regulated common carriers of general commodities for the years 1974 to 1979. The analysis focuses upon regulated general commodity carriers because these carriers concentrate on less-than-truckload (LTL) carriage and have been the most severely constrained by regulatory restrictions concerning routes, gateways, and so on. In addition, since these carriers serve small, rural shippers with relatively few other sources of transportation supply, there is considerable concern about the shipping costs and service levels that will face these shippers in a deregulated environment. The analysis focuses upon the mid- to late 1970s because this represents the recent past before substantial deregulation occurred. As such, it should permit a view of the fully regulated trucking industry and provide a benchmark for comparison with the less regulated environment following the Trucking Act of 1980, which has led to substantial deregulation.

Section 1 of this chapter discusses the measurement of technical change and productivity growth and describes the model that will be used to analyze the trucking industry. Section 2 then describes the data and reports on the estimation results. Section 3 discusses the sources and nature of technical change. The concluding section discusses the policy implications of the analysis.

1.   Measuring productivity growth and technical change

In recent years a number of studies have attempted to analyze the nature and extent of productivity growth in many regulated industries.[2] Because of the convenient duality principles of production, these have generally analyzed productivity growth and technical change using cost functions. Thus the basic approach is to introduce time into the cost function and to measure productivity growth as the derivative of the change of costs with respect to time. By examining the second derivative of this expression, one can decompose the productivity effects into their relevant components and determine whether technical change comes about through input effects or output effects. Perhaps the most general approach was that of Stevenson (1980), who used a truncated third-order approximation of a cost function whose arguments not only included output, factor prices, and time, but also included state variables that affected the structure of costs and production. By estimating a general cost

---

[2] See Cowing and Stevenson (1981) for a representative number of these studies.

function, Stevenson was able to decompose technological growth into three components: output effects, input effects, and state effects.

Following Stevenson, let us consider a general cost function with the following form:

$$C = (\mathbf{w}, \mathbf{y}, \mathbf{t}, T), \tag{1}$$

where C represent long-run total costs,[3] $\mathbf{w}$ represents a vector of factor prices, $\mathbf{t}$ represents a vector of "technological" variables or operating characteristics, and T represents time. To capture the effect of time, and thus of technical change upon the full range of these variables, we follow Stevenson and utilize a truncated third-order translog approximation in which we include the third-order terms that contain the time variable T, but omit the other third-order terms. Thus the estimating equation takes the following form[4]:

$$
\begin{aligned}
\ln C = {} & \alpha_0 + \sum_i \alpha_i \ln w_i + \sum_j \beta_j \ln t_j + \gamma_y \ln y + \delta_T T \\[6pt]
& + \tfrac{1}{2} \sum_i \sum_s a_{is} \ln w_i \ln w_s + \sum_i \sum_j b_{ij} \ln w_i \ln t_j + \sum_i c_{iy} \ln w_i \ln y \\[6pt]
& + \sum_i d_{iT} \ln w_i T + \tfrac{1}{2} \sum_j \sum_r e_{jr} \ln t_j \ln t_r + \sum_j f_{jy} \ln t_j \ln y \\[6pt]
& + \sum_j g_{jT} \ln t_j T + \tfrac{1}{2} h_{yy} (\ln y)^2 + k_{yT} \ln T + \tfrac{1}{2} m_{TT} T^2 \\[6pt]
& + \tfrac{1}{2} \sum_i \sum_s n_{isT} \ln w_i \ln w_s T + \sum_i \sum_j p_{ijT} \ln w_i \ln t_j T \\[6pt]
& + \sum_i q_{iyT} \ln w_i \ln y T + \tfrac{1}{2} \sum_j \sum_r s_{jrT} \ln t_j \ln t_r T + \sum_j u_{jyT} \ln t_j \ln y T \\[6pt]
& + \tfrac{1}{2} v_{yyT} (\ln y)^2 T + T + \varepsilon,
\end{aligned}
\tag{2}
$$

where ε represents a disturbance term.

This specification has several advantages over the more common second-order translog approximation as used in Friedlaender and Wang Chiang (1983) or Caves, Christensen, and Swanson (1980). In particular, in the second-order approximation, the parameters on the second-order terms are assumed to be constant over time. This implies, for example, that the effects

---

[3] Because trucking capital is relatively short lived and transferable, it is reasonable to utilize a long-run cost function in analyzing trucking costs.

[4] Note that all variables are estimated as deviations from the sample mean. In addition, we impose the usual symmetry and homogeneity conditions to ensure cost minimization.

of operating characteristics on the factor shares or upon the use of inputs are invariant over time or that the effect of operating characteristics upon output is also time invariant. Since, however, operating characteristics are one of the principal ways that regulatory policy can affect trucking costs, this is obviously a constraining assumption. Finally, the use of a second-order approximation constrains changes in the elasticity of substitution to come about through shifts over time in the factor shares of inputs rather than through technically induced shifts in the second-order relations among input prices. To the extent, however, that these interaction effects may not be constant over time, it is useful to incorporate this into the analysis.

Within the context of this model, measures of technical change and productivity growth can be analyzed as follows. First, the existence of Hicks neutral technical change can be determined by postulating separability between time and the other variables. In this case, the general cost function can be written as

$$C = g(T)h(\mathbf{y},\mathbf{w},\mathbf{t}). \tag{3}$$

This in turn implies that all of the coefficients on the terms containing interactions with time (T) and the other variables ($\mathbf{w}$, $\mathbf{y}$, and $\mathbf{t}$) are zero.[5] In view of the nonhomothetic nature of production, it is unlikely that these conditions will be satisfied.[6]

Productivity growth and technical change can be measured explicitly by differentiating the cost function with respect to time to obtain the following expression:

$$\frac{\partial \ln C}{\partial T} = \delta_T + \sum_i d_{iT}\ln w_i + \sum_j g_{jT}\ln t_j + k_{yT}\ln y + m_{TT}T$$

$$+ \tfrac{1}{2}\sum_i \sum_s n_{isT}\ln w_i \ln w_s \quad \sum_i \sum_j p_{ijT}\ln w_i \ln t_j$$

$$+ \sum_i q_{iyT}\ln w_i \ln y + \tfrac{1}{2}\sum_j \sum_r s_{jrT}\ln t_j \ln t_r$$

$$+ \sum_j u_{jyT}\ln t_j \ln y + \tfrac{1}{2}v_{yyT}(\ln y)^2. \tag{4}$$

This in turn can be divided into the pure productivity effect, the input effect, the output effect, and the characteristics effect. The pure productivity effect is

---

[5] In particular, the following coefficient restrictions must be imposed.

$$d_{iT} = 0 \ \forall i, \ g_{jT} = 0 \ \forall j, \ K_{yT} = 0, \ n_{isT} = 0 \ \forall i,s, \ p_{ijT} = 0 \ \forall i,j,$$
$$q_{iyT} = 0 \ \forall i, \ s_{jrT} = 0 \ \forall j,r, \ u_{jyT} = 0 \ \forall j, \ v_{yyT} = 0.$$

[6] This point will be discussed more fully subsequently.

given by the change in costs with respect to time, evaluated at mean factor prices, operating characteristics, and output levels. This measures the residual change in costs that is not explained by changes in factor prices, output, or operating characteristics; that is,

$$\left.\frac{\partial \ln C}{\partial T}\right|_{w = \bar{w}, t = \bar{t}, y = \bar{y}} = \delta_T + m_{TT} T. \tag{5}$$

The input effect, the output effect, and the characteristic effect are obtained by differentiating Eq. (4) with respect to each of the relevant arguments to yield the following expressions.

$$\frac{\partial^2 \ln C}{\partial T \partial \ln w_i} = d_{iT} + \sum_s n_{isT} \ln w_s + \sum_j p_{ijT} \ln t_j + q_{iyT} \ln y. \tag{6a}$$

$$\frac{\partial^2 \ln C}{\partial T \partial \ln y} = k_{yT} + \sum_i q_{iyT} \ln w_i + \sum_j u_{jyT} \ln t_j + v_{yyT} \ln y. \tag{6b}$$

$$\frac{\partial^2 \ln C}{\partial T \ln t_j} = g_{jT} + \sum_i p_{ijT} \ln w_i + \sum_r s_{jrT} \ln t_r + u_{jyT} \ln y. \tag{6c}$$

Note that these expressions also reflect the change in the relevant elasticity with respect to time. Thus the input effect measures the change in the factor price–cost elasticity with respect to time; the output effect measures the change in the output–cost elasticity with respect to time; the operating-characteristics effect measures the change in the characteristics–cost elasticity with respect to time.

Although it is in principle possible to decompose the sources of technical change into their various components, examination of Eqs. (6a–c), indicates that the identification of each of these effects is difficult because the same terms often appear in each expression. This suggests that a modified version of the Stevenson model would be useful, which would permit explicit hypothesis tests concerning the extent to which augmentation of inputs, output, or operating characteristics can account for productivity growth. This can be done by specifying a model in which each of these variables is assumed to be augmented over time and then using nested hypothesis tests to determine which form of augmentation appears to be dominant.

We thus modify the preceding model and specify costs as

$$C = C(\omega, \tau, \phi), \tag{7}$$

where each argument is assumed to be time augmented; that is,

$$\omega_i = w_i e^{\varepsilon_i T}, \qquad \tau_j = t_j e^{\eta_j T}, \qquad \phi = y e^{\theta_y T}. \tag{8}$$

We now utilize a third-order approximation to Eq. (7) and write

$$\ln C = \alpha_0 + \sum_i \tilde{\alpha}_i \ln\omega_i + \sum_j \tilde{\beta}_j \ln\tau_j + \tilde{\gamma}_\phi \ln\phi + \tfrac{1}{2}\sum_i \sum_s \tilde{a}_{is}\ln\omega_i\ln\omega_s$$

$$+ \sum_i \sum_j \tilde{b}_{ij}\ln\omega_i\ln\tau_j + \sum_i \tilde{c}_{i\phi}\ln\omega_i\ln\phi + \tfrac{1}{2}\sum_j \sum_r \tilde{e}_{jr}\ln\tau_j\ln\tau_r$$

$$+ \sum_j f_{j\phi}\ln\tau_j\ln\phi + \tfrac{1}{2}\tilde{h}_{\phi\phi}(\ln\phi)^2$$

$$+ \tfrac{1}{6}\sum_i \sum_s \sum_k \tilde{A}_{isk}\ln\omega_i\ln\omega_s\ln\omega_k + \tfrac{1}{2}\sum_i \sum_s \sum_j \tilde{B}_{isj}\ln\omega_i\ln\omega_s\ln\tau_j$$

$$+ \tfrac{1}{2}\sum_i \sum_s \tilde{C}_{is\phi}\ln\omega_i\ln\omega_s\ln\phi + \tfrac{1}{2}\sum_i \sum_j \sum_r \tilde{D}_{ijr}\ln\omega_i\ln\tau_j\ln\tau_r$$

$$+ \sum_i \sum_j \tilde{E}_{ij\phi}\ln\omega_i\ln\tau_j\ln\phi + \tfrac{1}{2}\sum_i \tilde{F}_{i\phi\phi}\ln\omega_i(\ln\phi)^2$$

$$+ \tfrac{1}{6}\sum_j \sum_r \sum_h \tilde{G}_{jrh}\ln\tau_j\ln\tau_r\ln\tau_h + \tfrac{1}{2}\sum_j \sum_r \tilde{H}_{jr\phi}\ln\tau_j\ln\tau_r\ln\phi$$

$$+ \tfrac{1}{2}\sum_j \tilde{I}_{j\phi\phi}\ln\tau(\ln\phi)^2 + \tfrac{1}{6}\tilde{J}_{\phi\phi\phi}(\ln\phi)^3. \tag{9}$$

Substituting Eq. (8) for ω_i, τ_j, and ϕ, collecting terms, and truncating the higher order terms other than those involving interactions between T and the other variables yields the following:

$$\ln C = \alpha_0 + \sum_i \tilde{\alpha}_i \ln w_i + \sum_j \tilde{\beta}_j \ln t_j + \tilde{\gamma}_\phi \ln y + \tilde{\delta}_T T + \tfrac{1}{2}\sum_i \sum_s \tilde{a}_{is}\ln w_i\ln w_s$$

$$+ \sum_i \sum_j \tilde{b}_{ij}\ln w_i\ln t_j + \sum_i \tilde{c}_{i\phi}\ln w_i\ln y + \sum_i \tilde{d}_{iT}\ln w_i T$$

$$+ \tfrac{1}{2}\sum_j \sum_r \tilde{e}_{jr}\ln t_j\ln t_r + \sum_j \tilde{f}_{j\phi}\ln t_j\ln y + \sum_j \tilde{g}_{jT}\ln t_j T + \tfrac{1}{2}\tilde{h}_{\phi\phi}(\ln y)^2$$

$$+ \tilde{k}_{\phi T}\ln yT + \tfrac{1}{2}\tilde{m}_{TT}T^2 + \tfrac{1}{2}\sum_i \sum_s \tilde{n}_{isT}\ln w_i\ln w_s T$$

$$+ \sum_i \sum_j \tilde{p}_{ijT}\ln w_i\ln t_j T + \sum_j \tilde{q}_{i\phi T}\ln w_i\ln yT + \tfrac{1}{2}\sum_j \sum_r \tilde{s}_{jrT}\ln t_j\ln t_r T$$

$$+ \sum_j \tilde{u}_{j\phi T}\ln t_j\ln yT + \tfrac{1}{2}\tilde{v}_{\phi\phi T}(\ln y)^2 T, \tag{10}$$

where

$$\tilde{\delta}_T \equiv \sum_i \tilde{\alpha}_i\varepsilon_i + \sum_j \beta_j\eta_j + \tilde{\gamma}_\phi\theta_y$$

$$\tilde{d}_{it} \equiv \sum_s \tilde{a}_{is} \varepsilon_s + \sum_j \tilde{b}_{ij} \eta_j + \tilde{c}_{i\phi} \theta_y$$

$$\tilde{g}_{jT} \equiv \sum_i \tilde{b}_{ij} \varepsilon_i + \sum_r \tilde{e}_{jr} \eta_r + \tilde{f}_{j\phi} \theta_y$$

$$\tilde{k}_{\phi T} \equiv \sum_i \tilde{c}_{i\phi} \varepsilon_i + \sum_j \tilde{f}_{j\phi} \eta_j + \tilde{h}_{\phi\phi} \theta y$$

$$\tfrac{1}{2} \tilde{m}_{TT} = \tfrac{1}{2} \sum_i \sum_s \tilde{a}_{is} \varepsilon_i \varepsilon_s \sum_i \sum_j \tilde{b}_{ij} \varepsilon_i \eta_j + \sum_i \tilde{c}_{i\phi} \varepsilon_i \theta_y + \tfrac{1}{2} \sum_j \sum_r \tilde{e}_{jr} \eta_j \eta_r$$

$$+ \sum_j \tilde{f}_{j\phi} \eta_j \theta_y + \tfrac{1}{2} \tilde{h}_{\phi\phi} (\theta_y)^2$$

$$\tilde{n}_{isT} \equiv \sum_k \tilde{A}_{isk} \varepsilon_k \sum_j \tilde{B}_{isj} \eta_j + \tilde{C}_{is\phi} \theta_y$$

$$\tilde{p}_{ijT} \equiv \sum_s \tilde{B}_{ijs} \varepsilon_s + \sum_r \tilde{D}_{ijr} \eta_r + \tilde{E}_{ij} \theta_y$$

$$\tilde{q}_{i\phi T} \equiv \sum_s \tilde{C}_{is\phi} \varepsilon_s + \sum_j \tilde{E}_{ij\phi} \eta_j + \tilde{F}_{i\phi\phi} \theta_y$$

$$\tilde{s}_{jrT} \equiv \sum_i \tilde{D}_{ijr} \varepsilon_i + \sum_h \tilde{G}_{jrh} \eta_h + \tilde{H}_{jr\phi} \theta_y$$

$$\tilde{u}_{j\phi T} = \sum_i \tilde{E}_{ij\phi} \varepsilon_i + \sum_r \tilde{H}_{jr\phi} \eta_r + \tilde{I}_{j\phi\phi} \theta_y$$

$$\tilde{v}_{\phi\phi T} = \sum_i \tilde{F}_{i\phi\phi} \varepsilon_i + \sum_j \tilde{I}_{j\phi\phi} \eta_j + \tilde{J}_{\phi\phi\phi} \theta_y. \tag{10a}$$

A comparison of Eqs. (2) and (10) indicates that they have an identical form and that Eq. (10) is in fact a restricted form of Eq. (2), with the coefficient restrictions being given in Eq. (10a). Hence this augmentation model is merely a restricted form of the Stevenson model.

The augmentation parameters $(\varepsilon_i, \eta_j, \theta_y)$ represent "average" augmentation effects of inputs, operating characteristics, and output. Thus if factor-augmenting technical change has taken place, we would expect each ε_i to be negative, indicating that the "real" cost of factor i has fallen relative to that of the base period. Intuitively, if a given input had the same nominal price in two periods, but its real price had fallen, this is equivalent to purchasing a better quality of the input. In contrast, a positive value of θ_y would imply technical change with respect to output, since the effective output would be greater for given factor prices and operating characteristics. The expected sign of the augmentation effects associated with operating characteristics is less clear, depending upon the expected sign of the derivative of costs with respect to operating characteristics. For those variables for which $\partial \ln C / \partial \ln t$ is negative (such as length of haul, average load), the augmentation effect should be positive in the presence of technical progress, indicating that the effective value of this variable has increased over time. Conversely, for those variables for which $\partial \ln C / \partial \ln t$ is positive (the percentage of fragile traffic, for example), the expected sign of the augmentation effect should be negative in the presence of technical progress.

The advantage of using the augmentation model over the Stevenson model lies in the additional explanatory power it provides, since it permits the explicit calculation of each augmentation rate associated with each argument of the cost function. Moreover, the augmentation model makes it possible to test explicitly whether technical change arises from input augmentation, characteristic augmentation, or output augmentation. Finally, by using this formulation, the "pure" productivity effects ($\tilde{\delta}_T$ and $\tilde{m}_{TT}$) can be decomposed into combinations of the various augmentation effects and the other parameters, indicating that there is no "unexplained" productivity growth. The specific structure of the hypothesis tests used to analyze the nature of technical change will be presented in the following section when we discuss the empirical tests.

2.   Data and estimation

In this section, we first discuss the data and variables used in the analysis. We then present the estimated cost function and discuss its implications for the structure of technology in the trucking industry and consider explicitly its nature of technical change and productivity growth.

2.1.   Data and variables

In choosing a database for this analysis, it was important to ensure that the underlying technology was the same across all firms. To this end, we limited the sample to relatively large general-commodity carriers who engage in intermediate- and long-haul service. In addition, to ensure that observed time-related differences in technology reflect technical change and productivity growth instead of firm-related differences, we limited the sample to firms for whom a continuous data set was available.[7] Because substantial deregulation

---

[7] Friedlaender and Spady (1981) have argued that the technology of small, localized regional carriers differs significantly from that of large regional or interregional carriers. Hence in this study an effort was made to exclude the small, localized regional carriers from the sample and to limit it to large regional and interregional

took place in 1980, we used 1979 as the last year of the analysis. Because of changes in the format of reporting, it was only possible to obtain a consistent data set back to 1974. Thus the database used in this analysis consisted of a time-series cross section of a matched sample of eighty-five large general-commodity carriers for the period 1974–79.

As discussed previously, the basic estimating equation was a long-run cost function whose arguments consisted of output (y), input prices ($\mathbf{w}$), operating characteristics or technological variables ($\mathbf{t}$), and time (T). Thus the basic cost function took the general form of $C = C(y,\mathbf{w},\mathbf{t},T)$.[8] The specific variables used in the cost function for the analysis of trucking productivity are as follows:

> C = TCOST = the total expenditures of the firm, measured to be the sum of (1) labor costs, (2) fuel expenditures and fuel taxes, (3) expenditures on revenue capital equipment, (4) "other" capital expenditures, (5) expenditures on purchased transportation
>
> w_1 = price of labor, a divisia index of prices for the following types of labor weighted by expenditure shares: supervisory and salaried clerical; line haul, pickup and delivery, and terminal; other
>
> w_2 = price of fuel, defined as fuel price (including tax) in dollars per gallon
>
> w_3 = price of revenue equipment; a divisia index of prices of the following types of revenue equipment weighted by expenditure shares: trucks, tractors, semitrailers, full trailers, and other equipment
>
> w_4 = price of general capital, measured as expenditures on general

carriers. The specific carriers included in the sample were based on data availability. Because the construction of the database required the merging of a number of disparate tapes from the Interstate Commerce Commission (Annual Report Tapes of Class I and II Motor Carriers), inconsistencies in reporting arose. Hence the eighty-five carriers used in this sample essentially represent the subset of firms that were in the ICC annual report tapes for each year and that provided a consistent set of data. In addition to the data contained in the annual reports, data on regional fuel prices were taken from *Platt's Oil Price Handbook*.

[8] In adjusting for the composition of output one can either use a direct hedonic adjustment on output (let $C = C(\psi,\mathbf{w})$, where $\psi = \psi(y,\mathbf{t})$) or use the more general technology specification given in the text. Since the hedonic formulation assumes separability between inputs and operating characteristics, the technology specification is more general. Although one can also include firm-specific dummy variables to adjust for the heterogeneity of output, the use of these dummy variables is not needed if the technological variables are sufficiently inclusive. For a full discussion of these and related points, see Friedlaender and Spady (1981) and Mundlak (1978).

capital divided by "carrier operating property–net," which was taken as a measure of the firm's capital

w_5 = price of purchased transportation; a divisia index of prices of rented transportation equipment and purchased transportation weighted by expenditure shares

y = physical output, defined as the total ton-miles carried by the firm

t_1 = alh = average length of haul, defined as total ton-miles divided by total tons

t_2 = load = average load per vehicle, defined as total ton-miles divided by total vehicle-miles

t_3 = ltl = percentage of freight in less-than-truckload lots, defined as total LTL tons divided by total tons

t_4 = size = average shipment size, defined as total tons divided by total shipments

t_5 = ins = unit insurance cost, defined as insurance costs per ton-mile

T = time defined as $T = 1 = 1974, T = 2 = 1975, \ldots, T = 6 = 1979$

Output was measured in terms of aggregate ton-miles. Although there have been a number of recent efforts to estimate a multiple-output cost function to take the heterogeneity of output explicitly into account (see, for example, Harmatuck [1981] and Wang Chiang and Friedlaender [1984]), data limitations prevented such disaggregation. Because, however, the inclusions of a sufficient range of technological variables or operating characteristics can serve to capture much of the heterogeneity of output, the following operating characteristics were included in the analysis: average length of haul (alh), average load (load), average shipment size (size), insurance costs per ton-mile (ins), and the percentage of LTL traffic carried by the firm (ltl).

The first three operating characteristics attempt to reflect the composition of output in physical terms and serve as proxies for the firm's network.[9] Small loads, small shipments, and short hauls tend to raise costs; therefore one would expect costs to be negatively related to these variables. The insurance variable serves as a proxy for the fragility and value of the commodities carried by the firm. Because fragile, valuable commodities tend to require

---

[9] Unfortunately, data on trucking networks are generally proprietary and are only available for 1976. Although the omission of these variables may lead to some specification error, the included variables on operating characteristics capture many of the qualitative aspects of each firm's network. For example, firms with a dense distribution of terminals should have relatively short hauls, low loads, and small shipment sizes. For a full discussion of the role of network effects upon trucking costs see Wang Chiang and Friedlaender (1984).

special handling, costs should be positively related to this variable. The LTL variable measures the distribution of traffic between LTL and TL traffic. LTL traffic being inherently more expensive to carry because it requires extensive consolidation and handling, costs should be positively related to this variable.

The inputs used in this analysis included labor, fuel, purchased transportation,[10] revenue-equipment capital, and general capital. The prices of labor, revenue-equipment capital, and purchased transportation were derived by using a divisia index of the prices of the different types of inputs given in the Interstate Commerce Commission Annual Reports, weighted by the expenditure shares within each category.[11] Fuel prices measured regional levels of fuel cost,[12] while the general capital costs included any residual costs that could not be explicitly attributed to the other factors plus depreciation, maintenance, and a 14 percent opportunity cost for capital.[13] Costs were defined to equal the sum of all factor payments: labor, fuel, purchased transportation, revenue equipment, and other capital. Note that because "other" capital includes a measure of the opportunity cost of capital, total costs also include the opportunity cost of capital.

2.2. Models of technical change

In the previous section we outlined two alternative models: the Stevenson model, which treated time as a technological variable; and the augmentation model, which treated time as an augmentation factor on the various arguments of the cost function: output, input prices, or operating characteristics. Because

---

[10] Trucking firms typically subcontract out a portion of their truckload operations to owner operators, whom they utilize to even out their traffic flows. For a full discussion of these activities, see Wyckoff and Maister (1977).

[11] The general form of the index used to aggregate input prices is given by

$$w_i = \sum_j S_{ij} w_{ij},$$

where w_i = index of input price i, S_{ij} = expenditure share of subcategory j of input type i, and w_{ij} = price of subcategory j of input type i.

For a full discussion of the construction of the input price, see Wang Chiang (1981).

[12] Data were obtained from *Platt's Oil Price Handbook*.

[13] These costs consisted of operating costs, less the costs of other categories, plus maintenance costs (which were assumed to represent payments for capital services), depreciation, and a measure of the opportunity cost of capital, which was assumed to equal 14 percent of "carrier operating property–net." Since carrier operating property–net was taken as a measure of the firm's value of capital, the price of capital was measured by "other" expenditures or carrier operating property–net.

the augmentation model is a restricted form of the Stevenson model, we can test to determine whether it is an acceptable representation of technical change. Moreover, since the augmentation model assumes that all of the arguments are affected by technical change, it is possible to use hypothesis tests to see which variables are, in fact, augmented over time.

Figure 2.1 presents the nested hypothesis tests and their associated test statistics. Moving through the hierarchy of tests, we first observe that we cannot reject the augmentation specification of the cost function. Moreover, we also cannot reject the hypothesis that augmentation affects two of the three different arguments of the cost function. However, moving to the third row, we observe that at reasonable levels of significance, we can reject the hypothesis that technical change is solely factor augmenting or output augmenting. But we cannot reject the hypothesis that technical change is solely augmenting in the operating characteristics. Finally, the last row indicates that we can firmly reject the hypothesis that costs are not affected by time, indicating that technical change has clearly taken place.

These findings are not entirely conclusive, but they suggest that technical change primarily comes about through operating characteristics, rather than through inputs or output. Specifically, although it is not possible to reject the hypothesis that technical change occurred jointly through a combination of inputs and outputs (or combinations of inputs and operating characteristics or of output and operating characteristics), it is possible to reject the hypothesis that technical change came about solely through inputs or output. Thus although technical change may have a joint effect upon inputs and output, it appears to have the strongest single effect through operating characteristics.

This finding is important for both methodologic and policy reasons. From the viewpoint of methodology, technical change is often thought of as being neutral (affecting all arguments of the cost function proportionately), as being factor augmenting (increasing the efficiency of the various factors in different proportions), or as being output augmenting (increasing the elasticities of scale associated with production). However, it is not generally thought of as having a strong effect through operating characteristics or other technological variables. Hence these findings suggest that this may be an important omission in industries in which technological variables may be important (such as the transportation industries or electric utilities).

From the viewpoint of policy, it is important to note that many of these technological variables are directly affected by regulation, in so far as it affects routings and equipment utilization. If technical change works by changing the ways in which operating characteristics affect the cost function and the underlying technology, this suggests that regulatory changes may have an even greater effect upon costs than is generally perceived. Of course, the specific impact of technical change upon these variables depends upon the estimated parameters in the cost function, to which we now turn.

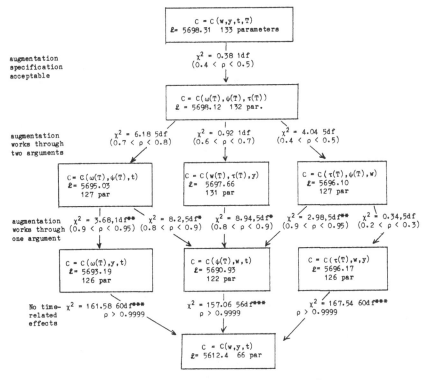

Figure 2.1. Nested hypothesis tests of technical change. $\mathscr{L}$ = log of likelihood function; ρ = level of significance of χ^2 statistic; * reject hypothesis at 80 percent confidence level; ** reject hypothesis at 90 percent confidence level; *** reject hypothesis at 99.9 percent confidence level.

2.3.   *Estimated model*

In estimating the augmentation specification of the cost function, a number of the parameters on the interaction and third-order terms were found to be highly insignificant. Thus these variables were deleted.[14] Table 2.1 gives the estimated coefficients for this "parsimonious" augmentation specification of the cost function $C = C(\tau(t,T),w,y,)$[15] and its associated factor share equa-

---

[14] Specifically, all third-order terms with a t-statistic under 0.3 were omitted except for variables that reflect the third-order interactions between input prices and time, which affect the elasticity of substitution. In addition, all second-order terms whose t-statistic was less than 0.3 were also omitted, unless their related third-order terms were retained.

[15] Note that for simplicity, we omit the tildas over the coefficients estimated in Eq. (10).

Table 2.1. Regression equation, augmentation model, $c(y,\mathbf{w},\tau(T))$

Parameter	Variable	Estimated coefficient	t-Stat
0	const	19.3242	430.127
1	w_1 (labor)	0.6261	119.514
2	w_2 (fuel)	0.0663	41.588
3	w_3 (revenue equipment)	0.0187	21.263
4	w_4 (general capital)	0.22128	70.628
5	w_5 (purchased transportation)	0.0670	11.610
1	t_1 (alh)	−0.2539	3.519
2	t_2 (load)	−0.9774	8.001
3	t_3 (ltl)	−0.1667	1.460
4	t_4 (size)	−0.3556	2.723
5	t_5 (ins)	0.7440	1.331
y	y (output)	0.9539	26.552
T	T (time)	0.0106	0.580
1	η_1 (alh-aug)	−0.0104	0.340
2	η_2 (load-aug)	−0.0088	0.677
3	η_3 (ltl-aug)	−0.0076	0.284
4	η_4 (size-aug)	0.0221	0.406
5	η_5 (ins-aug)	−0.1316	2.093
$\tfrac{1}{2}a_{11}$	w_1w_1	0.0285	14.592
a_{12}	w_1w_2	−0.0378	22.091
a_{13}	w_1w_3	−0.0079	4.703
a_{14}	w_1w_4	−0.0034	1.327
a_{15}	w_1w_5	−0.0080	3.023
$\tfrac{1}{2}a_{22}$	w_2w_2	0.0248	22.849
a_{23}	w_2w_3	−0.0042	2.940
a_{24}	w_2w_4	−0.0067	11.170
a_{25}	w_2w_5	−0.0009	−1.211
$\tfrac{1}{2}a_{33}$	w_3w_3	0.0069	9.403
a_{34}	w_3w_4	−0.0020	4.077
a_{35}	w_3w_5	0.0002	0.512
$\tfrac{1}{2}a_{44}$	w_4w_4	0.0030	2.735
a_{45}	w_4w_5	0.0060	3.330
$\tfrac{1}{2}a_{55}$	w_5w_5	0.0026	0.859

Parameter	Variable	Estimated coefficient	t-Stat
b_{11}	w_1t_1	−0.0276	3.365
b_{12}	w_1t_2	0.0104	1.299
b_{13}	w_1t_3	0.0769	6.812
b_{14}	w_1t_4	−0.0217	1.252
b_{15}	w_1t_5	−0.0223	3.995
b_{21}	w_2t_1	0.0143	7.228
b_{23}	w_2t_3	0.0079	1.772
b_{24}	w_2t_4	0.0069	1.830
b_{25}	w_2t_5	−0.0043	2.888
b_{31}	w_3t_1	−0.0047	3.058
b_{32}	w_3t_2	0.0025	1.372
b_{33}	w_3t_3	0.0040	1.503
b_{34}	w_3t_4	−0.0010	0.434
b_{35}	w_3t_5	−0.0027	3.644
b_{41}	w_4t_1	0.0129	2.427
b_{42}	w_4t_2	−0.0002	0.025
b_{44}	w_4t_4	0.0080	1.501
b_{45}	w_4t_5	0.0171	4.258
b_{51}	w_5t_1	0.0051	0.528
b_{52}	w_5t_2	−0.0127	1.366
b_{53}	w_5t_3	−0.0888	5.959
b_{54}	w_5t_4	0.0078	0.640
b_{55}	w_5t_5	0.0122	1.999
c_{1y}	w_1y	0.0016	0.433
c_{2y}	w_2y	−0.0029	2.904
c_{3y}	w_3y	0.0008	1.358
c_{4y}	w_4y	−0.0016	0.704
c_{5y}	w_5y	0.0021	0.487
d_{1T}	w_1T	0.0030	1.209
d_{2T}	w_2T	0.0002	0.351
d_{3T}	w_3T	0.0004	1.772
d_{4T}	w_4T	−0.0026	2.236
d_{5T}	w_5T	−0.0010	0.383
$\tfrac{1}{2}e_{11}$	t_1t_1	0.3749	5.934
e_{12}	t_1t_2	−1.0157	5.489
e_{13}	t_1t_3	−0.0359	0.155
e_{14}	t_1t_4	0.3959	2.021
e_{15}	t_1t_5	0.3143	3.988
$\tfrac{1}{2}e_{22}$	t_2t_2	0.0226	0.246

Table 2.1. *(Continued)*

Parameter	Variable	Estimated coefficient	t-Stat	Parameter	Variable	Estimated coefficient	t-Stat
e_{23}	t_2t_3	−0.4040	1.388	p_{23T}	w_2t_3T	−0.0007	0.405
e_{24}	t_2t_4	−0.9564	3.716	p_{24T}	w_2t_4T	−0.0012	0.795
e_{25}	t_2t_5	−0.6494	5.870	p_{25T}	w_2w_5T	−0.0006	0.913
$\frac{1}{2}e_{33}$	t_3t_3	−0.7144	3.673	p_{31T}	w_3t_1T	−0.0004	0.591
e_{34}	t_3t_4	−1.2928	5.425	p_{32T}	w_3t_2T	0.0024	2.405
e_{35}	t_3t_5	−0.2730	4.134	p_{33T}	w_3t_3T	−0.0004	0.583
$\frac{1}{2}e_{44}$	t_4t_4	−0.4287	3.946	p_{35T}	w_3t_5T	0.0005	1.507
$\frac{1}{2}e_{55}$	t_5t_5	0.0368	1.298	p_{41T}	w_4t_1T	−0.0011	0.448
f_{1y}	t_1y	−0.0902	1.714	p_{42T}	w_4t_2T	0.0040	0.826
f_{2y}	t_2y	0.1419	1.664	p_{45T}	w_4t_5T	−0.0013	0.749
f_{3y}	t_3y	−0.2309	2.680	p_{51}	w_5t_1T	0.0033	1.121
f_{4y}	t_4y	−0.2508	3.120	p_{52T}	w_5t_2T	−0.0105	2.065
f_{5y}	t_5y	−0.0747	1.841	p_{53T}	w_5t_3T	0.0011	0.5288
g_{1T}	t_1T	−0.0486	2.051	p_{54T}	w_5t_4T	0.0012	0.795
g_{2T}	t_2T	0.0956	1.735	p_{55T}	w_5t_5T	−0.0033	1.279
g_{3T}	t_3T	0.0794	1.672	q_{1yT}	w_1yT	−0.0012	0.908
g_{4T}	t_4T	0.332	0.797	q_{3yT}	w_3yT	0.0004	1.401
g_{5T}	t_5T	−0.0051	0.414	q_{4yT}	w_4yT	0.0007	0.684
K_yT	yT	0.0168	1.646	$\frac{1}{2}s_{11T}$	t_1t_1T	0.0828	2.945
$\frac{1}{2}h_{yy}$	yy	0.0028	0.182	s_{12T}	t_1t_2T	0.2838	3.145
m_{TT}	TT	−0.0006	0.236	s_{13T}	t_1t_3T	−0.1503	3.028
$\frac{1}{2}n_{11T}$	w_1w_1T	0.0015	1.379	s_{15T}	t_1t_5T	0.0606	2.820
n_{12T}	w_1w_2T	−0.0040	3.972	$\frac{1}{2}s_{22T}$	t_2t_2T	0.1190	1.536
n_{13T}	w_1w_3T	0.0009	1.043	s_{23T}	t_2t_3T	0.1036	1.460
n_{14T}	w_1w_4T	0.0015	1.081	s_{25T}	t_2t_5T	−0.0578	0.984
n_{15T}	w_1w_5T	−0.0015	0.919	$\frac{1}{2}s_{55T}$	t_5t_5T	−0.0148	1.105
$\frac{1}{2}n_{22T}$	w_2w_2T	0.0018	2.804	y_{1yT}	t_1yT	−0.0376	2.314
n_{23}	w_2w_3T	0.0005	0.637	u_{2yT}	t_2yT	0.0982	2.261
n_{24}	w_2w_4T	0.0001	0.309	u_{3yT}	t_3yT	0.0620	1.844
n_{25}	w_2w_5T	−0.0001	0.284	y_{4yT}	t_4yT	0.0216	1.026
$\frac{1}{2}n_{33}$	w_3w_3T	−0.0004	1.086				
n_{34}	w_3w_4T	−0.0004	1.606				
n_{35}	w_3w_5T	−0.0001	0.667				
$\frac{1}{2}n_{44}$	w_4w_4T	−0.0002	0.301				
n_{45}	w_4w_5T	−0.0008	0.859				
n_{55}	w_5w_5T	0.0026	1.429				
p_{12T}	w_1t_2T	0.0041	0.761				
p_{15T}	w_1t_5T	0.0047	1.977				
p_{21T}	w_2t_1T	−0.0018	2.969				

Table 2.2. *Hypothesis tests*

Hypothesis	Coefficient restrictions	L	DF	χ^2	ρ
(1) Second order	$n_{isT} = 0$ $\forall$ i,s $\quad$ $p_{ijT} = 0$ $\forall$ i,j $\quad$ $q_{iyT} = 0$ $\forall$ i $\quad$ $s_{jrT} = 0$ $\forall$ j,r $\quad$ $u_{jyT} = 0$ $\forall$ j $\quad$ $v_{yyT} = 0$	5,629.63	39	128.18	>0.999
(2) No time effect	Same as (1) plus $\eta_j = 0$ $\forall$ j	5,612.43	44	162.58	>0.999
(3) Full separability $C = I(\mathbf{w})J(y)h(\tau(t,T))$	$b_{ij} = 0$ $\forall$ i,j $\quad$ $c_{iy} = 0$ $\forall$ i $\quad$ $f_{jy} = 0$ $\forall$ j $\quad$ $n_{isT} = 0$ $\forall$ i,s $\quad$ $p_{isT} = 0$ $\forall$ i $\quad$ $q_{iyT} = 0$ $\forall$ j $\quad$ $u_{jyT} = 0$ $\quad$ $v_{yyT} = 0$	5,316.70	57	754.04	>0.999
(4) Partial separability $C = M(\mathbf{w},\tau(t,T))N(y,\tau(t,T))$	Same as (2) plus $c_{iy} = 0$ $\forall_i$ $\quad$ $q_{iyT} = 0$ $\forall_i$	5,676.13	7	35.18	>0.999

tions, defined as a restriction of Eq. (10).[16] The remaining coefficients were generally statistically significant.

In estimating cost functions it is useful to consider the general role of the operating characteristics, the time variable, and the question of separability. Table 2.2 presents the hypothesis tests used to evaluate these questions and their summary test statistics, which indicate the following. First, not only is the hypothesis that the operating characteristics are jointly equal to zero decisively rejected, but most of the parameters on the operating characteristics

[16] The share equation for input i is given by the following expression.

$$\frac{\partial \ln C}{\partial \ln w_i} = \tilde{\alpha}_i + \sum_s \tilde{a}_{is} \ln w_s + \sum_j \tilde{b}_{ij} \ln t_j + \tilde{c}_{i\phi} \ln y + \tilde{d}_{iT} T + \sum_s \tilde{n}_{isT} \ln w_s T$$

$$+ \sum_j \tilde{p}_{ijT} \ln t_j T + \tilde{q}_{i\phi T} \ln y T$$

These share equations were estimated jointly with the cost equation using the full-information maximum likelihood (FIML) estimation procedures. Because the sum of the share equations equals 1, the share equation for purchased transportation was dropped in the estimation. For a full discussion of the estimating procedure, see Friedlaender and Spady (1981).

are highly significant, indicating that these variables should clearly be included in the cost function. Second, although the augmentation factors on the individual operating characteristics were generally insignificant, the previous discussion indicated that the hypothesis that they are jointly equal to zero was decisively rejected. In addition, many of the third-order terms in the time variable were highly significant. Thus it would be incorrect to model the technology of general-commodity carriers as being constant over time. Third, the hypothesis that the cost function is separable was decisively rejected, indicating that technology is decidedly not homothetic. Thus global generalizations about returns to scale, elasticities of substitution, and technical change are not possible, because the specific values of input prices and operating characteristics will affect the values of these measures.

3.   Technical change

The previous analysis of the sources of technical change indicated that it comes about through its effect upon operating characteristics rather than through its effect upon inputs or outputs. Thus neither input prices nor output levels appear to be augmented by technical change. In contrast, operating characteristics are augmented so that in any given year T, the effective value of the operating characteristic is given by $\tau_j = t_j e^{\eta_j T}$, where t_j represents the physical values of the jth operating characteristic, η_j represents the augmentation effect, and T represents time. Consequently a positive value of η_j implies that the effective value of the operating characteristic is greater than its nominal value, whereas a negative value of η_j implies the opposite.

For those characteristics that have a positive impact upon costs, $\eta_j < 0$ implies technical progress, and conversely for those operating characteristics that have a negative impact upon costs. Because trucking technology is non-homothetic, however, it is generally difficult to determine the sign of $\partial C / \partial t_j$ by simple examination of the estimated coefficients and hence whether technical progress or regress has occurred with respect to a given operating characteristic. Consequently a detailed examination of the way in which the augmentation effects interact with the other variables to bring about technical change is necessary.

The η_j coefficients given in Table 2.1 measure the augmentation effects associated with each operating characteristic. All of these effects are estimated to be negative, indicating that the effective value of each operating characteristic becomes smaller over time. With the exception of the augmentation effect associated with insurance and handling, all of these estimated effects are statistically insignificant. Nevertheless, the previous analysis of the source of technical change indicates that they are jointly significant and the vehicle through which technical change operates.

The degree of technical change can be estimated by differentiating the cost function, Eq. (10), with respect to time. Differentiating and collecting terms yields the following expression.

$$
\frac{\partial \ln C}{\partial T} = \delta_T + \sum_i d_{iT} \ln w_i + \sum_j g_{jT} \ln t_j + k_{\phi T} \ln y + m_{TT} T
$$

$$
+ \tfrac{1}{2} \sum_i \sum_s n_{isT} \ln w_i \ln w_s + \sum_i \sum_j p_{ijT} \ln w_i \ln t_j
$$

$$
+ \sum_i q_{i\phi T} \ln w_i \ln y + \tfrac{1}{2} \sum_j \sum_r s_{jrT} \ln t_j \ln t_r + \sum_j u_{j\phi T} \ln t_j \ln y
$$

$$
+ \tfrac{1}{2} v_{\phi\phi T} (\ln y)^2 \tag{11}
$$

where

$$\delta_T \equiv \sum_j \beta_j \eta_j \qquad\qquad p_{ijT} \equiv \sum_r D_{ijr} \eta_r$$

$$d_{iT} \equiv \sum_j b_{ij} \eta_j \qquad\qquad q_{i\phi T} \equiv \sum_j E_{ij\phi} \eta_j$$

$$g_{jT} \equiv \sum_r e_{jr} \eta_r \qquad\qquad s_{jrT} \equiv \sum_h G_{jrh} \eta_h$$

$$h_{\phi T} \equiv \sum_j f_{j\phi} \eta_j \qquad\qquad u_{j\phi T} \equiv \sum_r H_{jr\phi} \eta_r$$

$$m_{TT} \equiv \sum_j \sum_r e_{jr} \eta_j \eta_r \qquad v_{\phi\phi T} \equiv \sum_j I_{j\phi\phi} \eta_j$$

$$n_{isT} \equiv \sum_j B_{isj} \eta_j$$

Note that all the time-related coefficients are linear combinations of the augmentation effects and the coefficients associated with the underlying cost function. Since input and output augmentation did not appear to be statistically significant, the crucial role of augmentation of the operating characteristics is apparent.

Table 2.3 gives the coefficients in Eq. (11) that are needed to calculate the percentage change in costs with respect to time. For the "representative" firm operating with the output, input prices, and operating characteristics of the sample mean, this elasticity is given by $\delta_T + m_{TT}(T - \bar{T})$. Because this does not depend upon the values of the firm-specific variables, it is tempting to treat this as a pure time effect. Because, however, each of these coefficients is a linear combination of the augmentation effects and the respective linear and interaction coefficients associated with the operating characteristics, it is

Table 2.3. *Coefficients required to estimate the elasticity of costs with respect to time*

Parameter	Variable	Estimated coefficient	t-Stat	Parameter	Variable	Estimated coefficient	t-Stat
T	T	0.0106	0.580	p_{42T}	$w_4 t_2 T$	0.0040	0.826
d_{1T}	$w_1 T$	0.0030	1.209	p_{45T}	$w_4 t_5 T$	-0.0013	0.750
d_{2T}	$w_2 T$	0.0002	0.351	p_{51T}	$w_5 t_1 T$	0.0033	1.121
d_{3T}	$w_3 T$	0.0004	1.772	p_{52T}	$w_5 t_2 T$	-0.0105	2.065
d_{4T}	$w_4 T$	-0.0026	2.236	p_{53T}	$w_5 t_5 T$	0.0011	0.5288
d_{5T}	$w_5 T$	-0.0010	0.383	p_{54T}	$w_5 w_4 T$	0.0012	0.795
g_{1T}	$t_1 T$	-0.0486	2.051	p_{55T}	$w_5 w_5 T$	-0.0033	1.279
g_{2T}	$t_2 T$	0.0956	1.735	q_{1yT}	$w_1 yT$	-0.0012	0.908
g_{3T}	$t_3 T$	0.0794	1.672	q_{3yT}	$w_3 yT$	0.0004	1.401
g_{4T}	$t_4 T$	0.0332	0.797	q_{4yT}	$w_4 yT$	0.0007	0.684
g_{5T}	$t_5 T$	-0.0051	0.414	$\frac{1}{2} s_{11T}$	$t_1 t_1 T$	0.0828	2.945
K_{yT}	yT	0.0168	1.646	s_{12T}	$t_1 t_2 T$	-0.2838	3.145
$\frac{1}{2} m_{TT}$	TT	-0.0006	0.236	s_{13T}	$t_1 t_3 T$	-0.1503	3.028
$\frac{1}{2} n_{11T}$	$w_1 w_1 T$	0.0015	1.379	s_{15T}	$t_1 t_5 T$	0.0605	2.820
n_{12T}	$w_1 w_2 T$	-0.0040	3.972	$\frac{1}{2} s_{22T}$	$t_2 t_2 T$	0.1190	1.537
n_{13T}	$w_1 w_3 T$	0.0009	1.043	s_{23T}	$t_2 t_3 T$	0.1036	1.460
n_{14T}	$w_1 w_4 T$	0.0015	1.081	s_{25T}	$t_2 t_4 T$	-0.0578	0.984
n_{15T}	$w_1 w_5 T$	-0.0015	0.919	$\frac{1}{2} s_{55T}$	$t_2 t_5 T$	-0.0148	1.105
$\frac{1}{2} n_{22T}$	$w_2 w_2 T$	0.0018	2.804	u_{1yT}	$t_1 yT$	-0.0376	2.314
n_{23T}	$w_2 w_3 T$	0.0005	0.637	u_{2yT}	$t_2 yT$	0.0982	2.261
n_{24T}	$w_2 w_4 T$	0.0001	0.309	u_{3yT}	$t_3 yT$	0.0620	1.844
n_{25T}	$w_2 w_5 T$	-0.0001	0.284	u_{4yT}	$t_4 yT$	0.0216	1.026
$\frac{1}{2} n_{33T}$	$w_3 w_3 T$	-0.0004	1.086				
n_{34T}	$w_3 w_4$	-0.0004	1.606				
n_{35T}	$w_3 w_5 T$	-0.0001	0.667				
n_{44T}	$w_4 w_4 T$	-0.0002	0.301				
n_{45T}	$w_4 w_5 T$	-0.0008	0.859				
n_{55T}	$w_5 w_5 T$	0.0026	1.429				
p_{12T}	$w_1 t_2 T$	0.0041	0.761				
p_{15T}	$w_1 t_5 T$	0.0047	1.977				
p_{21T}	$w_2 t_1 T$	-0.0018	2.962				
p_{23T}	$w_2 t_3 T$	-0.0007	0.405				
p_{24T}	$w_2 t_4 T$	-0.0012	0.795				
p_{25T}	$w_2 t_5 T$	-0.0006	0.913				
p_{31T}	$w_3 t_1 T$	-0.0004	0.591				
p_{32T}	$w_3 t_2 T$	0.0024	2.405				
p_{33T}	$w_3 t_3 T$	-0.0004	0.583				
p_{35T}	$w_3 t_5 T$	0.0005	1.507				
p_{41T}	$w_4 t_1 T$	-0.0011	0.448				

clear that they cannot be treated as unexplained residuals, but in fact reflect the impact of the augmentation effects associated with the operating charac- teristics. Nevertheless, because this expression is constant over firms, it is reasonable to treat this as a "pseudo" time effect.

The analysis of technical change for the nonrepresentative firms is made difficult by the nonhomothetic structure of technology. In order to determine the way in which the augmentation effects influence the structure of costs and technical change, it is useful to analyze the respective relations among costs, time, and the following variables: operating characteristics, output, and input prices.

3.1. Operating characteristics

The elasticity of cost with respect to the jth operating characteristics is given by the following expression.

$$\frac{\partial \ln C}{\partial \ln t_j} = \left[\beta_j + \sum_i b_{ij} \ln w_i + \sum_r e_{jr} \ln t_r + f_{j\phi} \ln y \right]$$
$$+ \left[\left(g_{jt} + \sum_i p_{ijT} \ln w_i + \sum_r s_{jrT} \ln t_r + u_{j\phi T} \ln y \right) T \right] \quad (12)$$

The first bracketed term reflects the technological relations between costs and the relevant operating characteristic, while the second bracketed term reflects the way in which time affects these relations. Note that the expression within the parenthesis in the second bracket is equal to $\partial^2 \ln C / \partial T \partial \ln t_j$ and therefore measures the direct effect of operating characteristics upon technical change.

Table 2.4 presents the coefficients required to estimate the elasticity of cost with respect to each operating characteristic, evaluated at the input prices at the sample mean. Since the coefficients on the interaction terms between input prices and operating characteristics are numerically small, little infor- mation is lost by this simplification. Within Table 2.4, the coefficients above the line reflect technological relationships between cost and operating charac- teristics (that is, $\partial \ln C / \partial \ln t_j$ for $T = \bar{T}$), while the coefficients below the line reflect the direct effect of operating characteristics upon technical change.

For the representative firm operating at the sample mean, increase in length of haul reduces costs. Moreover, as the average load increases beyond its value at the sample mean, these costs savings will increase substantially. However, increases in the other operating characteristics beyond the value at their sample mean will tend to offset these cost reductions. On balance, these conflicting influences tend to offset each other, indicating that the net effect of increase in average length of haul upon costs is negative.

The time-related effects of average length of haul also have an ambiguous impact upon costs. For the representative firm operating at the sample mean,

Table 2.4. *Coefficients required to estimate the derivative of costs with respect to operating characteristics, with input prices evaluated at the sample mean*

Parameter[a]	Variable	Average length of haul (t_1)		Average load (t_2)		% LTL (t_3)		Average ship size (t_4)		Insurance (t_5)	
		Coef.	t-Stat	Coef.	t-Stat	Coef.	t-Stat	Coef.	t-Stat	Coef.	t-Stat
β_j	t_j	-0.2539	3.519	-0.9774	8.001	-0.1667	1.046	-0.3356	2.723	0.0744	1.331
η_j	t_j-augment	-0.0104	0.340	-0.0088	0.677	-0.0076	0.284	-0.0221	0.406	-0.1316	2.093
e_{1j}	$t_1 t_j$	0.3749	5.934	-1.0157	5.489	-0.0359	0.155	0.3959	2.021	0.3143	3.988
e_{2j}	$t_2 t_j$	-1.0157	5.489	0.0226	0.246	-0.4040	1.388	-0.9564	3.716	-0.6494	5.870
e_{3j}	$t_3 t_j$	-0.0359	0.155	-0.4040	1.388	-0.7144	3.673	-1.2928	5.425	-0.2730	4.134
e_{4j}	$t_4 t_j$	0.3959	2.021	-0.9564	3.716	-1.2928	5.425	-0.4287	3.946	—	
e_{5j}	$t_5 t_j$	0.3143	3.988	-0.6494	5.870	-0.2730	4.134	—		0.0368	1.298
f_{jy}	$t y_j$	-0.0902	1.714	0.1419	1.664	-0.2309	2.680	-0.2508	3.120	-0.0747	1.841
g_{jT}	$t_j T$	-0.0486	2.051	0.0956	1.735	0.0794	1.672	-0.0332	0.797	-0.0051	0.414
s_{1jT}	$t_1 t_j T$	0.0828	2.945	-0.2832	3.145	-0.1503	3.028	—		0.0605	2.820
s_{2jT}	$t_2 t_j T$	-0.2838	3.145	0.1190	1.537	0.1036	1.460	—		-0.0578	0.984
s_{3jT}	$t_3 t_j T$	-0.1503	3.208	0.1036	1.460	—		—		—	
s_{4jT}	$t_4 t_j T$	—		—		—		—		—	
s_{5jT}	$t_5 t_j T$	0.0605	2.820	-0.0578	0.984	—		—		0.0148	1.105
u_{jyT}	$t y_j T$	-0.0376	2.314	0.0982	2.261	0.0620	1.844	0.0216	1.026	—	

[a] Note that e_{ii} and s_{ii} terms are really $\frac{1}{2} e_{ii}$ and $\frac{1}{2} s_{ii}$. Dashes mean coefficients were dropped in the final estimation.

the time-related coefficient is negative (-0.0486) indicating that, ceteris paribus, increases in average length of haul will increase productivity growth. Moreover, the time-related interaction coefficients between average length of haul and other operating characteristics are generally numerically large and negative. Thus firms whose average length of haul and other operating characteristics are 10 percent beyond their values at the sample mean should experience marked technical progress.

The coefficients on the linear and interaction terms associated with average load (t_2) imply that costs should fall as average load increases beyond its sample mean. Moreover, increases in the values of the other operating characteristics will enhance the cost-reducing effects of increases in average load.

Although an increase in average load has an unambiguous effect upon costs, its effect upon productivity growth is ambiguous. Nevertheless, it is reasonable to argue that it should generally be associated with technical regress. For the representative firm operating at the sample mean, the time-related effect of average load is positive, indicating that an increase in average load beyond its sample mean is associated with technical regress. Moreover, further increases in average load or increases in the percentage of LTL traffic tend to exacerbate the tendency toward technical regress. Although an increase in average length of haul can offset this tendency toward technical regress, its magnitude would have to be quite large to provide a full offset.

It is interesting to note that the representative firm operating at the sample mean not only experiences cost reductions from increases in the percentage of LTL traffic, but that firms whose operating characteristics take on values beyond the mean experience even greater cost savings. Since LTL shipments require extensive pickup-and-delivery operations and terminal consolidations, both of which are costly, these findings are somewhat surprising. Nevertheless, they make sense in the context of the firms in the sample, which tend to be large, interregional LTL carriers with large investments in terminal facilities and pickup-and-delivery equipment. Consequently, as their proportion of LTL traffic rises, they are able to make more efficient utilization of their terminal facilities and pickup-and-delivery equipment. Moreover, the ability to utilize above average loads and shipment sizes enhances these efficiencies.

Although the direct effect of increases in LTL upon technical change implies technical regress, the time-related interaction between LTL and length of haul is sufficiently great to indicate that firms with above average lengths of haul may experience technical progress as the percentage of LTL traffic increases. While the effects of the interactions between the percentage of LTL traffic and average load output tend to offset these effects somewhat, it is likely that increases in the percentage of LTL should be accompanied by technical progress for firms whose length of haul is higher than the sample mean.

Increases in shipment size tend to reduce costs while having very little effect upon technical change. The representative firm operating at the sample mean obtains clear benefits from increases in shipment size. Although these benefits will be mitigated if the firm operates with above average lengths of haul, they will be substantially enhanced if average load and the percentage of LTL are above average. For these firms, increases in shipment size imply reduced handling costs and consequent economies. Although increases in shipment size have marked effects upon costs, they appear to have very minor impact upon technical change, which is highly insensitive to the magnitudes of shipment size utilized by the firm.

Increases in insurance costs have a positive impact upon costs for the representative firm; and these impacts are greater for firms whose average length of haul is above the sample mean. These secondary effects associated with average length of haul are offset, however, for firms whose average load and percentage of LTL traffic are above the sample mean. Thus large, fragile loads carried in LTL shipments may be somewhat less costly to carry. Because increases in insurance costs are associated with increases in total costs, the negative augmentation coefficient (η_5) associated with this variable indicates that technical progress has occurred in the handling of fragile, high-value commodities. Moreover, the time-related effects associated with insurance are generally negative (although numerically small), indicating that the direct augmentation effects tend to be enhanced by the indirect effects of the time-related interactions between insurance costs and the other operating characteristics.

To summarize, while the direct augmentation effects appear to have had the greatest impact upon insurance, reducing the cost penalty associated with this variable over time, technical change has also had a strong effect in operating through the percentage of LTL traffic and average length of haul. Thus firms with greater than average lengths of haul, LTL traffic, and insurance costs have tended to exhibit more technical change than other firms.

3.2.   Scale effects

The relations among costs, output, and time can be clarified by considering the elasticity of cost with respect to output, which is given by the following expressions.

$$\frac{\partial \ln C}{\partial \ln y} = \left[\gamma_y + \sum_i c_{iy} \ln w_i + \sum_j f_{jy} \ln t_j + h_{yy} \ln y \right]$$
$$+ \left[\left(K_{yT} + \sum_i q_{iyT} \ln w_i + \sum_j u_{jyT} \ln t_j + v_{yy} \ln y \right) T \right] \quad (13)$$

The first bracket reflects the technological relationships between output and costs and thus abstracts from technical change. The second bracket reflects the time-related relationships between costs and output, with the expression within the parentheses being equal to $\partial^2 \ln C / \partial \ln y \partial T$. Thus this expression indicates how the change in output affects technical change. Note that all of the coefficients in this expression are themselves linear combinations of the augmentation effects and the relevant coefficients in the interaction terms in the underlying cost function (for example, $K_{yT} \equiv \sum_i f_{jy} \eta_j$, where f_{jy} represents the coefficient on the interaction terms between output and operating characteristics and η_j represents the augmentation effects on the operating characteristics).

Table 2.5 gives the coefficients needed to calculate the elasticity of cost with respect to output, evaluated at the input prices of the sample mean. As was true in the discussion of operating characteristics, the coefficients above the line reflect the technological relations between cost and output; the coefficients below the line reflect the way time effects this. Again, the interactions between output and input prices are not considered because they are numerically small.

Table 2.5 indicates that the representative firm exhibits mild economies of scale. Moreover, these scale economies increase substantially as the value of the following variables increases beyond the sample mean: average length of haul, the percentages of LTL traffic, shipment size, and insurance costs.[17] Although these effects could be offset by increases in size of average load, on balance it would appear that firms with a high percentage of LTL traffic, carrying larger than average loads and hauls would exhibit strong economies of scale. Interestingly, variation in output appears to have relatively small effects upon scale economies. Although h_{yy} is positive, indicating a U-shaped average cost curve, its value is both small and statistically insignificant, indicating that one cannot reject the hypothesis of an asymptotically falling average cost curve.

The coefficients below the line give the impact of variations in output upon technical change (and conversely, the impact of technical change upon scale economies). The generally positive values of these coefficients indicate that increases in output have been associated with technical regress, and that firms with above average levels of average load, percentage of LTL, and shipment size have experienced greater technical regress for increases in output.

Because of the significance of scale economies for policy purposes, it is

---

[17] Note that because changes in most of the operating characteristics are associated with changes in trucking operations and network utilization (and possibly network configuration), these measured economies reflect economies of scale rather than economies of density.

Table 2.5. *Coefficients required to calculate the elasticity of cost with respect to output, evaluated with input prices at the sample mean*

Parameter	Variable	Coefficient	t-Statistic
γ_y	y	0.9539	26.552
f_{1y}	$t_1 y$	−0.0902	1.714
f_{2y}	$t_2 y$	0.1419	1.664
f_{3y}	$t_3 y$	−0.2309	2.680
f_{4y}	$t_4 y$	−0.2508	3.120
f_{5y}	$t_5 y$	−0.0747	1.841
$\frac{1}{2} h_{yy}$	yy	0.0028	0.182
K_{yT}	yT	0.0168	1.646
u_{1yT}	$t_1 yT$	−0.0376	2.314
u_{2yT}	$t_2 yT$	0.0982	2.261
u_{3yT}	$t_3 yT$	0.0620	1.844
u_{4yT}	$t_4 yT$	0.0216	1.026
u_{5yT}	$t_5 yT$	—	—
v_{yyT}	yyT	—	—

Note: Dashes mean coefficients were dropped in the final estimation.

useful to analyze explicitly how scale economies have changed over time for a number of large and small firms in the sample. These are shown in Table 2.6. In 1974 all but one of the largest carriers had cost elasticities in excess of 1, indicating that they were experiencing mild diseconomies of scale. In contrast, a number of the smaller carriers showed some evidence of significant scale economies. It is interesting to note, however, that by 1979 the majority of the large carriers showed some evidence of scale economies, while the bulk of the small carriers exhibited mild diseconomies of scale. Apparently, during this period technological change affected the larger carriers differentially, enabling them to reap relatively greater benefits from longer hauls. Thus during the 1970s the advantages of size appear to have benefited the largest carriers relatively more than other carriers. This may help explain the concern that these carriers may continue to grow at the expense of smaller carriers in a deregulated environment.

3.3. Input effects and elasticities of substitution

Although technical change is often thought of as occurring through input augmentation, the empirical findings of this chapter have indicated that inputs are not a vehicle for technical change in the trucking industry. The analysis of augmentation effects indicated that it is possible to reject decisively the hy-

Table 2.6. *Elasticity of costs with respect to output,*
eight largest and eight smallest firms, by year

Firm[a]	1974 Ton-miles (mil)	Elasticity	1975 Ton-miles (mil)	Elasticity	1976 Ton-miles (mil)	Elasticity
Largest						
Yellow Freight	4,547.9	1.036	4,286.7	1.031	5,100.8	1.027
Roadway Express	4,883.8	0.985	4,242.6	0.994	4,740.4	1.004
McLean Trucking	2,680.6	1.073	2,418.3	1.075	2,998.0	1.075
Ryder Truck Lines	2,132.8	1.086	2,010.8	1.070	2,651.3	1.085
Spector Freight	1,766.0	1.060	2,053.1	1.028	2,303.1	1.074
Pacific Intermountain Express	2,216.3	1.144	2,070.4	1.154	2,242.0	1.123
Transcon Lines	2,096.6	1.095	1,756.4	0.982	2,080.7	0.989
Time-DC	2,570.7	1.067	1,862.9	1.067	1,708.4	1.053

Firm[a]	1977 Ton-miles (mil)	Elasticity	1978 Ton-miles (mil)	Elasticity	1979 Ton-miles (mil)	Elasticity
Largest						
Yellow Freight	5,900.9	0.990	6,301.0	0.981	6,603.0	0.957
Roadway Express	5,560.2	0.994	6,343.2	0.988	7,057.3	0.983
McLean Trucking	3,289.8	1.041	3,518.7	1.031	3,686.4	1.009
Ryder Truck Lines	3,334.7	1.047	4,113.9	1.029	4,384.0	0.997
Spector Freight	2,465.3	1.049	2,703.3	1.025	2,601.1	0.997
Pacific Intermountain Express	2,628.9	1.105	3,077.7	1.055	3,308.6	1.031
Transcon Lines	2,267.7	0.915	2,516.8	0.906	2,316.4	0.884
Time-DC	1,706.2	1.021	1,733.6	0.924	1,464.3	0.874

Firm[a]	1974 Ton-miles (mil)	Elasticity	1975 Ton-miles (mil)	Elasticity	1976 Ton-miles (mil)	Elasticity
Smallest						
Barber Transportation	61.8	1.019	53.6	1.025	65.6	1.013
Crouse Cartage	62.8	1.087	58.2	1.119	74.2	1.067
New-Penn Motor Express	87.0	0.931	77.0	0.938	81.4	0.988
Dorn's Transportation	99.8	0.993	79.4	1.046	89.6	1.099
Salt Creek Freightways	74.4	1.051	76.8	1.066	90.7	1.069

Table 2.6. *(Continued)*

Firm[a]	1974 Ton-miles (mil)	Elasticity	1975 Ton-miles (mil)	Elasticity	1976 Ton-miles (mil)	Elasticity
Estes Express	81.0	1.008	71.6	1.033	96.5	1.120
Georgia Highway	115.8	0.932	85.4	0.992	99.5	1.016
Schuster Express	108.5	0.971	92.8	1.005	102.1	0.975

Firm[a]	1977 Ton-miles (mil)	Elasticity	1978 Ton-miles (mil)	Elasticity	1979 Ton-miles (mil)	Elasticity
Smallest						
Barber Transportation	80.1	1.015	87.4	1.005	86.6	1.018
Crouse Cartage	93.2	1.040	117.4	1.050	146.0	0.965
New-Penn Motor Express	92.0	0.977	111.4	0.948	118.7	0.974
Dorn's Transportation	95.1	1.110	95.0	1.142	85.2	1.169
Salt Creek Freightways	105.5	1.064	115.1	1.056	110.5	1.078
Estes Express	123.7	1.027	138.2	1.050	145.4	1.056
Georgia Highway	140.0	1.022	177.1	0.985	192.1	0.962
Schuster Express	121.7	0.931	113.1	0.959	102.6	1.073

[a]Firms were ranked and selected based on 1976 ton-mile outputs.

pothesis that technical change arises solely through input augmentation. Moreover the analysis of the impact of operating characteristics and of output upon technical change indicated that the time-related interaction terms between each of these variables and input prices were numerically small and only marginally statistically significant. This implies that the time-related effects of inputs are minimal. The impact of input prices upon technical change is given by the following expression.

$$\frac{\partial^2 \ln C}{\partial T \partial \ln w_i} = d_{iT} + \sum_s n_{isT} \ln w_s + \sum_j p_{ijT} \ln t_j + q_{iy} \ln y \qquad (14)$$

The previous analysis of operating characteristics and output argued that the p_{ijT} and q_{iy} coefficients were numerically small and generally insignificant. Because the time-related factor-price coefficients may have an effect upon technical change and elasticities of substitutes, however, it is useful to examine them explicitly.

These are given in Table 2.7. The d_{iT} coefficients reflect the impact of input price i upon technical change for the representative firm operating at the sample mean. With the exception of general capital and purchased transportation, these were small and positive, indicating that slight technical regress has been associated with most inputs. In the case of general capital, however, technical progress appears to have taken place. This is consistent with our previous findings concerning the role of LTL and terminal operation in technical change. General capital largely represents terminals and other structures. Since the amount of capital embodied in terminals affects the way shipments are handled and routed, it makes sense that operating characteristics affect technical change through this form of capital.

The coefficients on the interaction terms among factor prices and time (n_{isT}) are generally small and statistically insignificant, indicating that the time-related behavior of the representative firm is a reasonably good representation of industry behavior. There are a few notable exceptions, however. The negative coefficient on the labor-fuel price interaction indicates that although technical regress is associated with increases in fuel prices for the representative firm, high fuel prices could be associated with technical progress for firms with above average labor costs. This suggests that firms with high fuel and labor costs will structure their shipments in such a way as to enhance technical change.

In addition to analyzing the impact of input prices upon technical change, it is useful to analyze the way technical change has affected the elasticities of substitution and the own-price elasticity of demand of each of the inputs. Within the context of the translog cost function used in this analysis, the elasticities of substitution and the own-price elasticities are respectively given by the following expressions for the representative firm operating with mean levels of output, input prices, and operating characteristics.[18]

$$\sigma_{is} = \frac{a_{is} + n_{isT}T + S_iS_s}{S_iS_s} \qquad i \neq s \tag{15a}$$

$$E_{ii} = \frac{a_{ii} + n_{iiT}T - S_i + S_i^2}{S_i} \tag{15b}$$

where S_i and S_s are the fitted shares of the ith and the sth inputs. For firms operating at the sample mean, these are given in Table 2.8 and indicate that

[18] See Uzawa (1962). Uzawa has shown that the partial elasticity of substitution σ_{ii} between factors i and s is given by CC_{is}/C_iC_s, where the subscripts reflect differentiation of the cost function with respect to input i and s. The conventional own-price elasticity E_{ii} is given by $S_i\sigma_{ii}$ where S_i is the share of the ith input. Performing the relevant differentiation on Eq. (10) yields Eq. (15). For a full discussion see Berndt and Wood (1975) and Friedlaender and Spady (1981).

Table 2.7. *Impact on technical change from change in factor prices, by type of factor price*

Parameter	Variable	Labor (w_1) Coef.	t-Stat	Fuel (w_2) Coef.	t-Stat	Revenue equipment (w_3) Coef.	t-Stat	General capital (w_4) Coef.	t-Stat	Purchased transportation (w_5) Coef.	t-Stat
d_{iT}	$w_1 w_i T$	0.0030	1.209	0.0002	0.351	0.0004	1.772	−0.0026	2.236	−0.0010	0.383
n_{1iT}	$w_1 w_i T^a$	0.0015	1.379	−0.0040	3.972	0.0009	1.043	0.0015	1.081	−0.0015	0.919
n_{2iT}	$w_2 w_i T$			0.0018	2.804	0.0005	0.637	0.0001	0.309	−0.0001	0.284
n_{3iT}	$w_3 w_i T$					−0.0004	1.086	−0.0004	1.606	−0.0001	0.667
n_{4iT}	$w_4 w_i T$							−0.0002	0.301	−0.0008	0.859
n_{5iT}	$w_5 w_i T$									0.0026	1.429

[a]Coefficients in $w_i w_s T$ are all symmetric; coefficients on the terms $w_i w_i T \ i \leq 4$ are $\frac{1}{2} n_{iiT}$.

Table 2.8. *Elasticities of substitution and own-price elasticity,*
evaluated at the mean

	Labor	Fuel	Revenue equipment	General capital	Purchased transportation
Labor	−0.2827	0.0892	0.3299	0.9754	0.8096
	(0.008)[a]	(0.047)	(0.147)	(.019)	(0.067)
Fuel		−0.1871	−2.3468	0.5456	0.8083
		(0.035)	(1.139)	(0.046)	(0.160)
Revenue equipment			−0.2448	0.5289	1.1425
			(0.085)	(0.121)	(0.280)
General capital				−0.7510	1.4048
				(0.011)	(0.123)
Purchased transportation					−0.8935
					(0.045)

[a]Standard errors in parentheses.

the own-price elasticity of each input is relatively low, ranging from a value
of −0.1871 for fuel (s.e., 0.035) to a high of −0.8935 (s.e., 0.045) for
purchased transportation. These figures are not surprising, since purchased
transportation is often treated as a residual input by LTL trucking firms to
carry peak loads, while fuel is an essential input for the line-haul journey.

The elasticities of substitution indicate that most inputs are substitutes for
one another, with the notable exception of fuel and revenue equipment, which
are strong complements for each other. The latter finding is also not surprising, since the basic ingredients for the line-haul journey are truck and fuel.
The substitutability of these inputs with labor is indicative of the dual role that
labor plays in the terminal and line-haul operations. Whereas line-haul labor
is doubtless a complement of fuel and revenue equipment, terminal labor is
not. Because terminal operations are very labor intensive, however, when the
price of fuel or of revenue equipment goes up, there is a substitution away
from line-haul operations and toward terminal operations, thus leading to a
net substitution toward labor. Although the elasticities of substitution are
generally low, this is not the case for purchased transportation, which appears
to be highly substitutable with revenue equipment and other capital. Again
this is not unexpected, given the residual role of purchased transportation.
Indeed, the degree of substitutability of purchased transportation with all of
the other inputs appears to be higher than that of the remaining inputs with one
another.

In addition to considering the elasticities of inputs at the sample mean, it is
useful to consider how they have changed over time in response to technical
change. This can be shown in two ways: first by calculating the derivatives of

Table 2.9. *Mean derivatives of elasticities of substitution and own-price elasticities with respect to time, evaluated at the sample mean*[a]

	Labor	Fuel	Revenue equipment	General capital	Purchased transportation
Labor	0.0074	−0.0891	0.0954	0.0107	−0.0368
	(0.0001)	(0.0025)	(0.0078)	(0.0002)	(0.0014)
Fuel		0.0509	0.4711	0.0028	−0.0255
		(.0005)	(0.0360)	(0.0000)	(0.0011)
Revenue equipment			−0.0600	−0.0951	−0.1162
			(0.0041)	(0.0023)	(0.0018)
General capital				−0.0038	−0.0462
				(0.0000)	(0.0045)
Purchased transportation					0.0377
					(0.0020)

[a]Standard deviations of derivatives are in parentheses.

the input elasticities with respect to time; and second, by calculating the input elasticities over the sample period to see how they have changed.

The derivatives of the own-price elasticities and the elasticities of substitution are given by the following expressions for a typical firm, whose factor prices, outputs, and operating characteristics are at the sample mean.

$$\frac{\partial \sigma_{is}}{\partial T} = \frac{1}{S_i^2 S_s^2}(n_{isT}S_iS_s - (a_{is} + n_{isT}T)(S_id_{sT} + S_sd_{iT})) \qquad (16a)$$

$$\frac{\partial E_{ii}}{\partial T} = \frac{1}{S_i^2}(n_{iiT}S_i - d_{iT}(a_{ii} + n_{iiT}T) + S_i^2d_{iT}) \qquad (16b)$$

where S_i and S_s represent the fitted factor shares.

Table 2.9 gives the mean value of the derivatives of the input elasticities with respect to time evaluated at the sample mean and shows that over time, labor and fuel have become less substitutable as have purchased transportation and all other inputs.[19] In contrast, fuel and revenue equipment have become less complementary. Thus, in general, technical change appears to have reduced the responsiveness of the cross effects among inputs.

The effect of technical change upon the own-price elasticities appears to have been minimal, with the exception of fuel (whose elasticity appears to

[19] Indeed, by the end of the sample period, labor and fuel actually appear to have become complements for the typical firm operating at the sample mean. This implies that during the sample period, the labor employed in the line-haul journey became the dominant component of the total labor force employed by the firms in the sample.

have become noticeably lower), and revenue equipment (whose elasticity has become noticeably higher). In view of the large fuel price increases that occurred over the sample period, the fall in the price elasticity of fuel is surprising; apparently firms have substituted against other inputs instead of fuel.

3.4.   Measures of technical change

Having analyzed the determinants of technical change, it is interesting to see the extent to which different types of trucking firms have experienced productivity growth. This is given in Table 2.10 for the eight largest and eight smallest firms in the sample for each year. It is interesting to note that most of these firms have exhibited technical progress over most years in the sample. Consequently, although the operating characteristics may imply a lack of technical change at the sample mean, when the operating characteristics interact with the other variables, the net effect is one of technical progress rather than one of technical regress. Moreover, it is interesting to note that there do not appear to be any systematic differences in the technical change experienced by large and small firms. As we have indicated, operating characteristics appear to be the main force through which technical change operates, and these do not appear to be systematically related to firm size.

4.   Summary and conclusions

In terms of policy there are two principal findings associated with this analysis. First, technical change appears to occur primarily through operating characteristics rather than through inputs or output; and second, the net impact of the augmentation effects is extremely difficult, if not impossible, to predict. This poses an obvious dilemma for policy, because it indicates that the way in which changes in operating characteristics may affect costs over time is very difficult to trace and predict. For example, if one considered the augmentation effect on average length of haul alone, one would predict that as hauls increased over time, the cost saving associated with these increases would fall rather than rise. However, when the full interactions of length of haul with the other variables are taken into account, the opposite conclusion may be reached.

The basic problem with analyzing the impact of technical change upon trucking costs is that the structure of technology is extremely nonhomothetic. Not only does technical change appear to affect the relation of costs and operating characteristics at the sample mean, but it also affects the values of this relation throughout the range of the sample. Thus the interactions between any given operating characteristic and the other variables not only have

Table 2.10. *Percentage change in cost with respect to time, eight largest and eight smallest firms, by year*[a]

Firm	1974 Ton-miles (mil)	% change in cost	1975 Ton-miles (mil)	% change in cost	1976 Ton-miles (mil)	% change in cost
Largest						
Yellow Freight	4,547.9	−2.56	4,286.7	−2.68	5,100.8	−3.01
Roadway Express	4,883.8	0.69	4,242.6	0.05	4,740.4	0.25
McLean Trucking	2,680.6	−2.02	2,418.3	−2.79	2,998.0	−3.54
Ryder Truck Lines	2,132.8	−3.63	2,010.8	−2.99	2,651.3	−4.19
Spector Freight	1,766.0	−1.88	2,053.1	−1.45	2,303.1	−2.88
Pacific Intermountain Express	2,216.3	−4.47	2,070.4	−5.48	2,242.0	−5.08
Trancon Lines	2,096.6	−5.62	1,756.4	−2.05	2,080.7	−1.96
Time-DC	2,570.7	−1.62	1,862.9	−3.97	1,708.4	−5.02

Firm	1977 Ton-miles (mil)	% change in cost	1978 Ton-miles (mil)	% change in cost	1979 Ton-miles (mil)	% change in cost
Largest						
Yellow Freight	5,900.9	−1.94	6,301.0	−1.78	6,603.0	−1.56
Roadway Express	5,560.2	0.60	6,343.2	0.51	7,057.3	0.16
McLean Trucking	3,289.8	−2.01	3,518.7	−1.14	3,686.4	−1.03
Ryder Truck Lines	3,334.7	−4.05	4,113.9	−4.61	4,384.0	−4.49
Spector Freight	2,465.3	−2.51	2,703.3	−1.36	2,601.1	−1.21
Pacific Intermountain Express	2,628.9	−5.98	3,077.7	−5.99	3,308.6	−7.20
Trancon Lines	2,267.7	−1.37	2,516.8	−0.17	2,316.4	1.08
Time-DC	1,706.2	−5.64	1,733.6	0.42	1,464.3	1.53

Firm	1974 Ton-miles (mil)	% change in cost	1975 Ton-miles (mil)	% change in cost	1976 Ton-miles (mil)	% change in cost
Smallest						
Barber Transportation	61.8	−1.10	53.6	−1.46	65.6	−1.16
Crouse Cartage	62.8	−4.18	58.2	−1.43	74.2	−3.28
New-Penn Motor Express	87.0	−2.91	77.0	−4.11	81.4	−2.19

(*continued*)

Table 2.10. *(Continued)*

Firm	1974		1975		1976	
	Ton-miles (mil)	% change in cost	Ton-miles (mil)	% change in cost	Ton-miles (mil)	% change in cost
Dorn's Transportation	99.8	1.24	79.4	0.23	89.6	0.03
Salt Creek Freightways	74.4	−3.27	76.8	−2.30	90.7	−0.78
Estes Express	81.0	−0.02	71.6	−0.38	96.5	1.39
Georgia Highway	115.8	−3.99	85.4	−1.41	99.5	−1.09
Schuster Express	108.5	−2.65	92.8	−0.95	102.1	−1.43

Firm	1977		1978		1979	
	Ton-miles (mil)	% change in cost	Ton-miles (mil)	% change in cost	Ton-miles (mil)	% change in cost
Smallest						
Barber Transportation	80.1	−0.10	87.4	−1.33	86.6	−3.17
Crouse Cartage	93.2	−2.25	117.4	−2.09	146.0	−2.33
New-Penn Motor Express	92.0	−2.08	111.4	−3.40	118.7	−2.88
Dorn's Transportation	95.1	−1.18	95.0	−1.80	85.2	−3.30
Salt Creek Freightways	105.5	−2.70	115.1	−3.05	110.5	−3.79
Estes Express	123.7	−1.59	138.2	−0.71	145.4	−0.74
Georgia Highway	140.0	−1.40	177.1	−3.00	192.1	−3.73
Schuster Express	121.7	−2.95	113.1	−2.05	102.6	−2.22

[a]Firms were ranked and selected based on 1976 ton-mile outputs.

a significant impact upon costs, but they also have a significant impact upon how these costs can be expected to change over time. Because the numerical value of these effects is quite sensitive to the actual values of the operating characteristics, the input prices, and the level of output, however, generalizations are virtually impossible to make. Indeed, what appears to be true for the representative firm at the sample mean (technical regress), does not appear to be true at either end of the size spectrum of the sample.

In spite of the rather pessimistic analytical finding for policy, it is useful to note that the bulk of the firms in this sample did exhibit technical progress during the sample period. Thus, as a result of whatever combinations of operating characteristics, input prices, and output level that may have occurred, most of the firms did appear to become more efficient over time. Of course, whether this will continue to occur is problematical, given the sensitivity of the degree of technical progress to the actual values of the operating characteristics, input prices, and the level of output.

In view of the large number of bankruptcies that have occurred in the trucking industry since 1980, the question of continued technical progress is an extremely important one. Thus whether large firms are differentially efficient, whether increases in load and length of haul should lead to greater or lesser degrees of technical progress are important questions to answer for the continued health of the industry.

References

Berndt, E., and D. O. Wood (1975). "Technology, Prices, and the Derived Demand for Energy." *Review of Economics and Statistics*, 57: 259–68.

Caves, D., L. Christensen, and J. Swanson (1980). "Productivity in U.S. Railroads, 1951–1974." *Bell Journal of Economics*, 11, no. 1 (Spring): 166–81.

Cowing, T., and R. Stevenson, eds. (1981). *Productivity Measurement in Regulated Industries*. New York: Academic Press.

Friedlaender, A. F., and R. H. Spady (1981). *Freight Transport Regulation: Equity, Efficiency and Competition in the Rail and Regulated Trucking Industries*. Cambridge, Mass.: MIT Press.

Friedlaender, A. F., and J. S. Wang Chiang (1983). "Productivity Growth in the Regulated Trucking Industry." *Research in Transportation Economics*, 1: 149–84.

Harmatuck, D. J. (1981). "A Multiproduct Cost Function for the Trucking Industry." *Journal of Transport Economics and Policy*, 14, no. 1: 54–67.

Koenker, R. (1977). "Optimal Scale and the Size Distribution of American Trucking Firms." *Journal of Transport Economics and Policy*, 14, no. 1: 54–67.

Mundlak, Yair (1978). "On the Pooling of Time Series and Cross Section Data." *Econometrica*, 46, no. 1, January: 69–86.

Platt's Oil Price Handbook, 1967–77 editions.

Schur, S. J. (1982). Technological Change and Productivity Growth in the U.S. Trucking Industry. Unpublished MS Thesis, Department of Civil Engineering, Massachusetts Institute of Technology, Cambridge, Mass.

Spady, R. H., and A. F. Friedlaender (1978). "Hedonic Cost Functions for the Regulated Trucking Industry." *The Bell Journal of Economics* 9, no. 1 (Spring): 159–79.

Stevenson, R. (1980). "Measuring Technological Bias." *American Economic Review*, 70, no. 1: 162–73.

Trinc's Transportation Consultants. *Trinc's Blue Book of the Trucking Industry*, 1974–79 editions.

Uzawa, H. (1962). "Production Functions with Constant Elasticity of Substitution." *Review of Economic Studies*, 44: 291–99.

Wang Chiang, S. J. (1981). Economies of Scale and Scope in Regulated Industries: A Case Study of the U.S. Trucking Industry. Unpublished PhD dissertation, Department of Civil Engineering, Massachusetts Institute of Technology, Cambridge, Mass.

Wang Chiang, S. J., and A. F. Friedlaender (1984). "Output Aggregation, Network Effects, and the Measurement of Trucking Technology." *The Review of Economics and Statistics*, 64, no. 2, May: 267–76.

Wyckoff, D. D., and D. Maister (1977). *The Motor Carriers Industry*, Lexington, Mass.: Lexington Books.

CHAPTER 3

An econometric analysis of the cost and production structure of the trucking industry

ANDREW F. DAUGHETY, FORREST D. NELSON, AND WILLIAM R. VIGDOR

An understanding of the structure of technology and the cost-generation process is a necessary step in the analysis of many policy issues. Questions of regulation, deregulation, merger, pricing, and investment all require extensive information on the affected firms' cost and production functions. The recent explosion of interest in issues of deregulation of transportation industries has generated a number of cost analyses of railroads, airlines, and, most recently, motor carriers. The purpose of this chapter is to help further sharpen the emerging image that studies of the motor carrier industry are providing.[1] Our approach will involve emphasizing the heterogeneity of motor carrier technology, the source of the heterogeneity being the spatial context (or environment) within which production takes place. Our main goal is to find a unified and convenient characterization of the subtechnologies, with special emphasis on the role of the spatial environment in generating the subtechnologies.

We proceed as follows. We first pose a family of technologies indexed by a vector of attributes reflecting spatial and market characteristics. We shall see that one way to think of this vector is as a vector of lumpy inputs, some of which may or may not have meaningful notions of markets in which to purchase the lumpy inputs. We then proceed to consider the attribute-indexed cost function dual to the family of technologies. This leads to an econometric model that is estimated using a panel database consisting of over 3,000 yearly observations on firms from 1953 to 1958.

This is a particularly useful period of time to use. During that period very little substantial technological change occurred. Furthermore, regulation was

The research reported in this chapter has been supported by National Science Foundation grant SES-8218684. Support from The Transportation Center, Northwestern University is also appreciated. We thank Ann Friedlaender, Joel Horowitz, Richard Spady, and Sam Wu for their comments.

[1] See, for example, Spady and Friedlaender (1978), Friedlaender and Spady (1981), Harmatuck (1981), Friedlaender, Spady, and Wang Chiang (1981), and Wang Chiang and Friedlaender (1984).

very stable during the period. There was little or no entry and operating ratio regulation was mechanically and consistently applied. In particular, if the industry met a 93 percent operating ratio criterion (if industry operating costs were at least 93 percent of industry operating revenues, that is), then rate increases that maintained the ratio were, essentially, automatically accepted by the Interstate Commerce Commission independent of other regulatory criteria (see Dobesh, 1973). Thus, the period chosen provides a unique opportunity to study the industry in a stable technological and regulatory environment, especially since this uniformity holds both temporally and spatially (across states and regions). This is not as true of the 1960s and 1970s, which are the periods used in most other trucking studies. During those years the regulatory environment was substantially less calm and stable than was true in the 1950s.

The estimated-cost model is then used to examine issues of functional structure. In particular, we reject a hedonic model and accept a model wherein the attributes act mainly through the input variables. This then leads to an analysis of average cost functions for the subtechnologies which reveals that technological attributes, as opposed to factor prices, are the primary determinants of cost differences across firms.

1.   Modeling the technology of motor carrier firms

We view a trucking firm as a combination of various types of trucks, labor and fuel, matched with facilities and routes, so as to serve a collection of spatially separated markets. Thus the technology of a trucking firm (and of all transport firms) not only involves the usual inputs of capital, labor, fuel, and so on, but also must reflect the fact that output is the delivery of goods to a specific place at a specific time. This means that part of the proper specification of the technology of the firm involves the environment in which it operates, including its network and any legal constraints it faces. This is no less true of a trucking firm (which generally does not own the roads, though it may own spatially distributed terminal facilities) than it is of a railroad or pipeline system.

To be specific, let the origins and destinations a firm serves be nodes in a network, with the firm selecting (subject to regulatory approval in the form of operating rights) a set of routes to link the nodes. Given such a network, various forms of capital (such as trucks and terminal facilities), labor and fuel are factors of production for the firm. Note that the network is viewed as a collection of routes and locations, not routes and facilities. It is also important to observe that the collection of markets and routes is fixed by the regulator in the form of "operating rights," as discussed in Spady and Friedlaender (1978). Once these operating rights are defined, the network of the firm is only adjustable over a long period, despite major adjustments in the spatial environment (such as changes in the spatial distribution of demand).

Let us assume that we can represent the spatial setting of the firm (the spatial environment and network) by a vector of attributes $\mathbf{a} \in R^k$. We think of the attribute vector as an index on the technology and thus if inputs are $\mathbf{x} \in R^n_+$ and outputs are $\mathbf{z} \in R^m_+$, we write the technology[2] as $T(\mathbf{z},\mathbf{x}|\mathbf{a})$, with feasibility written as $T(\mathbf{z},\mathbf{x}|\mathbf{a}) \leq 0$. Thus, changes in the network (in $\mathbf{a}$) may be viewed as shifts in the technology that relate the generation of outputs to the acquisition of inputs. For example, consider two networks that we shall call A and B. Let A consist of two nodes (moderately close together) and one arc linking the two nodes while B consists of a large number of nodes (say 1,000) spread over a large area with many arcs linking the various nodes together, though not necessarily linking each node directly to each other node.

In general we would expect to see a number of differences between a firm operating over A and a firm operating over B. The main source of these differences is that the markets served by the firms will generally differ in terms of transport services demanded both with respect to levels and types. For example, it is unlikely that any given market pair (in either network) will want to exchange in *both directions* equal quantities of the same commodities, or even equal quantities of different commodities. In other words, spatially distributed markets introduce a "lumpiness" in the intermarket flow of goods, which means that full utilization of truck capacity may not be possible. Of course, the multiplicity of hauling opportunities implicit in the B network helps reduce this effect (this is known as "balanced loads").

Larger networks will be associated with greater capital utilization, which may be viewed as a difference in technology used (as opposed to technical inefficiency). Moreover, the more extensive the network, the greater the opportunity to utilize specialty equipment efficiently (for example, equipment specially designed for certain commodity characteristics, such as refrigerated units). Larger, more extensive networks also afford longer hauls, generally associated with more efficient use of fuel and trucks. Both longer hauls and the ability to consolidate freight (or to otherwise match shipments so as to increase average loads) alter the technological relations between inputs and outputs; both reflect the network over which the firm applies input resources.

Let $\mathbf{q}$ be the vector of input prices ($\mathbf{q} \in R^n_{++}$). Then if the firm takes input prices as exogenous and minimizes expenditure, the cost function can be written as $C(z,\mathbf{q}|\mathbf{a})$. In other words the family of technologies (indexed by the attribute vector $\mathbf{a}$) give rise to a family of cost functions, also indexed by the attribute vector $\mathbf{a}$.

---

[2] See McFadden (1978), where this approach is called a "technology shift parameter."

Estimating and using a cost function to describe technology presumes that the firms being examined are efficient or else that potential inefficiencies are accounted for by the model. Because the firms under study were regulated, this is a particularly important point; there is a long literature on regulation-induced inefficiencies (see Joskow and Noll, 1981). Four types of inefficient firm operation are possible.

1. Firms simply do not minimize costs because they are protected by regulation.
2. Firms suffer Averch–Johnson (AJ) effects; that is, they face asymmetric incentives for use of inputs.
3. Firms suffer input biases due to required service levels.
4. The industry itself is inefficiently structured; that is, the distribution of output over firms is different from what would emerge from unregulated competition.

Point 1 is a problem all analyses face, which is addressed by a variant of Stigler's survival principle: While there was not free entry into the industry, firms that were inefficiently operated could be bought out. Since regulation was not confiscatory, it would pay someone to buy an inefficiently managed firm and run it more efficiently. Thus, we will assume that any inefficiencies of type 1 are not systematic and that in general firms do minimize cost.

Cost and production duality for rate-of-return regulated firms (the Averch–Johnson case) has recently been developed by Färe and Logan (1983). Operating ratio regulation, while interpretable as AJ-like in nature (see Moore, 1978), is not applied in the trucking industry at the level of an individual firm. Instead, it is applied at the level of the industry, thereby generally ameliorating or totally eliminating any AJ-like biases in input choices (see Daughety, 1984).

Point 3 is a lumpiness argument. Consider a railroad required to provide service between two points (say A and B). It is the nature of a railroad that some minimal amount of way and structure must therefore be present. Hence, an industry unable to eliminate low-density routes is likely to have more capital than it would prefer. This argument does not transfer to the trucking industry. Trucks run on roads provided by the state. Moreover, terminal facilities can be expanded and contracted. There is no minimal terminal facility since consolidation and deconsolidation ("break-bulk") activity could be accomplished inside the truck itself (via the routing of pickups and deliveries), if volume were low enough.

Finally, as pointed out in Daughety (1984), the type of regulation that the motor carrier industry *did* face provided incentives for an inefficient distribution of firm types to evolve. It is precisely this issue that the cost function proposed previously is capable of addressing, if the attribute vector acts as an index of firm types in the distribution of output.

Thus, if we assume that firms take input prices as parametric,[3] that they minimize expenditures and suffer no input biases as discussed, then it is valid to use $C(\mathbf{z},\mathbf{q}|\mathbf{a})$ to characterize $T(\mathbf{z},\mathbf{x}|\mathbf{a})$. A convenient way to think of such cost functions is to view the role of the attributes as that of affecting the parameters of the cost function. Thus, if for given vector $\mathbf{a}$, T is Cobb–Douglas in $\mathbf{z}$ and $\mathbf{x}$, then we might write the cost model in logarithmic terms as

$$\ln C(z,q|\mathbf{a}) = \alpha_0(\mathbf{a}) + \alpha_1(\mathbf{a}) \ln z + \alpha_2(\mathbf{a})\ln q,$$

where for convenience we have considered a technology with one input x and one output z.

Because of the duality between cost and production representations (see, for example, McFadden, 1978), the structure of $C(\mathbf{z},\mathbf{q}|\mathbf{a})$ can be used to infer structure in $T(\mathbf{z},\mathbf{x}|\mathbf{a})$. In particular, we will be interested in the role of the attribute vector $\mathbf{a}$. For example, if one could write the cost function as $C^1(h(\mathbf{z},\mathbf{a}),\mathbf{q})$, where C^1 and h are appropriately defined, then this would imply that the vector $\mathbf{a}$ could be thought of as part of an output description (see Spady and Friedlaender, 1978). Structural tests on the role of the $\mathbf{a}$ vector will be discussed.

Our approach will be as follows. We will assume that, for given $\mathbf{a}$, a translog approximation of the cost function is satisfactory (see Christensen, Jorgenson, and Lau, 1973):

$$\ln C(\mathbf{v}|\mathbf{a}) = \alpha_{00}(\mathbf{a}) + \sum_i \alpha_{i0}(\mathbf{a})\ln v_i + \tfrac{1}{2}\sum_i \sum_j \alpha_{ij}(\mathbf{a})\ln v_i \ln v_j \qquad (1)$$

with $\mathbf{v} = (\mathbf{z},\mathbf{q})$. For convenience, we can represent (1) as

$$\ln C(\mathbf{v}|\mathbf{a}) = \sum_{i=0}^{m+n} \sum_{j=0}^{i} \alpha_{ij}(\mathbf{a})\ln v_i \ln v_j \Delta_{ij}, \qquad (2)$$

where $\ln v_0 \equiv 1$ and

$$\Delta_{ij} = \begin{cases} \tfrac{1}{2} & i = j, \ j \geq 1, \\ 1 & \text{otherwise.} \end{cases}$$

Thus, in particular, the attribute vector only affects the α values and not the transformations of the variables themselves.

---

[3] Kennan (1984) shows that the theoretical notion of parametric prices does not mean that prices are exogenous in econometric analyses using industry data, especially when firms are subject to common, marketwide shocks. Rather, a simultaneous-equations bias occurs. In the case at hand, however, we assume that one of the main benefits of regulation (to the regulatees) is insulation from marketwide shocks (except of the most intense sort, such as major recession). This assumption, in conjunction with the large number of firms in the industry, can be shown to result in the bias being trivial.

Various methods for introducing the attributes suggest themselves. For example, if all parameters are constant in the attribute vector, then the resulting model simply ignores the attribute vector (as did studies before Spady and Friedlaender [1978]). As another possibility, each α could be expressed as a logarithmic expansion of $\mathbf{a}$:

$$\alpha_{ij}(\mathbf{a}) = \beta_{ij}^{00} + \sum_{r=1}^{k} \beta_{ij}^{r0}\ln a_r + \sum_{r=1}^{k} \sum_{s=1}^{r} \beta_{ij}^{rs}\ln a_r \ln a_s, \qquad (3)$$

which can be conveniently written as

$$\alpha_{ij}(\mathbf{a}) = \sum_{r=0}^{k} \sum_{s=0}^{r} \beta_{ij}^{rs}\ln a_r \ln a_s, \qquad (4)$$

where $\ln a_0 \equiv 1$.

Unfortunately, such an assumption necessitates estimation of

$$\left[\frac{(m + n + 1)(m + n + 2)}{2} \right]\left[\frac{(k + 1)(k + 2)}{2} \right]$$

parameters. Thus, for example, if $n = 4$, $m = 2$, and $k = 3$, then such a model contains 280 parameters to be estimated. Eliminating the quadratic terms in the expansion of α_{ij} reduces the parameter requirement (down to 112) but eliminates the ability to examine second-order effects. As a comparison we elect to use a quadratic expansion of $\alpha_{00}(\mathbf{a})$, a quadratic expansion of the $\alpha_{i0}(\mathbf{a})$ and to let $\alpha_{ij}(\mathbf{a})$ be linear in $\mathbf{a}$. In the example from before ($n = 4$, $m = 2$, $k = 3$), this amounts to 154 parameters, while preserving important interaction effects and own second-order effects. Note that this amounts to setting $\beta_{ij}^{rs}=0$ for (jointly) $i,j,r,s \geq 1$.

The approach here differs from the approach taken by Spady and Friedlaender (1978; hereafter SF). They estimate the cost model $C(\psi(\mathbf{z},\mathbf{t}),\mathbf{q})$ where $\mathbf{t}$ is a vector of quality variables and $\psi(\mathbf{z},\mathbf{t})$ is effective output. The purpose of their approach is to replace the potentially large vector of outputs (subscripted by commodity and service characteristics) with a manageable representation of output. The role of $\mathbf{t}$ in the SF model is thus different from the role of $\mathbf{a}$ in the model we use. In the SF model firms produce a value of $\mathbf{t}$ as part of output. Thus, values of $\mathbf{t}$ are drawn from a distribution, with some value associated with an "average firm." In our model the $\mathbf{a}$ vector will be used to distinguish firms: The industry as a whole is viewed as a heterogeneous collection of firms, indexed by $\mathbf{a}$.

In a different analysis (Friedlaender and Spady, 1981; hereafter FS) a reduced form that is a subcase of the one we will use is estimated, with the $\mathbf{t}$-vector viewed as "operating characteristics." In that model technological heterogeneity is specifically incorporated via regional differences. In our model we will use the elements of the attribute vector to separate the technologies.

In the appendix to this chapter (Appendix 3A) we discuss the data and variable selection issues. To summarize, we have chosen to use four prices, three attributes, and two variables to represent the potential range of outputs. The variables and their mnemonic representations are as follows, starting with output.

$$\text{Output} \begin{cases} y: & \text{Total ton-miles (OTM)} \\ i: & \text{Average cargo loss-and-damage insurance (INS)} \end{cases}$$

Output z is viewed as represented by the traditional output measure OTM and by a proxy for commodity mix, the average (per ton-mile) cost of cargo loss-and-damage insurance; thus, $z = (y,i)$. An ideal representation of z would be commodity and origin–destination (OD) specific tons moved. The lack of OD data occasions the use of the ton-mile measure, while the lack of commodity disaggregation occasions the use of the cargo loss-and-damage insurance expenditure per ton-mile, based on the notion that higher INS should reflect a mix of commodities carried that is more heavily weighted toward very-high-value manufactured parts and the like. Thus we replace the unobservable, very-high-dimension output vector z with the simple representation (y,i).

$$\text{Prices} \begin{cases} q_1: & \text{Price of fuel (PF)} \\ q_2: & \text{Price of labor (PL)} \\ q_3: & \text{Price of purchased transportation (PT)} \\ q_4: & \text{Price of capital (PK)} \end{cases}$$

We take fuel, labor, purchased transportation, and capital as the factors of production (x in the technology model) for motor carrier firms. Appendix 3A provides detail on the construction of the four prices PF, PL, PT, and PK. Because of data limitations, no further disaggregation of the four factors of production was possible.

$$\text{Attributes} \begin{cases} a_1: & \text{Average length of haul (AH)} \\ a_2: & \text{Average load (AL)} \\ a_3: & \text{Average shipment size (AS)} \end{cases}$$

The three attributes are used to grossly differentiate firms on the basis of the network that they operate over, the markets they face and the operating rights restrictions they operate under. Average length of haul, measured as total ton-miles divided by total tons, is ton-weighted average miles. In general, AH should be larger the greater the spatial extent of the system operated by a firm. Admittedly, this is a crude measure of the size of a network, and it is certainly likely to be insensitive to small variations in network design.

Average load (total ton-miles divided by total miles, that is, mile-weighted average tons) should increase in value as a firm engages in more truckload traffic or as a firm is able to "balance" its loads. Both of these factors reflect the types of demands faced and the network owned by the firm. Since the spatial distribution of demand (and the type of demand – that is, availability of truckload shipments, availability of backhauls, and so on) influence the utilization of capital, average load acts to link the spatial environment of the firm to the choice of types and levels of inputs. Moreover, in a loose sense, inflexibility in the regulatory controls on operating rights should also be reflected by such a variable.[4]

Average shipment size (in tons per shipment) again links choice of inputs and input/output relationships to the nature of the demand faced by the firm. This is relevant since, unlike a manufacturing firm, a transportation firm's output is its throughput. Average shipment size will tend to rise as a function of the degree of truckload activity, which is a reflection of the nature of demand the firm faces.

The cost equation was estimated simultaneously with factor share equations for fuel, labor, and purchased transportation (see Christensen and Green, 1976). Additive disturbances, assumed to be normally distributed and uncorrelated across years and firms, were appended to the cost equation and factor shares. As is now standard practice, linear homogeneity in prices and symmetry [which is implicit in the $\frac{1}{2}$ terms used in Eq. (1)] were enforced. The system of equations estimated involved dividing (standardizing) each variable (other than the factor shares) by their sample mean, taking logarithms, and then dividing the standardized cost, fuel price, labor price, and purchased transportation price by the standardized price of capital so as to automatically enforce homogeneity in prices.

Substituting (4) into (2), and appending factor share equations, error terms, and observation superscripts (t) yields the following system of equations to be estimated.

$$\ln c^t = \sum_{i=0}^{m+n-1} \sum_{j=0}^{i} \sum_{r=0}^{k} \sum_{s=0}^{r} \beta_{ij}^{rs}\ln a_r^t \ln a_s^t \ln v_i^t \ln v_j^t \Delta_{ij} + \varepsilon_0^t \qquad (5)$$

$$s_i^t = \sum_{j=0}^{m+n-1} \sum_{r=0}^{k} \sum_{s=0}^{r} \beta_{ij}^{rs}\ln a_r^t \ln a_s^t \ln v_j^t + \varepsilon_i^t \qquad i = 3,4,5 \qquad (6)$$

---

[4] Note that since AH is OTM/tons and AL is OTM/miles, the potential exists for some confusion between these attributes and y (OTM). In fact, as we shall show, this may be occurring, since we find that AH and AL are strongly related to input usage and weakly related to output level through the structure of the cost function.

$$\Delta_{ij} = \begin{cases} \frac{1}{2} & i = j, \quad j \ge 1, \\ 1 & \text{otherwise,} \end{cases}$$

$$\beta_{ij}^{rs} = 0 \text{ for } i,j,r,s \text{ all } \ge 1,$$

where

$v_0^t = e,$	$a_1^t = AH^t/\overline{AH},$
$v_1^t = OTM^t/\overline{OTM},$	$a_2^t = AL^t/\overline{AL},$
$v_2^t = INS^t/\overline{INS},$	$a_3^t = AS^t/\overline{AS},$
$v_3^t = (PF^t/\overline{PF}) \div (PK^t/\overline{PK}),$	$c^t = (C^t/\bar{C}) \div (PK^t/\overline{PK}),$
$v_4^t = (PL^t/\overline{PL}) \div (PK^t/\overline{PK}),$	$s_3^t = (EX_F^t/C^t)$
$v_5^t = (PT^t/\overline{PT}) \div (PK^t/\overline{PK}),$	$s_4^t = (EX_L^t/C^t)$
$a_0^t = e$	$s_5^t = (EX_T^t/C^t)$

with EX_F^t, EX_L^t, EX_T^t are the expenditures on fuel, labor, and purchased transportation acquired for use during period t, and where a bar over a variable name indicates the mean of the sample values.

The system of equations was estimated using SAS on an IBM 3033 at the University of Iowa, using Zellner's Seemingly Unrelated Regression (ZSUR) technique (see Judge et al., 1980). The estimation process was iterated until parameter estimates converged. Such a procedure produces maximum likelihood estimates that are invariant with respect to which factor share equation is dropped (see Barton, 1967).

2. The estimated-cost model

Tables 3.1 to 3.3 present the ZSUR estimates of Eqs. (5) and (6). The estimated model, with homogeneity constraints imposed, involves eight primary right-hand-side variables (two outputs, three prices, and three attributes), 120 coefficients, and three factor share equations. The homogeneity restrictions can be used to solve for coefficients relating to the one additional price; that is, β_{6j}^{rs}, $(j = 0, \ldots, 6)$, so the tables contain results for all nine variables, 154 coefficients, and four share equations.

The data are organized in three tables to emphasize and illustrate the interpretation of the role of attributes **a** advocated, namely that the attributes affect the parameters of the cost function. Estimates of the parameters β_{ij}^{rs} are organized as follows: Table 3.1 contains terms β_{ij}^{00}, $0 \le j \le i \le 6$, with subscript i varying across rows and j varying across columns. These terms are interpreted as cost-function parameters for outputs and prices when attribute

Table 3.1. *Estimated cost model: zero-order coefficients of output and price variables*

Variable (i)	First order $\beta_{i\cdot0}^{00}$	Second order β_{ii}^{00}	Interaction with					$F_{24,\infty}$
			PK $\beta_{i\cdot6}^{00}$	PT $\beta_{i\cdot5}^{00}$	PL $\beta_{i\cdot4}^{00}$	PF $\beta_{i\cdot3}^{00}$	INS $\beta_{i\cdot2}^{00}$	
1 OTM	1.0506 (.0119)[a] [88.1]	.0316 (.0105) [3.0]	-.0101 (.0014) [-7.5]	-.0016 (.0022) [-.7]	.0145 (.0019) [7.4]	-.0028 (.0006) [-5.0]	.0352 (.0137) [2.6]	1,730.2
2 ACL	.1609 (.0233) [6.9]	.0571 (.0262) [2.2]	.0046 (.0023) [2.0]	.0053 (.0037) [1.4]	-.0036 (.0032) [-1.1]	-.0062 (.0009) [-6.8]		14.1
3 PF	.0724 (.0009) [83.6]	.0232 (.0015) [15.5]	-.0065 (.0006) [-10.8]	.0114 (.0006) [19.9]	-.0281 (.0015) [-18.6]			1,505.9
4 PL	.5005 (.0031) [163.7]	.0153 (.0037) [4.2]	-.0171 (.0021) [-8.1]	.0299 (.0022) [13.7]				7,574.1

5 PT	.1097	−.0701	.0288	337.1
	(.0034)	(.0023)	(.0013)	
	[31.9]	[−30.8]	[22.3]	
6 PK	.3175	−.0053		5,042.5
	(.0021)	(.0016)		
	[149.4]	[−3.2]		
0 Intercept	.2152			
	(.0136)			
	[15.8]			

Equation	$R^2(Y, \hat{Y})$	RMSE	F(eq.)	(df)	F(X eq.)	(df)
Cost	.969	.2053	778.8	(119,∞)	22.1	(90,∞)
Fuel	.324	.0175	50.5	(29,∞)	5.5	(30,∞)
Labor	.519	.0616	113.7	(29,∞)	5.9	(30,∞)
Transportation	.503	.0722	106.6	(29,∞)	14.2	(30,∞)
Capital	.227	.0446	30.9	(29,∞)		
System	.905		1004.5	(119,∞)		

[a] Entries in parentheses are standard errors; entries in brackets are t-ratios.

Table 3.2. *Estimated cost model: linear effects of output and prices and their interactions with attributes*

Variable	Intercept β_{i0}^{00}	AH β_{i0}^{10}	AL β_{i0}^{20}	AS β_{i0}^{30}	AH × AH β_{i0}^{11}	AL × AL β_{i0}^{22}	AS × AS β_{i0}^{33}	AH × AL β_{i0}^{21}	AH × AS β_{i0}^{31}	AL × AS β_{i0}^{32}
0 Intercept	.2152 (.0136)[a]	−.4428 (.0243)	−.3033 (.0416)	−.0929 (.0149)	.1327 (.0294)	.2282 (.0769)	.0292 (.0098)	−.1815 (.0764)	.1072 (.0283)	−.0253 (.0444)
1 OTM	1.0506 (.0119)	−.0376 (.0201)	.0241 (.0396)	.0096 (.0156)	.0640 (.0169)	.0645 (.0436)	.0019 (.0056)	−.0179 (.0460)	.0109 (.0170)	.0131 (.0227)
2 INS	.1609 (.0233)	−.0622 (.0424)	.0210 (.0720)	.0893 (.0258)	.0074 (.0298)	.0994 (.0610)	.0018 (.0076)	−.0708 (.0711)	.0198 (.0219)	.0332 (.0300)
3 PF	.0724 (.0009)	.0147 (.0015)	−.0197 (.0026)	.0003 (.0010)	−.0017 (.0026)	.0177 (.0061)	−.0037 (.0008)	−.0099 (.0036)	−.0027 (.0012)	.0046 (.0017)
4 PL	.5005 (.0031)	−.0759 (.0051)	.0158 (.0092)	−.0460 (.0035)	.0477 (.0084)	.0301 (.0207)	−.0035 (.0028)	−.0923 (.0117)	−.0093 (.0042)	.0122 (.0059)
5 PT	.1097 (.0034)	.0368 (.0057)	−.0012 (.0103)	.0426 (.0040)	.0060 (.0078)	−.0593 (.0195)	.0131 (.0031)	.0407 (.0122)	.0223 (.0047)	−.0057 (.0068)
6 PK	.3175 (.0021)	.0245 (.0036)	.0051 (.0064)	.0030 (.0025)	−.0520 (.0058)	.0115 (.0139)	−.0060 (.0020)	.0615 (.0082)	−.0103 (.0030)	−.0110 (.0042)
$F_{39,i}$		78.7	32.2	52.5						

[a]Entries in parentheses are standard errors.

levels are at their population means. Table 3.2 contains terms β_{i0}^{rs} for $i = 0$, $1, \ldots, (m + n)$ and $0 \leq s \leq r \leq k$, with i (output and price variables) varying across rows and r and s (attributes) across columns. Note that the first column repeats some of the entries from Table 3.1. All remaining terms, β_{ij}^{r0} for $1 \leq j \leq i \leq 6$ and $r = 0, \ldots, 3$, appear in a similar arrangement in Table 3.3. Again, entries in the first column repeat the remainder of the terms in Table 3.1. (Recall that 126 terms β_{ij}^{rs} with $i,j,r,$ and s all greater than zero were restricted to be zero.) In all three tables, coefficient standard errors appear in parentheses immediately below the coefficient, and (in Table 3.1) t-ratios appear in brackets below the standard errors. F-statistics for testing the overall significance of output and price variables (that is, that all thirty of the coefficients associated with an output or price variable are zero) appear in the last column of Table 3.1. Similar statistics for the three attribute variables (each of which involves forty-nine coefficients) appear in the last row of Table 3.2. All nine variables are resoundingly significant.

Additional entries in Table 3.1 provide summary measures of the fit of the model. The overall R-square is difficult to interpret in this context of an equation system, but similar statistics [labeled $R^2(Y,\hat{Y})$] computed for each equation separately (as the square of the simple correlation between the observed and predicted values of the dependent variable in the equation) are informative. As they show, the cost equation fits quite well, with 96.9 percent of the variance of cost explained by the model. Fits for the share equations, ranging from 22.7 percent for capital to 51.9 percent for labor, are weaker but still quite significant. Two F-statistics are reported for each equation. The first, labeled F(eq.), is the standard statistic for testing the overall fit of the equation; all are resoundingly and unsurprisingly significant. The second F-statistic, labeled $F(x$ eq.), serves for a test of whether the data disagree with the across-equation constraints imposed on coefficients in that equation. The significance of these latter statistics is somewhat discomforting. A test of the other major constraint on the model, price homogeneity, was not conducted but would likewise lead to rejection.[5]

---

[5] These results are not so easy to interpret as might first appear. In addition to the interpretation of testing the a priori constraints, taking the specification of the model as given, the statistics can be read as assessing the specification of the model. That is, measurement error, omitted variables, or incorrect functional form might all lead to biases in coefficient estimates in directions that conflict with the across-equation constraints. Our confidence in the economic theory that dictates those constraints, the otherwise reasonable fit of the model, and the reasonableness of substantive implications of the estimates compel us to accept the latter interpretation. Want of additional and better measures on relevant variables and sufficiently flexible alternative forms, on the other hand, prevent us from taking the obvious steps to correct the biases.

Table 3.3. Estimated cost model: quadratic output and price effects and attribute reactions

Variable Pair (i,j)	Interaction with			
	Intercept β_{ij}^{00}	AH β_{ij}^{10}	AL β_{ij}^{20}	AS β_{ij}^{30}
OTM × OTM	.0316	−.0583	.0065	.0070
	(.0105)[a]	(.0157)	(.0363)	(.0137)
INS × INS	.0571	−.0242	−.0274	.0664
	(.0262)	(.0489)	(.0742)	(.0225)
PF × PF	.0232	.0064	−.0255	.0065
	(.0015)	(.0025)	(.0046)	(.0015)
PL × PL	.0153	.0095	−.0507	.0009
	(.0037)	(.0055)	(.0111)	(.0042)
PT × PT	−.0701	−.0217	.0257	−.0302
	(.0023)	(.0035)	(.0069)	(.0028)
PK × PK	−.0053	−.0109	.0018	−.0054
	(.0016)	(.0025)	(.0051)	(.0020)
OTM × INS	.0352	.0127	−.0036	−.0044
	(.0137)	(.0200)	(.0409)	(.0142)
OTM × PF	−.0028	.0004	−.0004	−.0017
	(.0006)	(.0008)	(.0018)	(.0007)
OTM × PL	.0145	−.0082	.0363	−.0023
	(.0019)	(.0029)	(.0062)	(.0025)
OTM × PT	−.0016	−.0046	−.0087	.0034
	(.0022)	(.0031)	(.0069)	(.0028)
OTM × PK	−.0101	.0214	−.0272	.0005
	(.0014)	(.0020)	(.0044)	(.0017)

Variable Pair (i,j)	Interaction with			
	Intercept β_{ij}^{00}	AH β_{ij}^{10}	AL β_{ij}^{20}	AS β_{ij}^{30}
INS × PF	−.0062	−.0011	.0022	−.0024
	(.0009)	(.0015)	(.0025)	(.0008)
INS × PL	−.0036	−.0036	−.0022	.0252
	(.0032)	(.0054)	(.0089)	(.0030)
INS × PT	.0053	.0170	−.0251	−.0095
	(.0037)	(.0061)	(.0101)	(.0034)
INS × PK	.0046	−.0124	.0251	−.0134
	(.0023)	(.0038)	(.0063)	(.0021)
PF × PL	−.0281	−.0113	.0280	−.0113
	(.0015)	(.0024)	(.0044)	(.0016)
PF × PT	.0114	.0059	−.0045	.0057
	(.0006)	(.0009)	(.0018)	(.0007)
PF × PK	−.0065	−.0011	.0019	−.0010
	(.0006)	(.0009)	(.0019)	(.0007)
PL × PT	.0299	.0028	.0026	.0143
	(.0022)	(.0033)	(.0066)	(.0026)
PL × PK	−.0171	−.0010	.0201	−.0039
	(.0021)	(.0032)	(.0065)	(.0025)
PT × PK	.0288	.0129	−.0238	.0102
	(.0013)	(.0020)	(.0039)	(.0016)

[a] Entries in parentheses are standard errors.

Estimates of the shares of labor and fuel are in rough agreement with other studies, suggesting that the present model is properly capturing these effects on cost. The estimated share of labor (at the mean of the sample) is the first-order coefficient on PL, 0.5005. This corresponds reasonably well with estimates by both SF and Moore (1978), albeit for different time periods than the data at hand. The share of fuel (7.2 percent) is slightly higher than that estimated by SF (4 percent), but this may be accounted for by the significant operating changes that are likely to have accrued due to the development of the interstate highway system which occurred, in large part, between the time period of concern in this chapter and the one of concern to SF (1972).

Note that the coefficient on OTM is slightly greater than 1, suggesting slight diseconomies of scale[6] ($S = 0.9518$) at the point of means. This result is extremely close to the estimate in SF (0.9646), who find essentially constant returns to scale indicated by the first-order coefficient on ψ. In the case of SF, the standard error on the first-order coefficient of ψ is large enough so as not to be able to reject constant returns to scale. In our case we can reject constant returns to scale. The difference is likely to be the fact that we are using almost thirty times as many observations, thereby generating much smaller standard errors. The closeness of the economies-of-scale point estimates in the two studies is certainly noteworthy.

Increases in INS generate increases in cost. Thus, holding ton-miles fixed but adjusting the product mix to reflect commodities of higher and higher value results in increased costs of production. Although this is not a particularly precise method for measuring economies of scope – that is, cost advantages due to transporting a mix of commodities (see Baumol, Panzar and Willig, 1982) – the sign of the coefficient on INS suggests that such economies are unlikely to be present in a more commodity-disaggregate cost model.

To see this, consider the following simple model. Let u_1 and u_2 be the ton-miles of low-value goods and high-value goods respectively[7]; thus $y = u_1 + u_2$. Moreover, assume that total of loss and damage insurance payments I is simply $u_1 + pu_2$, where for convenience we have assumed that low-value goods premiums are \$1 per ton-mile while high-value goods premiums are \$$p$ per ton-mile ($p > 1$). The output representation we have used in our estimation model is (y, i) where $i = I/y$ is the variable INS. Cost complementarities

---

[6] In keeping with the literature in transportation, this coefficient is actually measuring economies of *density*, since for a given **a**-vector, system size is fixed. Note that such an analysis also holds INS constant, thereby fixing the product mix. Thus the diseconomy of density is a *ray* diseconomy (see Baumol, Panzar, and Willig, 1982). Here we use the standard measure $S = (C/y)/(\partial C/\partial y)$.

[7] "Low value" is a relative term, since most of the goods being carried are manufactured goods, as opposed to bulk agricultural commodities such as corn or wheat, which moved via unregulated trucks during this time period.

involve examining the derivative $\partial^2 C/\partial u_1 \partial u_2$, which can be shown to be as follows:

$$\frac{\partial^2 C}{\partial u_1 \partial u_2} = \frac{\partial^2 C}{\partial y^2} + \frac{\partial^2 C}{\partial y \partial i}\left(\frac{\partial i}{\partial u_1} + \frac{\partial i}{\partial u_2}\right) + \frac{\partial C}{\partial i}\left(\frac{\partial^2 i}{\partial u_1 \partial u_2} + \frac{\partial^2 i}{\partial y \partial u_1}\right)$$
$$+ \frac{\partial^2 C}{\partial i^2}\left(\frac{\partial i}{\partial u_1}\frac{\partial i}{\partial u_2}\right).$$

Using Tables 3.1–3.3, it can be shown that $\partial^2 C/\partial y^2 > 0$ and $\partial^2 C/\partial i^2 < 0$. The model of insurance payments implies that $(\partial i/\partial u_1)(\partial i/\partial u_2) < 0$ and thus the last term is positive. The middle two terms are negligible; the portions in brackets are of magnitudes (ton-miles)$^{-1}$ and (ton-miles)$^{-2}$ respectively. The data therefore suggest that $\partial^2 C/\partial u_1 \partial u_2 > 0$.

Thus, there appear to be no cost complementarities. Note that adjusting INS amounts to a movement along a transray ($y = u_1 + u_2$; see Baumol, Panzar, and Willig, 1982) that does not appear to be convex. Therefore the model suggests that economies of scope with respect to commodity types is unlikely. Again, we note some caution in this since a disaggregate model has not been used to actually examine economies of scope. However, the analysis does suggest that extension of the model to allow for multiple commodities is likely to result in a low ratio of insight to effort in this regard.

All three of the attributes have significant, negative coefficient estimates (in the first-order terms). Increases in average length of haul (AH), average load (AL), and average shipment size (AS) all yield reductions in cost. From the perspective developed earlier, this is taken to imply that increases in network size, the number and types of markets served, the degree of spatial balance in demands, and the degree of truckload demands contribute to ameliorating the lumpiness of spatially distributed demand and supply by improving opportunities (by reducing search costs, for instance) to mix and match loads so as to utilize capital and labor more efficiently.

Table 3.4 provides estimates of demand and substitution elasticities for the four factors: fuel (F), labor (L), capital (K), and purchased transportation (T). Estimates are provided in two subtables in Table 3.4. The upper table, labeled "Evaluated at sample means," provides estimates of demand and substitution elasticities as is traditionally done by using the formulas for demand elasticities (η_i) and substitution elasticities (σ_{ij}) evaluated at the sample means of the data. The general formulas for estimating η_i and σ_{ij} are as follows:

$$\hat{\eta}_i = \frac{\hat{\alpha}_{ii}(\mathbf{a})}{\hat{S}_i(\mathbf{a})} + \hat{S}_i(\mathbf{a}) - 1, \tag{7}$$

$$\hat{\sigma}_{ij} = \frac{\hat{\alpha}_{ij}(\mathbf{a})}{\hat{S}_i(\mathbf{a})\hat{S}_j(\mathbf{a})} + 1, \tag{8}$$

Table 3.4. *Demand and substitution elasticities*

	F	L	K	T
	Evaluated at sample means			
	F	L	K	T
F	−0.6074 (0.0204)[a]	0.2260 (0.0406)	0.7178 (0.0264)	2.4296 (0.0825)
L		−0.4690 (0.0069)	0.8923 (0.0132)	1.5445 (0.0445)
K			−0.6991 (0.0057)	1.8287 (0.0440)
T				−1.5295 (0.0358)
	Population averages[b]			
	F	L	K	T
F	−0.634,−0.654 (−0.700,−0.587)	0.345, 0.446 (0.287, 0.570)	0.712, 0.732 (0.691, 0.764)	2.183, 2.097 (1.799, 2.537)
L		−0.450,−0.441 (−0.485,−0.403)	0.896, 0.905 (0.875, 0.927)	1.539, 1.469 (1.331, 1.675)
K			−0.692,−0.686 (−0.709,−0.670)	1.905, 1.781 (1.537, 2.128)
T				−1.550,−1.465 (−1.758,−1.257)

[a]Standard errors are in parentheses.

[b]Entry: $\dfrac{a,b}{(c,d)}$, where a = mean, b = median, c = lower quartile, d = upper quartile.

where $\hat{S}_i$ (**a**) is the estimated factor share; see Eq. (6). At the point-of-means

$$\hat{S}_i(\mathbf{a}) = \beta^{00}_{i0}, \quad i = 3, \ldots ,6$$

and

$$\hat{\alpha}_{ij}(\mathbf{a}) = \beta^{00}_{ij}, \quad i = 3, \ldots ,6, \, j = 3, \ldots ,i.$$

The second subtable, labeled "Population averages," was constructed by computing (7) and (8) at every point in the sample; [$\hat{S}_i(\mathbf{a})$ is computed from Eq. (6) and the $\hat{\alpha}_{ij}(\mathbf{a})$ are computed from (3)]. Each cell contains the mean, median, lower, and upper quartile values. Note that in both subtables, η_i is along the diagonal while $\hat{\sigma}_{ij}$ is in the upper triangle. The purpose of including both subtables is that, although the lower subtable in Table 3.4 is generally more informative, the upper subtable permits ease of comparison with traditional estimates. Note that the standard errors in the upper subtable reflect sampling error on the coefficients, while the interquartile range displayed in the lower subtable reflects variation over firms in the sample, ignoring sampling error.

All values appear reasonable; note that all factors are substitutes, though the degrees of substitution between fuel and labor and between fuel and capital appear to be low. The elasticities on F, K, and L versus T all suggest the very intuitive model of a trucking firm's *line-haul* technology involving two fixed-proportions production processes, one internal to the firm and one external. The internal process takes F, K, and L and produces output. The external process is called "purchased transportation" and packages F, K, and L for firms to buy. The firm then substitutes between the two processes to accomplish line-haul activity. When coupled with terminal activity, overall production elasticities are nonzero (not Leontief), since there is no reason to expect terminal activity to be Leontief.

3.   Testing the role of the attributes vector

The cost model in Tables 3.1–3.3 allows us to examine the role of the **a**-vector in the description of motor carrier technology. In this section we will focus on the role that the attributes play in the transformation of inputs into output. The main result is that a degree of separability appears to be present; the attributes affect the marginal rates of substitution between inputs but contribute little to scale effects.

To examine structure, recall that since $\mathbf{z} = (y, i)$, technology can be represented as $T(y, i, \mathbf{x} | \mathbf{a})$, where feasibility is represented by $T(y, i, \mathbf{x} | \mathbf{a}) \leq 0$. If output was a scalar, then to test for homotheticity (that marginal rates of substitution are constant along rays from the origin in input space) in a translog model, one simply examines the hypothesis that interaction terms between output and the input prices are zero. If these interactions are zero, the cost function is multiplicatively separable in output and input prices. This occurs if and only if technology is homothetic (see Shephard, 1970), and thus testing for homotheticity in a single output model is straightforward.

In the multiple-output case, however, homotheticity need not involve technological separability of the output vector from the input vector (see McFadden, 1978 and Hanoch, 1970 for a definition of input homotheticity). Unfortunately, the standard test of multiplicative separability of the cost function described previously is a joint test of both technological separability – that technology could be written as $T(h(y, i), \mathbf{x} | \mathbf{a})$ – and homotheticity; there seems to be no way around this confusion of hypotheses within the translog model.

In the case at hand, a review of Tables 3.1–3.3 suggests that the test of multiplicative separability of the cost function will be rejected; it was, resoundingly so. This implies that global statements about returns to scale, substitution elasticities, and so forth are not possible since changes in input prices *may* affect such computations. The reason for the foregoing qualification is that rejection of the joint hypothesis could be consistent with acceptance of homotheticity. The rejection result may reflect the failure of the input/output technological separability hypothesis rather than the homotheticity hypothesis.

Though the main avenue for finding structure via homotheticity is not open, a second structural route exists and has reasonable, intuitive properties. As indicated earlier, we have viewed the attribute vector **a** as representing the spatial and legal environment within which the firm chooses input levels and produces output. This was the reason for the ''|'' notation in the transformation and cost functions; the **a** vector was viewed as indexing technology (T) and cost (C). Thus, the claimed role of **a** can be examined by testing the estimated version of (1): are the attributes *output augmenting* as a hedonic model would assume (**a** is a vector of quality variables associated with the vector of output variables as in SF); is it *factor augmenting* (is its main role to affect marginal rates of substitution and the choice of input levels); or is it *universal* (no finer resolution of structure than $T(\mathbf{z},\mathbf{x}|\mathbf{a})$ is possible, as in FS)?

The appropriate test amounts to one of whether the coefficients on interactions between attributes and certain other variables are zero. Table 3.5 displays F-statistics for various sets of coefficients involving attributes AH, AL, and AS. In all cases the implicit hypothesis is that all coefficients in the set are zero. All ninety-nine attribute-related coefficients are represented in the table to provide a clear picture of the patterns of influence of attributes, but the last four lines are the most informative for the issue at hand. The role of the attributes would be described as factor augmenting, and the cost function could be represented as $C(y,i,\mathbf{q}|\mathbf{a}) = C_1(y,i,\mathbf{q})\ C_2(\mathbf{q}|\mathbf{a})$, if all interaction terms involving attributes (**a**) and output or INS (y,i) had zero coefficients. It would be described as output augmenting, with cost representation $C(y,i,\mathbf{q}|\mathbf{a}) = C_1(y,i,\mathbf{q}) \cdot C_2(\dot{y},i,|\mathbf{a})$, if all interactions between attributes and prices had zero coefficients. Both of these models would be rejected at conventional significance levels as the last three lines of Table 3.5 reveal. Still, the relative importance of the various groups is quite suggestive. The most significant affect of attributes is through the intercept term, as seen from line 18. (Note that this statistic is for the joint test that all coefficients other than β_{00}^{00} in row 1 of Table 3.2 are zero). Interactions with prices (line 19) have the next largest F ratio; and the three-way output by price by attribute terms as a group have the third largest. The weakest effect is seen to be in the output, (y,i), by attribute terms. Indeed if one allows for the very large sample size[8] and for the fact that the attributes used here are only proxy measures of network effects and may be contaminated by output (see footnote 4), this F ratio of 5.1 can be

---

[8] As Leamer (1978, esp. pp. 114–16) argues, the significance level should decrease with the sample size. In a Bayesian analysis with a diffuse prior he suggests a critical value of around 7 for a problem with dimensions as encountered here.

Table 3.5. *Tests of attribute interactions*

	H_0	Numerator degrees of freedom[a]	F
1	$\beta_{00}^{r0} = 0,\quad r = 1, \ldots, 3$	3	210.3
2	$\beta_{00}^{rs} = 0,\quad r = 1, \ldots, 3,\quad s = 1, \ldots, r$	6	7.3
3	$\beta_{i0}^{r0} = 0,\quad i = 3, \ldots, 6,\quad r = 1, \ldots, 3$	9	69.7
4	$\beta_{ij}^{r0} = 0,\quad i = 3, \ldots, 6,\quad j = 3, \ldots, i,\quad r = 1, \ldots, 3$	18	18.2
5	$\beta_{i0}^{rs} = 0,\quad i = 3, \ldots, 6,\quad r = 1, \ldots, 3,\quad s = 1, \ldots, r$	18	12.8
6	$\beta_{1j}^{r0} = 0,\quad j = 3, \ldots, 6,\quad r = 1, \ldots, 3$	9	8.7
7	$\beta_{2j}^{r0} = 0,\quad j = 3, \ldots, 6,\quad r = 1, \ldots, 3$	9	14.0
8	$\beta_{10}^{r0} = 0,\quad r = 1, \ldots, 3$	3	1.6
9	$\beta_{11}^{r0} = 0,\quad r = 1, \ldots, 3$	3	8.1
10	$\beta_{10}^{rs} = 0,\quad r = 1, \ldots, 3,\quad s = 1, \ldots, r$	6	6.5
11	$\beta_{20}^{r0} = 0,\quad r = 1, \ldots, 3$	3	7.3
12	$\beta_{22}^{r0} = 0,\quad r = 1, \ldots, 3$	3	4.7
13	$\beta_{20}^{rs} = 0,\quad r = 1, \ldots, 3,\quad s = 1, \ldots, r$	6	1.4
14	$\beta_{12}^{r0} = 0,\quad r = 1, \ldots, 3$	3	0.3
15	(8) + (9) + (10) : [y × a]	12	3.6
16	(11) + (12) + (13) : [i × a]	12	3.0
17	(14) : [y × i × a]	3	0.3
18	(1) + (2) : [a]	9	187.3
19	(3) + (4) + (5) : [q × a]	45	35.1
20	(6) + (7) : [(y,i) × q × a]	18	12.0
21	(8) + (9) + (10) + (11) + (12) + (13) + (14) : [(y,i) × a]	27	5.1

[a]Denominator degrees of freedom = ∞. Note also that indicated degrees of freedom for terms involving prices reflect enforced linear homogeneity.

viewed as suggesting a relatively minor conflict between the data and the hypothesis of a factor-augmenting role for attributes.

Thus, Table 3.5 indicates that the principal role of the attributes is in influencing the choice of input mix and level: Elasticities of substitution are strongly influenced by $\mathbf{a}$, while degree of returns to scale is relatively insensitive to $\mathbf{a}$. To a first approximation, then, the cost function can be written as

$$C(y,i,\mathbf{q}|\mathbf{a}) = C_1(y,i,\mathbf{q}) \times C_2(\mathbf{q}|\mathbf{a}) \qquad (9)$$

with the interpretation as given. In other words, a firm's cost function can be thought of as having a form in common among firms, (C_1), multiplied by an $\mathbf{a}$-specific function (C_2). An alternative way of viewing Eq. (9) is in terms of average cost functions, where average cost is taken to be

$$\frac{C(y,i,\mathbf{q}|\mathbf{a})}{y} = \frac{C_1(y,i,\mathbf{q})}{y} \cdot C_2(\mathbf{q}|\mathbf{a}).$$

This shows that the average cost curve for the firm involves a nonattribute average cost function (for a hypothetical standardized firm) multiplied by the attribute-specific shift function $C_2(\mathbf{q}|\mathbf{a})$. From the signs on β_{00}^{r0} in Table 3.2, we see that increases in $\mathbf{a}$ will be associated with subtechnologies that exhibit progressively lower average cost. Moreover, note that, under the standard definition of returns to scale (S), $\mathbf{a}$ does not influence S:

$$S = \frac{C(y,i,\mathbf{q}|\mathbf{a})}{yC_y(y,i,\mathbf{q}|\mathbf{a})} = \frac{C_1(y,i,\mathbf{q})}{yC_{1y}(y,i,\mathbf{q})},$$

where the y subscript in the denominator denotes derivative (Note: again, S is the scale measure for fixed INS; that is, the measure of ray economies of scale since fixed INS means fixed commodity mix.)

4. Average cost functions for subtechnologies

As we have indicated, the attribute-specific function $C_2(\mathbf{q}|\mathbf{a})$ scales the standard model $C_1(y,i,\mathbf{q})$ so as to provide attribute-specific cost and average cost functions. Recall that, in a crude sense, AH and AL reflect the spatial environment the firm is in, whereas AS reflects the nature of the commodities moved. Although clearly all three significantly influence cost, we propose to focus on AH as the most important of these in what follows. This is based on observing the relative importance (in terms of t-values) of the $\mathbf{a}$ first-order terms in Tables 3.1–3.3. The following analysis could also be performed for AL or AS or combinations of variables.

Let $\mathbf{v}^t = (y^t,\ i^t,\ \mathbf{q}^t)$ be the vector of outputs and input prices for an observation, (one firm, one year) and let $\mathbf{a}^t$ be the associated attribute vector. Then $AC^t = C(\mathbf{v}^t|\mathbf{a}^t)/y^t$ is the average cost for that observation. While AH is a continuous variable, a simple way to examine its role in indexing the subtechnologies is to induce a dichotomization of the population according to AH and compare mean values of average cost across observations for the two resulting groups. Since output is a vector (y,i), we will also dichotomize INS (i) so as to be able to examine the impact of AH on average cost in a two-dimensional representation [varying y continuously for each of two levels of i rather than (y,i) continuously]. Thus for each observation we form a dummy for AH and for INS as follows:

$$DAH^t = \begin{cases} 1 \text{ if } AH^t > \text{median (AH)} \\ 0 \text{ otherwise} \end{cases}$$

$$DINS^t = \begin{cases} 1 \text{ if } INS^t > \text{median (INS)} \\ 0 \text{ otherwise} \end{cases}$$

Thus, each observation is now categorized by long- versus short-haul (DAH = 1 or 0) and high- versus low-value mix of goods (DINS = 1 or 0).

Table 3.6 contains mean values of average cost within each of the four groups of observations determined by DAH and DINS. That both AH and INS have pronounced effects on average cost is clearly shown in that table. First,

Table 3.6. *Average costs for subtechnologies*

		DINS		
		0	1	
DAH	0	$\overline{AC}_{00} = 0.0935$ $n = 402$ $s_{\overline{AC}} = 0.0015$	$\overline{AC}_{01} = 0.1419$ $n = 1,141$ $s_{\overline{AC}} = 0.0018$	$\overline{AC}_{0.} = 0.1293$ $n = 1,543$ $s_{\overline{AC}} = 0.0015$
	1	$\overline{AC}_{10} = 0.0563$ $n = 1,140$ $s_{\overline{AC}} = 0.0005$	$\overline{AC}_{11} = 0.0743$ $n = 402$ $s_{\overline{AC}} = 0.0009$	$\overline{AC}_{1.} = 0.0610$ $n = 1,542$ $s_{\overline{AC}} = 0.0005$
		$\overline{AC}_{.0} = 0.0660$ $n = 1,542$ $s_{\overline{AC}} = 0.0007$	$\overline{AC}_{.1} = 0.1243$ $n = 1,543$ $s_{\overline{AC}} = 0.0016$	

the on-diagonal entries for $\overline{AC}_{00}$ and $\overline{AC}_{11}$ (short-haul, low-value and long-haul, high-value) are not significantly different. Second, the off-diagonal cells (which account for approximately 75 percent of the industry) are the extremes of the AC averages and are quite different with $\overline{AC}_{01}$ being almost three times the value of $\overline{AC}_{10}$.

Figure 3.1 displays the average cost functions for the four cases computed by using cell average values for prices, AL and AS. For each curve, the range of output is determined by the 10–90 percentile range of observations on OTM within that cell. As can be readily observed, the insignificant difference between the on-diagonal cells in Table 3.6 carries over to the two average cost functions in the middle portion of the graph. Similarly, the two extreme functions (01 and 10) indicate the same result as Table 3.6: Short-haul, high-value firms face average costs 2.5 to 3 times those of the long-haul, low-value firms.

It is important to observe that only two subtechnologies are actually being presented: long- versus short-haul firms. A three-dimensional diagram, with the third axis providing INS would entail two surfaces (one for DAH = 0 and one for DAH = 1) with the surfaces sloping upward as one travels away from the origin along the INS-axis. Finally, the fact that AH is a continuous variable means that we would observe a family of surfaces between (and above and below) the DAH = 0 and DAH = 1 surfaces. Put another way, shifts in the product mix will involve movements along a cost surface, while changes in the attribute vector involve shifts of the cost surfaces.

What accounts for the differences between the two cost surfaces (the surface for DAH = 0 and the surface for DAH = 1)? There are only two possible sources of the difference: input prices and technology. It is possible that firms

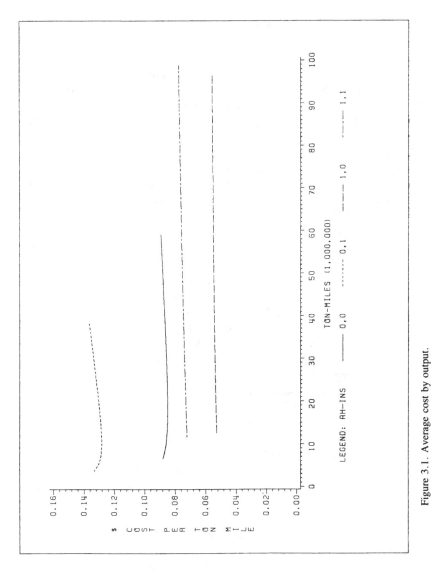

Figure 3.1. Average cost by output.

in the different cells of Table 3.6 somehow face different prices for factors of production. For example, since long-haul firms must send drivers greater distances, perhaps they employ a different quality of driver, who may cost a little more but has a significantly higher marginal product. Such a hypothesis is difficult to justify theoretically, because there does not seem to be any reason to assume that short-haul firms cannot hire such labor (or, equivalently, have poorer access to capital markets, have to pay more for fuel, and so on).

To estimate the impact of a difference in prices, the elasticity of average cost with respect to change in factor price was multiplied by the difference between the factor price paid by short-haul, high-value firms and the factor price paid by long-haul, low-value firms. This turns out to account for 2 to 3 percent of the difference between the two average cost curves. Thus, almost the entire difference in average costs between short and long haul (controlling for commodity mix) is attributable to differences in technology and *not* to differences in input prices.

There are various ways to characterize technology; one approach would be to examine the demand and substitution elasticities for the two subtechnologies. This is done in Table 3.7, which provides population averages of elasticities for the two subtechnologies. Thus, the two subtables in Table 3.7 can be compared with the lower subtable in Table 3.4. Again population means, medians, and interquartile ranges are provided for $\hat{\eta}_i$ on the diagonal and $\hat{\sigma}_{ij}$ in the upper triangle of each subtable.

Table 3.8 provides a rough means of comparison for the two subtables in Table 3.7. Each entry in Table 3.8 is the ratio of the corresponding element in the upper subtable in Table 3.7 to the corresponding element in the lower subtable of Table 3.7. Thus, since mean $\hat{\eta}_F = -0.609$ when DAH = 0, while mean $\hat{\eta}_F = -0.660$ when DAH = 1, the ratio is 0.92, which appears in the upper left portion of the first cell on the diagonal of Table 3.8. Thus, values below 1 indicate (respectively) a fall in mean, median, lower quartile value, and upper quartile value, while values of the ratio above 1 represent increases in mean, and so forth.

Note that the largest shifts in values are associated with σ_{FL}, σ_{FT}, and η_L, with lesser shifts for σ_{KT} and η_T, and even smaller effects for the rest of the elasticities. Thus long-haul (as compared to short-haul) firms appear to have less elastic labor demands, and are less elastic in fuel-labor substitution and are more elastic in fuel-purchased transportation substitution. In fact, the distributions of σ_{LT} and σ_{KT} have shifted slightly rightward (more elastic) while σ_{LK} and σ_{FK} have shifted slightly leftward. Furthermore, the distributions associated with η_F, η_L and η_K have all shifted leftward, in contrast to that for η_T. Thus, except for σ_{FL} and σ_{FT}, long-haul firms appear to be slightly more Leontief with regards to F, L, and K, and more elastic with

Table 3.7. *Subtechnology demand and substitution elasticities (population averages)[a]*

DAH = 0, N = 1,543			
	F	L	K	T

	F	L	K	T
F	−0.609,−0.628 (−0.683,−0.551)	0.404, 0.474 (0.337, 0.597)	0.709, 0.725 (0.692, 0.753)	2.058, 1.939 (1.550, 2.384)
L		−0.415,−0.408 (−0.439,−0.381)	0.882, 0.890 (0.860, .0.912)	1.572, 1.477 (1.324, 1.698)
K			−0.678,−0.674 (−0.690,−0.662)	2.019, 1.836 (1.570, 2.189)
T				−1.624,−1.479 (−1.785,−1.301)

DAH = 1, N = 1,542			
	F	L	K	T

	F	L	K	T
F	−0.660,−0.673 (−0.713,−0.624)	0.286, 0.416 (0.216, 0.541)	0.715, 0.743 (0.687, 0.774)	2.309, 2.214 (1.982, 2.655)
L		−0.486,−0.477 (−0.519,−0.443)	0.910, 0.920 (0.898, 0.937)	1.506, 1.463 (1.337, 1.654)
K			−0.707,−0.701 (−0.726,−0.682)	1.790, 1.722 (1.508, 2.075)
T				−1.476,−1.443 (−1.730,−1.211)

[a]Entry: $\dfrac{a,b}{(c,d)}$, where a = mean, b = median, c = lower quartile, d = upper quartile.

Table 3.8. *Relative distribution effects*

	F	L	K	T
F	.92,.93 .96,.88	1.41,1.14 1.56,1.10	.99,.98 1.01,.97	.89, .88 .78, .90
L		.85, .85 .85, .86	.96,.97 .96,.97	1.04,1.01 .99,1.03
K			.96,.96 .95,.97	1.13,1.07 1.04,1.05
T				1.10,1.02 1.03,1.07

	a (DAH = 0) $\quad b$ (DAH = 0)
Entry:	a (DAH = 1) $\quad b$ (DAH = 1)
	c (DAH = 0) $\quad d$ (DAH = 0)
	c (DAH = 1) $\quad d$ (DAH = 0)

regard to trade-offs between internal transportation (F, L, and K) and purchased transportation (T).

5.   Conclusions

This chapter has two main results. First, motor carrier technology is heterogeneous in a fundamental manner: The spatial environment of the firm is a crucial determinant of the technology the firm employs. This is not simply an issue of regional, geographic differences between firms. There are basic differences between firms in the long-haul and the short-haul business, between firms with balanced or unbalanced system designs, and between firms with large versus small shipments (facing markets with such characteristics).

Moreover, the role of such attributes is in the selection of input mix and input level and is only incidentally related to the nature and mix of outputs. The role of the attributes is seen in Tables 3.4 and 3.7. The attributes are factor augmenting, as was seen by the multiplicative separability of the cost function in y and **a.** This means that the attributes were not output augmenting, and thus we rejected the hedonic model. This does not mean that there are no quality variables associated with output. This means only that the attribute variables used in this analysis are not quality of output measures.

Second, the technological differences generate significant cost differences. Controlling for product mix, short-haul technology generates average costs 60 percent higher than long-haul technology. These cost differences are fully attributable to what appear to be mild adjustments in the ease of substitution of inputs.

To the degree that the distribution of types of technologies over firms is simply a reflection of the spatial distribution of demand, deregulation may have little effect upon the distribution of cost, save possibly to shift the distribution. However, to the degree that the distribution of types of technologies is artificially induced, deregulation is likely to have very significant effects. In particular, to the degree that inflexible regulation of operating rights contributes to the maldistribution of technologies by hampering firm network growth or adjustment in the face of shifting spatial demand, then relaxation of operating rights restrictions is likely to engender significant redistributions of firm types. Whether or not this is a significant source of the recent simultaneous waves of bankruptcies and entry that the industry has undergone since the enactment of the Motor Carrier Reform Act of 1980 is an important issue for future research.

Appendix 3A

The source of the data used in this study is *Trinc's Bluebook of the Trucking Industry* (1954–59). That database includes all class I carriers of general

Table 3A.1. *Distribution of observations by region and year*

Region	Year						Total
	1953	1954	1955	1956	1957	1958	
1 New England	0	70	69	76	36	38	289
2 Middle Atlantic	139	138	139	134	91	100	741
3 Central	151	149	162	171	120	127	880
4 Southern	0	83	83	81	66	70	383
5 Northwestern	0	39	39	38	29	29	174
6 Midwestern	0	45	43	45	27	29	189
7 Southwestern	0	37	39	34	31	30	171
8 Rocky Mountain	0	16	21	15	13	13	78
9 Pacific	0	41	44	40	26	29	180
Total	290	618	639	634	439	465	3085

freight reporting to the ICC for the years 1953–58. Firms are identified by name in each of nine regions. From the full set of 6,060 records, we collected 3,085 usable observations, distributed as indicated in Table 3A.1.

Variables included in the analysis, and their 10, 50 and 90 percentile values, were as follows:

		10%	Median	90%
(C)	Total cost ($1,000)	693.5	1,930.00	8,372.7
(INS)	Average cargo loss and damage insurance exp ($/TM)	0.05	0.11	0.25
(OTM)	Total ton-miles (1,000)	931.00	24,006.00	125,215.00
(PF)	Fuel price (¢/gallon)	13.5	15.39	18.4
(PL)	Labor price ($1,000/person/year)	4.30	5.19	6.11
(PT)	Purchased transportation price ($/mile)	0.15	0.54	1.02
(PK)	Capital price ($/$ of operating property net)	0.81	1.41	2.90
(AH)	Average length of haul (miles/movement)	86.96	208.00	508.97
(AL)	Average load (tons/movement)	5.78	9.40	13.27
(AS)	Average shipment size (tons/shipment)	0.33	0.56	1.42
(FF)	Fraction of expenses due to fuel	0.044	0.069	0.094
(FL)	Fraction of expenses due to labor	0.401	0.533	0.612
(FT)	Fraction of expenses due to purchased transportation	0.011	0.069	0.238
(FK)	Fraction of expenses due to capital	0.238	0.294	0.358

C was computed as the product of "operating ratio" and total "operating revenues," and OTM was taken directly from the Trinc's tables. INS was computed as "insurance expenditure: cargo, loss, and damage" divided by OTM. The tables contain expenses for "fuel expenditure: revenue equipment" (FE) and taxes for "gas, fuel and oil" (FT). Average fuel tax rates

($t = $ ¢/gal) were computed from data from the American Petroleum Institute (1971). Regional tax rates were computed as the simple average of gasoline tax rates across all states within the region for each year. Using this information, the price of fuel was computed as

$$PF = (FE/FT)t + t$$

PL was computed as personnel "compensation" divided by "average number" of personnel, where both numerator and denominator are the simple sum of entries for daily and hourly employees.

PT is, in principle, easy to compute as the ratio of "purchased transportation" expenses to the number of "miles rented." But many firms report zero purchased transportation expenses, and many others report expenses that include rail and water shipments. Accordingly, we chose to estimate PT as the mean of the foregoing ratio across firms within year and region with some adjustment for firm-specific variables. Specifically, we took PT to be the predicted value of expenditure/rented mile from the log regression of this variable on region and year dummies and the following three variables: fraction of miles rented (FMR = miles rented/total miles + 1), fraction of fleet in trucks [FFT = number of trucks/(trucks + tractors) + 1] and the fraction of miles rented with driver (FRW = miles rented with driver/total miles rented + 1). The value of 1 was added to all three fractions to allow logarithms when the fraction was zero. FMR was included after inspection of the data revealed a very strong correlation between rented transportation activity and this variable. The suggestion is that firms purchasing large amounts of transportation can arrange long-term contracts at quite favorable terms, relative to spot prices. FFT was included to allow for differences in the type of transportation purchased. Finally, rented transportation with drivers is more expensive than that driven by employees of the firm, so FRW was included to capture this difference. Table 3A.2 reports the results of this auxiliary regression on the 2,079 observations with all required data. As noted above, PT was generated as the prediction from this regression equation. When values of the required right-hand-side variables were not available, average values across all other firms were used.

For want of a better measure, PK was computed as residual expenses (total costs less expenditures on fuel and fuel taxes, cargo loss and damage insurance, purchased transportation and labor) divided by "operating property net."

AH was computed as the ratio of total ton miles (OTM) to total tons shipped. Since the numerator is the sum across "movements" of ton miles and the denominator is the sum across movements of tons, AH measures the weighted average length of haul, with tons moved serving as the weight. This variable serves to indicate the "size" of the network over which the firm

Table 3A.2. *Purchased transportation regression*

Dependent variable: ln (purchased transportation expense/miles rented)		
Variable	Coefficient	t-Ratio
Intercept	−0.725	−15.526
Region 1	−0.290	−3.900
Region 2	0.029	0.661
Region 4	−0.293	−5.279
Region 5	−0.066	−0.749
Region 6	0.139	1.796
Region 7	−0.002	−0.019
Region 8	−0.555	−5.015
Region 9	−0.056	−0.761
Year 1	−0.129	−2.039
Year 2	−0.107	−2.105
Year 3	−0.035	−0.686
Year 5	0.123	2.149
Year 6	0.031	0.549
ln(FMR)	−2.915	−34.944
ln(FFT)	−0.317	−2.256
ln(FRW)	0.956	16.508

$$R^2 = .483$$

operates. While there is no obvious reason to choose a weighted measure, the data source did not include records of the number of freight movements, so no unweighted measures could be computed. AL was similarly computed as OTM divided by total miles and thus is an average load size per freight movement, weighted by miles. AS was computed as total tons divided by the number of shipments. Note that "number of shipments" reflects the number of "bills of lading" not freight movements. Thus AS indicates the average size of shipping contracts while AL measures the size of consolidated freight movements. The simple correlation of these two variables is 0.098. (Other relevant correlations are 0.567 between AH and AL and −0.052 between AH and AS.)

The calculation of factor shares, FF, FL, FT, and FK, was straightforward. In each case it amounted to dividing the total expenditure on the relevant factor input by the sum of expenditures across the four categories.

The original database included 6,060 firms by year observations, but half of these were unuseable because of incomplete records, suspicious entries, or inappropriate firm type. The latter was the single most common cause of data omission; we included only those firms reporting at least 75 percent of their revenue from intercity traffic, and total revenues of at least $200,000. Examples of deletions due to suspicious data are factor shares outside the range of zero to one, expenditures on fuel taxes greater than expenditures on fuel, rented miles greater than total miles, and labor price less than $1,500/year. Elimination of observations involves a trade-off: A sacrifice of estimator efficiency if valid data is discarded, versus errors-in-variables biases if erroneous data are included. We viewed the latter as the more serious problem, given the ampleness of the database and the natural suspicion of accounting data reported to Trinc's. Thus we felt justified in our heavyhanded treatment of suspicious data. Note that since data screening based on the value of the dependent variable will introduce estimator bias, only exogeneous variables or their underlying components were screened for outliers.

SF included one additional variable, the percentage of truckload shipments, which we chose to omit; its distribution is extremely skewed, with 75 percent of the firms showing less than 6 percent of their traffic in truckload shipments while only 5 percent of the firms have truckload shipments exceeding one-third of their traffic. Thus any affect of this variable would be due to these very few firms in the tail of the distribution, and that imposes the risk of undue influence of outliers. Moreover, the correlation between this variable and AS was 0.82.

References

American Petroleum Institute (1971). "State Tax Rates of Gasoline." *Facts and Figures:* p. 476.

Barton, A. (1967). "Maximum Likelihood Estimation of Complete Systems of Demand Equations." *European Economic Review,* May: 7–73.

Baumol, W., J. Panzar, and R. Willig (1982). *Contestable Markets and the Theory of Industry Structure.* New York: Harcourt, Brace, Jovanovich.

Christensen, L., D. Jorgenson, and L. Lau (1973). "Transcendental Logarithmic Production Functions." *The Review of Economics and Statistics,* 55, February: 28–45.

Christensen, L., and W. Greene (1976). "Economies of Scale in U.S. Electric Power Generation." *Journal of Political Economy,* 84, no. 4: 655–76.

Daughety, Andrew F. (1984). "Regulation and Industrial Organization." *Journal of Political Economy,* 92, no. 5, October: 932–53.

Dobesh, Larry J. (1973). Earnings Control Standards for Regulated Motor Carriers. Unpublished PhD dissertation, Washington State University, Pullman, Wash.

Färe, Rolf, and James Logan (1982). "The Rate-of-Return Regulated Firm: Cost and Production Quality." *The Bell Journal of Economics,* 14, no. 2, Autumn: 405–14.

Friedlaender, A. F., and R. H. Spady (1981). *Freight Transport Regulation: Equity, Efficiency and Competition.* Cambridge, Mass.: MIT Press.

Friedlaender, A. F., R. H. Spady, and S. J. Wang Chiang (1981). "Regulation and the Structure of Technology in the Trucking Industry." In T. G. Cowing and R. E. Stevenson, eds., *Productivity Measurement in Regulated Industries.* New York: Academic Press.

Hanoch, G. (1970). "Homotheticity in Joint Production." *Journal of Economic Theory*, 2, no. 4: 423–26.

Harmatuck, D. J. (1981). "A Motor Carrier Joint Cost Function." *Journal of Transport Economics and Policy*, 15, no. 1: 135–53.

Kennan, John (1984). "Simultaneous Equations Bias in Estimates of Supply and Demand Functions Using Disaggregated Data." Working Paper 84–5, College of Business Administration, University of Iowa, Iowa City.

Joskow, Paul L., and Roger C. Noll (1981). "Regulation in Theory and Practice: An Overview." In Gary Fromm, ed., *Studies in Public Regulation*, Cambridge, Mass.: MIT Press.

Judge, G., W. Griffiths, R. Hill, and T.-C. Lee (1980). *The Theory and Practice of Econometrics*. New York: John Wiley and Sons.

LaMond, Annette M. (1980). *Competition in the General-Freight Motor-Carrier Industry*. Lexington, Mass.: Lexington Books.

Leamer, E. (1978). *Specification Searches*. New York: Wiley.

McFadden, D. F. (1978). "Cost, Revenue and Profit Functions." In *Production Economics: A Dual Approach to Theory and Applications*. Amsterdam: North Holland.

Moore, Thomas G. (1978). "The Beneficiaries of Trucking Regulation." *The Journal of Law and Economics*: 327–43.

Shephard, Ronald W. (1970). *Theory of Cost and Production Functions*. Princeton, N.J.: Princeton University Press.

Spady, R. H., and A. F. Friedlaender. (1978). "Hedonic Cost Functions for the Regulated Trucking Industry." *The Bell Journal of Economics*, 9, no. 1, Spring: 159–79.

Trinc's Incorporated. 1954–59. "Basic Accounts and Statistics." In *Trinc's Bluebook of the Trucking Industry*.

Wang Chiang, S. J., and A. F. Friedlaender (1984). "Output Aggregation, Network Effects, and the Measurement of Trucking Technology." *The Review of Economics and Statistics*, 66, no. 2, May: 267–76.

CHAPTER 4

Network effects and the measurement of returns to scale and density for U.S. railroads

DOUGLAS W. CAVES, LAURITS R.
CHRISTENSEN, MICHAEL W. TRETHEWAY,
AND ROBERT J. WINDLE

From the earliest days of railroad service, the nature and extent of scale economies in rail operations have provided grounds for ongoing study and debate. Recent attempts to define and quantify scale economies have recognized that it is important to distinguish returns to traffic density from returns to scale (or firm size). Returns to density reflect the relationship between inputs and outputs with the rail network held fixed. Returns to scale reflect the relationship between inputs and the overall scale of operations, including both outputs and network size.

The dominant view is that the rail industry is characterized by increasing returns to density but constant returns to scale. Certainly there are plausible theoretical grounds for this view, and the empirical evidence has been convincing to some observers. For example, in a recent review Keeler (1983) stated: "Studies of railroad costs from the 1970's tell a . . . consistent story about returns to traffic density. They all give *strong evidence* of increasing returns, up to a rather high traffic density . . ." (p. 51 [emphasis added]). He commented that "there are constant or mildly decreasing returns to larger firm sizes, when route density is held constant" (p. 164).

Keeler bases his conclusions primarily on five studies: Caves, Christensen, and Swanson (1981), Friedlaender and Spady (1981), Harmatuck (1979), Harris (1977), and Keeler (1974). While Keeler's view may have been justifiable in the light of the published evidence available to him at the time, we have examined the literature in more detail (including some unpublished results by Caves, Christensen, and Swanson), and have concluded that there is a genuine lack of such "strong evidence," especially in the two most recent

The research reported in this chapter was supported by the National Science Foundation. The authors wish to express their gratitude to Joseph A. Swanson for assistance in sample selection, to Carl Degen for research assistance, and to Ken McClelland for data processing. The paper has benefited greatly from the comments of Andrew Daughety, Ted Keeler, and Forrest Nelson.

and sophisticated studies.[1] Earlier studies of Keeler (1974), Harris (1977), and Harmatuck (1979) all pointed to substantial returns to density. The more recent studies of Friedlaender and Spady (1981) and Caves, Christensen, and Swanson (1981) both used more thorough cost accounting, more advanced theoretical specifications, and more modern functional forms, and they found far less evidence of increasing returns to density. The Caves, Christensen, and Swanson (1981) variable-cost function includes no network variable and thus provides no information on returns to density. Friedlaender and Spady include two network variables, low-density route mileage and total route mileage. Of the two, only low-density route mileage had a significant first-order coefficient (Friedlaender and Spady, 1981:233) Based on these two recent studies, it appears to us that the strongest defensible statement at this point is that there is no strong evidence against the hypothesis of increasing returns to density.

We believe the lack of clear-cut findings regarding economies of density results from the failure to account for unobserved network effects. It is quite likely that the cost effects of route structure differences are not adequately represented by entering route-miles or track-miles in the equations as is commonly done in recent rail studies. Such a procedure obviously leaves numerous aspects of network unaccounted for and raises the possibility that statistical estimates of cost-function coefficients will be biased.

Mundlak (1978) provides a careful analysis of the type of bias that can occur in the presence of unobserved firm effects, and outlines the appropriate procedures for obtaining unbiased estimates. A principal result is that typical regression procedures applied to combinations of time-series and cross-section (or panel) data will, in general, lead to biased coefficients, hence to biased estimates of returns to density and scale. However, Mundlak's results can be used to show that, when the data come either from a single cross section, or from a panel in which the time-series variation is heavily dominated by the cross-section variation, the individual (biased) coefficients can be added to obtain unbiased estimates of sums of the underlying coefficients.

In this chapter we show that it is the individual coefficients that are required for measurement of returns to density, and the sums that are required for returns to scale. Thus, it is highly likely that previous work, being

---

[1] The thrust of the Caves, Christensen, and Swanson study was the proper treatment of quasi-fixed factors. Returns to density was not addressed in the paper because unpublished work, of which Keeler was not aware, had shown the network variable to be insignificant. In addition, there is a peculiarity of the Friedlaender and Spady model, which implies a discrete decline in cost when density on a particular route crosses the threshold of 1 million gross ton-miles per route-mile. As Keeler (1983, p. 161) argues, this can be viewed as consistent with increasing returns to density. But we believe this peculiarity of the discrete decline on individual routes makes it difficult to draw strong conclusions.

based on cross-section data or very short time-series of cross sections, has yielded biased estimates of returns to density but unbiased estimates of returns to scale. This explains why existing studies have led to mixed findings on returns to density but consistent findings on returns to scale: The density results, being biased, were heavily subject to the characteristics of individual samples, models, and statistical procedures.[2]

To obtain unbiased estimates of returns to density for the rail industry we have developed a panel data set consisting of observations on forty-three carriers that operated for all or part of the twenty-five-year period 1951–75. We apply Mundlak's recommended statistical procedures to this data set. The results show returns to scale to be similar to estimates in prior studies: There are increasing returns to scale for small carriers, but for medium to large railroads returns to scale are nearly constant. As expected, it is in estimating returns to density that we obtain the most interesting findings. Our estimates indicate substantial increasing returns to density that persist over a larger range of output than has been found in any prior study. To demonstrate the importance of appropriate econometric techniques in measuring returns to density, we show that application of typical regression procedures to our data fails to show substantial economies of density.

1.   Methodology

1.1.   Incorporating network in the cost function

The transformation of a vector of inputs, **M**, into a vector of outputs, **Y**, is usually represented by the implicit function

$$f(\mathbf{Y}, \mathbf{M}, \mathbf{T}) = 0 \tag{1}$$

where the vector **T** represents shifts in the function due to changes in efficiency. McFadden (1978) has shown that if the transformation function has a strictly convex input structure, then all of the properties of the production structure can be inferred from the dual cost function:

$$C = g(\mathbf{Y}, \mathbf{W}, \mathbf{T}), \tag{2}$$

where **W** is a vector of prices at which the inputs can be purchased, and C is total cost:

[2] Some evidence along the line for the rail industry is found in Braeutigam, Daughety, and Turnquist (1984). Using time-series data from a single railroad and thereby avoiding the bias due to firm effects, they find substantial returns to density. Despite the interest of this result, it cannot be taken as definitive because of the small sample and the extremely short-run nature of the observations (thirty-five monthly data points).

$$C = \sum_i W_i M_i \tag{3}$$

The cost function (2) is homogeneous of degree 1, nondecreasing and concave in the factor prices.

Traditionally the level of output has been used to represent firm size in industry cost studies. Recently, however, writers have begun to distinguish between firm size and level of output. It is particularly important to make such a distinction for industries in which services are provided over a network of geographically distributed points.

The concept of firm size may be more closely tied to the size of the network and its configuration than to the output provided over that network. Thus cost per unit of output may vary substantially among firms, depending on the nature of the network. For example, one would expect a lower level of unit costs if a given level of rail output were provided over a more compact route structure. Thus we include a variable N in Eq. (2) to represent the effect of the network.

$$C = g(\mathbf{Y}, N, \mathbf{W}, \mathbf{T}). \tag{4}$$

Returns to scale has typically been taken to mean the percentage increase in output made possible by a one percent increase in all inputs. But the presence of both output ($\mathbf{Y}$) and network (N) in Eq. (4) requires us to specify whether an increase in input causes an increase in output alone or an increase in both output and network. This leads us to distinguish returns to density from returns to scale.

We define returns to density as the proportional increase in output made possible by a proportional increase in all inputs, with network and input prices held fixed. This is equivalent to the inverse of the sum of the elasticities of total cost with respect to the outputs:[3]

$$\text{RTD} = \frac{1}{\Sigma E_{yi}}, \tag{5}$$

where ΣE_{yi} denotes elasticity of total cost with respect to output Y_i. Returns to density are said to be increasing, constant, or decreasing, when the sum of the elasticities of total cost with respect to the outputs is less than unity, equal to unity, or greater than unity, respectively.

We define returns to scale as the proportional increase in both output and network made possible by a proportional increase in all inputs, with input prices fixed. This is equivalent to the inverse of the sum of the elasticities of total cost with respect to the outputs and network:

---

[3] See Caves, Christensen, and Swanson (1981) and Panzar and Willig (1977), for derivations of relationships between the structure of production and elasticities of cost.

$$\text{RTS} = \frac{1}{E_n + \Sigma E_{yi}}. \tag{6}$$

Returns to scale are said to be increasing, constant, or decreasing, when this sum of the elasticities is less than unity, equal to unity, or greater than unity, respectively.

It is difficult to quantify a railroad network in terms of observable quantities. Some aspects of network are observable, such as total route-miles, but it is easy to conceive of vastly different networks that add up to the same total route-miles. Thus it is useful to think of network as being represented partly by an observable variable, route-miles being the leading contender in prior work, and partly by unobserved effects. Accordingly, we rewrite the cost function (4), replacing network N with two variables: R for total route-miles, and F for unobserved network effects. The unobserved network effects F are constant over time for a given firm, but vary across firms.[4] Thus, we have

$$C = g(Y, R, W, T, F). \tag{7}$$

Mundlak (1978) has examined the properties of various estimators for (7). To review the pertinent results of Mundlak's analysis, we specify an estimating equation for (7) of the following form:

$$C = X\beta + ZF + U, \tag{8}$$

where β is a vector of coefficients, and X is the matrix of observations on input prices, outputs, and the observable network variable route-miles. Z is a matrix of binary variables, F is the vector of unobserved network effects, and U is the vector of disturbances, distributed according to the classical regression model.

Mundlak points out that there can be a relationship between the regressors X and the unobserved effects F. He specifies that the effects realized in the sample can be decomposed into a nonsystematic portion, and a systematic portion that depends upon the mean of the observed variables: That is,

$$ZF = Z\bar{X}\pi + Q, \tag{9}$$

where $\bar{X}$ is the matrix containing the mean for each firm for each of the variables in X ($\bar{X} = (Z'Z)^{-1}Z'X$). The relationship between the effects and the means of the explanatory variables is given by the π vector. The Mundlak specification clearly shows the relationship between the effects and the "typical" values of the observed explanatory variables.

---

[4] If a railroad substantially alters its network, we would expect its network effect (F) to change. We recognize this possibility in our model by treating substantial changes in network, such as acquisitions and mergers, as new firms with different effects.

The model in Eqs. (8) and (9) leads to two types of inference, which conveniently correspond to the notions of returns to scale and density. Conditional inference takes the network effects in the sample as given and bases predictions of change solely on the β coefficients:

$$E[C|\mathbf{X}^1,\mathbf{ZF}] - E[C|\mathbf{X}^0,\mathbf{ZF}] = (\mathbf{X}^1 - \mathbf{X}^0)\beta. \qquad (10)$$

Conditional inference is exactly what is required for estimating returns to density: It allows us to predict the effect of a change in output, while holding both the observed and unobserved components of network constant.

Measurement of returns to scale is not conditional on the unobserved network effect. Instead, returns to scale includes the variation in the unobserved effects that occurs systematically with changes in output and the observed component of route miles. Thus measurement of returns to scale must be based on unconditional inference (not conditioned on the unobserved effects). Substituting (9) into (8) we find the unconditional equation:

$$C = \mathbf{X}\beta + \mathbf{Z}\bar{\mathbf{X}}\pi + \mathbf{Q} + \mathbf{U}. \qquad (11)$$

Unconditional inference permits us to determine the change in C when $\mathbf{X}$ and $\mathbf{Z}\bar{\mathbf{X}}$ move together. Thus,

$$E(C|\mathbf{X}^1) - E(C|\mathbf{X}^0) = (\mathbf{X}^1 - \mathbf{X}^0)(\beta + \pi). \qquad (12)$$

We conclude that estimates of returns to density require unbiased estimates of the β coefficients, while estimates of returns to scale require unbiased estimates of $\beta + \pi$. In the following section we specify conditions under which unbiased estimates of returns to density and scale may be obtained.

1.2.   Estimation

If we are interested in both conditional and unconditional inference, then we must obtain estimates of both the β and the π coefficients in Eqs. (8) and (9). Mundlak (1978) shows that the best linear unbiased estimator of β is the "within" estimator, which results from applying least squares to (8).[5] To obtain the best linear unbiased estimator of π, we first compute the "between" estimator, which results from replacing each observation by its firm mean. Then we obtain π by subtracting the within estimator from the between estimator. Given panel data, the Mundlak results can readily be applied to obtain unbiased estimates of β and π and hence of returns to scale and density.

---

[5] This estimator is identical to one that results from replacing each observation on each variable by the deviation from the mean of that variable for the firm to which the observation corresponds.

An important question concerns the interpretation that can be placed on results obtained via procedures other than those recommended by Mundlak. Previous rail studies rely upon an estimator such as

$$\mathbf{b}_r = (\mathbf{X}'\mathbf{X})^{-1}\mathbf{X}'\mathbf{C} \tag{13}$$

The estimator $\mathbf{b}_r$ is simply the least squares estimator of (8), constraining the effects $\mathbf{F}$ to be zero.[6] Mundlak shows that the expectations of $\mathbf{b}_r$ is given by

$$E(\mathbf{b}_r) = \beta + \lambda\pi, \tag{14}$$

where $\lambda = (\mathbf{X}'\mathbf{X})^{-1}\mathbf{X}'\mathbf{Z}\bar{\mathbf{X}}$. Thus in general $\mathbf{b}_r$ is a biased estimator of β and yields biased estimates of returns to density. Furthermore it is a biased estimator of $\beta + \pi$ and therefore yields biased estimates of returns to scale.

An important special case arises when λ is an identity matrix. Then we have

$$E(\mathbf{b}_r) = \beta + \pi \tag{15}$$

This will occur when $\mathbf{Z}$ is an identity matrix, which happens if the $\mathbf{X}$ matrix consists of observations from a single cross section (or an average of several cross sections). Furthermore, λ will be close to an identity matrix if the data are from several cross sections in which the within firm variation is small relative to the between firm variation. Thus we conclude that the use of a single cross section yields unbiased estimates of $\beta + \pi$ and can therefore be employed to estimate returns to scale. However, the use of a single cross section does not yield unbiased estimates of β and cannot be used to obtain unbiased estimates of returns to density. The same statements are approximately true for estimates based on panel data when the between-firm variation dominates the within-firm variation in the $\mathbf{X}$'s.

Among the recent rail studies, Friedlaender and Spady (1981), Harris (1977) and Keeler (1974) employ multiple cross sections and hence are subject to the bias shown in Eq. (14). None of these three studies provides unbiased estimates of returns to density. But it is likely that the cross-section variation dominates the time-series variation, so that the estimates are nearly unbiased for $\beta + \pi$ and can be used to infer returns to scale. Harmatuck (1979) averages across three cross sections to convert his data to a single cross section. Thus he obtains between estimates that are unbiased for $\beta + \pi$ and can be used to infer returns to scale – but not returns to density.[7] The same

---

[6] Most studies actually employ a GLS version of $\mathbf{b}_r$ designed to correct for a variety of error covariance structures. These corrections are irrelevant to the points being discussed here.

[7] Keeler also uses averaged data in addition to multiple cross sections, thereby achieving unbiased estimates of $\beta + \pi$.

conclusion applies to Caves, Christensen, and Swanson (1981). Their use of several cross sections, widely separated in time with different samples in each cross section, can be regarded as equivalent to a single large cross section once time effects are controlled for.

In conclusion, we find that none of the existing studies yields unbiased estimates of returns to density. All potentially suffer from the bias due to failure to account for unobserved aspects of network. In contrast all studies provide unbiased or nearly unbiased estimates of returns to scale. This explains why the previous studies yield very similar estimates of returns to scale but differ sharply on estimates of returns to density. The estimates of returns to density are all biased and thus differ substantially among studies depending on the samples and the details of model specification and estimation.

2.   Data description

Our data are for 1951 through 1975 for railroads designated Class I by the U.S. Interstate Commerce Commission. We have been able to construct satisfactory data for a total of 820 observations, representing forty-three carriers that existed for all or part of the sample period. A list of firms in the sample is given in Appendix 4A.

Our procedures for data development are discussed in detail in Caves, Christensen, and Swanson (1981), which also displays a considerable amount of aggrgate data for the U.S. Class I Railroads. These procedures were refined, updated, and extended to our 1951–75 panel of railroad carriers in Caves, Christensen, Swanson, and Tretheway (1981). In order to keep the cost function to a manageable size, we specify three input aggregates, whose prices appear in the cost function. These are labor, fuel, and a capital and materials aggregate.

An important aspect of our data development is the development of economic rather than accounting costs of capital. We used a perpetual-inventory method to construct stocks of structures and equipment capital for each railroad. Expenditures for right-of-way replacement were capitalized rather than treated as a maintenance expense, as was the standard accounting practice during the sample period. This correction eliminates the problems created by deferred maintenance in measuring total costs. We developed capital service costs that account for economic depreciation, real interest costs, and taxes.

We specify two outputs – freight ton-miles and passenger-miles. In addition, we include average length of freight haul and average length of passenger trip as separate variables. By including these variables we recognize that output increases can arise either from increases in the number of tons or passengers or increases in the distance each ton or passenger is carried. As we shall show, this distinction is important in determining returns to scale.

Route-miles is included in the cost function as the observed measure of network size. Each firm is assigned its own firm effect to represent unobserved network effects. In addition the firm effect is permitted to vary whenever a firm undergoes a restructuring during the sample period.

3. Estimating methods and functional form

We employ the generalized translog multiproduct cost function to represent the total cost function. This generalization of the translog form involves using the Box–Cox metric rather than the natural log metric for output and route miles.[8]

We write the multiproduct generalized translog cost functions for firm F as

$$\ln C = \beta^0 + \beta^T T + \sum_i B_i^Y Y_i^* + \tfrac{1}{2} \sum_i \sum_j \beta_{ij}^{YY} Y_i^* Y_j^*$$

$$+ \sum_i \sum_j \beta_{ij}^{YY} Y_i^* \ln W_j + \beta^R R^* + \tfrac{1}{2} \beta^{RR} R^* R^*$$

$$+ \sum_i \beta_i^{RW} R^* \ln W_j + \sum_i \beta_i^W \ln W_i + \tfrac{1}{2} \sum_i \sum_j \beta_{ij}^{WW} \ln W_i \ln W_j$$

$$+ \sum_j \beta_{jY}^R R^* Y_j^* + F, \tag{16}$$

where T is a linear time trend, F is the unobserved network effects for firm F, and the asterisks represent the Box–Cox transformation: $Y_i^* = (Y_i^2 - 1)/\lambda$. In Caves, Christensen, and Tretheway (1980) we estimated the generalized translog multiproduct cost function for a 1963 cross section of U.S. Class I Railroads. In that study we estimated the value of the Box–Cox parameter, λ, to be 0.115 with a standard error of (0.051). Since nonlinear estimation with the panel data set in the study would be prohibitively expensive, we have fixed the value of λ at 0.10. Prior to making the natural logarithmic and Box–Cox transformation, each observation on each variable is divided by its sample mean μ; thus the transformed variables are all equal to zero when evaluated at the sample mean.

Without loss of generality, we impose symmetry, $\beta_{ij}^{WW} = \beta_{ji}^{WW}$ and $\beta_{ij}^{YY} = \beta_{ji}^{YY}$. A cost function must be homogeneous of degree 1 in input prices, which implies the following restrictions:

[8] The generalized translog multiproduct cost function is discussed in Caves, Christensen, and Tretheway (1980). Its features are similar to those of the translog, but it allows individual outputs to be zero for some observations. This is particularly important in rail application since passenger service is zero for a substantial number of observations.

$$\sum_i \beta_i^W = 1, \qquad \sum_i \beta_{ij}^{WW} = 0, \text{ for all } j, \qquad \sum_j \beta_{ij}^{YW} = 0, \text{ for all } i,$$

and $\quad \sum_i \beta_i^{RW} = 0.$ (17)

Shephard's (1953) lemma implies that the input shares (S_i) can be equated to the logarithmic partial derivatives of the cost function with respect to the input prices:

$$S_i = \beta_i^W + \sum_j \beta_{ij}^{WW} \ln W_j + \sum_j \beta_{ij}^{YW} Y_j^* + \beta_i^{YW} R^*.$$ (18)

It has become standard practice to specify classical disturbances for (17) and (18) and to estimate the parameters of the cost function via multivariate regression. We follow this procedure, using a modification of Zellner's (1962) technique for estimation. To overcome the problem of singularity of the contemporaneous covariance matrix, we delete one of the share equations prior to carrying out the second stage of Zellner's technique. The resulting estimates are asymptotically equivalent to maximum likelihood estimates. Moreover, the use of all equations at the first stage ensures that the estimates are invariant to the choice of equation to be deleted at the second stage.

Estimation of (16) as described provides the within estimates, the estimates of the β vector in Eq. (8). To obtain the π estimates of Eq. (9) we reestimate (16), replacing each observation by its firm mean. This provides the between estimates. Subtracting the within from the between estimates yields the π estimates.

4.   Results

There are eighty-seven independent parameters in Eq. (16). Full details of the regression are shown in Appendix 4B. The estimated model meets all of the required monotonicity and concavity properties at every point in the sample.

To summarize the results, we present the first-order coefficients in Table 4.1. There are three sets of results in Table 4.1. The first column provides the estimates β from Eq. (16). Since this model includes firm effects, these estimates provide conditional inference. Unconditional inference is based on the sum of the β estimates and the π estimates. This sum is shown in column 2. To illustrate the importance of the unobserved network effects, we present column 3, which was obtained by reestimating (16) with the firm effects omitted.

The estimated coefficients in Table 4.1 can be interpreted as cost elasticities at the sample mean (see Table 4.2 for sample means). This follows from the elasticity equation:

Table 4.1. *Generalized translog total cost function for U.S. Class 1 Railroads, 1951–75*

	Estimates of β, conditional inference (1)	Estimates of $\beta + \pi$, unconditional inference (2)	Restricted estimates of β omitting firm effects (3)
	First-order coefficients		
Ton-miles	.468	.756	.718
	(.020)	(.096)	(.013)
Passenger-miles	.101	.196	.184
	(.009)	(.088)	(.010)
Route-miles	.404	.066	.107
	(.110)	(.151)	(.020)
Length of haul	−.153	−.079	−.094
	(.044)	(.124)	(.020)
Length of trip	−.086	−.063	−.081
	(.016)	(.050)	(.007)
Price of labor	.486	.479	.484
	(.002)	(.012)	(.002)
Price of fuel	.044	.043	.044
	(.001)	(.003)	(.001)
Price of capital and materials	.470	.478	.472
	(.003)	(.013)	(.003)
	Properties of the cost structure at the sample mean		
RTD fixed haul and trip	1.76		1.11
	(.07)		(.02)
RTS fixed haul and trip		.98	.99
		(.07)	(.01)
RTS increase haul and trip		1.09	1.13
		(.08)	(.01)

$$\frac{\partial \ln C}{\partial \ln Y_i} = E_{Yi} = \left(\beta_i^Y + \sum_j \beta_{ij}^{YY} Y_j^* + \sum_j \beta_{ij}^{YW} \ln W_j + \beta_j^{RYR*} \right) Y_i^\lambda, \quad (19)$$

or

$$\frac{\partial \ln C}{\partial \ln Y_i} = E_{Yi} + \beta_i^Y. \quad (20)$$

at the sample mean.

All of the estimated first-order effects have the expected signs, and the standard errors are in general quite small. There is a strong positive relation between total cost and either ton-miles or passenger-miles, but a negative relation between total cost and either length of haul or length of trip.

Table 4.2. *Sample means*

Freight output	16.1 billion ton-miles
Passenger output	425 million passenger-miles
Average length of haul	282 miles
Average length of trip	201 miles
Route-miles	4766 miles

The lower portion of Table 4.1 presents estimates of returns to density and scale at the sample mean. Returns to density are obtained by using the conditional estimates (column 1) to evaluate Eq. (5),

$$\text{RTD} = (E_{\text{TM}} + E_{\text{PM}})^{-1}, \tag{21}$$

where E_{TM} and E_{PM} are the ton-mile and passenger-mile elasticities. The estimates of returns to density in Table 4.1 are based only on the ton-mile and passenger-mile elasticities; that is, we are presuming that length of haul and trip are constant, given the fixed network. This yields an estimate of returns to density of 1.76 at the sample mean. We have also computed returns to density by applying (19) and (5) to all the observations in our sample. No observation falls outside of the range 1.5 to 2.1; thus opportunities for reducing costs by increasing density appear to be widespread.

Conditional inference is not appropriate for assessing returns to scale, since changes in scale include changes in both the observed and unobserved network effects. Thus we rely upon column 2 ($\beta + \pi$) for assessing returns to scale. Because network is permitted to change in the returns to scale calculation, it is possible that length of haul and trip also change. The estimates of RTS will depend upon the variation of length of haul and trip with ton-miles and passenger-miles. If we hold length of haul and trip fixed, we use the following formula:

$$\text{RTS} = (E_{\text{TM}} + E_{\text{PM}} + E_N)^{-1}, \tag{22}$$

where E_N is the network elasticity. This presumes that the network expansion enables the railroad to carry more traffic, but that the average distance carried does not change. For this case we find returns to scale at the sample mean of 0.98 with a standard error of 0.07.

An alternative measure holds passengers and tons constant and provides for output growth by increasing haul and trip lengths. We augment Eq. (22) as

$$\text{RTS} = (E_{\text{TM}} + E_{\text{PM}} + E_N + E_T + E_H)^{-1}, \tag{23}$$

where E_T and E_H are the cost elasticities of length of haul and trip. This yields an estimate of RTS at the sample mean of 1.14 with a standard error of 0.12

(not shown in Table 4.1), indicating the economies available from longer hauls and trips.[9]

The RTS measures in (22) and (23) represent extreme cases. In (22) output growth arises solely from increases in quantities carried; in (23) output growth arises solely from distance carried. A more representative measure would reflect the industry's actual variation of quantity and distance carried. In logarithmic terms the range of sample variation in length of haul is about one-half as great as the range of sample variation for output, trip length, and network variables. Accordingly we modify equation (23) as

$$\text{RTS} = (E_{\text{TM}} + E_{\text{PM}} + E_N + E_T + \tfrac{1}{2}E_H)^{-1}. \tag{24}$$

This yields an estimate of returns to scale of the sample mean of 1.09 with a standard error of 0.08 (shown at the bottom of Table 4.1).

To provide a more complete picture of the structure of rail costs we present average cost curves in Figure 4.1. The curve denoted by + denotes changes in average cost resulting from changes in scale with haul and trip allowed to vary as in the RTS measure in Eq. (24). The point numbered 1.0 on the horizontal axis corresponds to the sample mean values for output, network, haul, and trip (see Table 4.2). Other points denote values relative to the mean for all of these variables except length of haul. Consistent with Eq. (22), length of haul varies with the square root of the indicators on the axis. The curve is constructed on the basis of the unconditional ($\beta + \pi$) estimates. It has the classic L shape and reflects the slight increasing returns to scale at the sample mean.

The other curve in the figure is based on the conditional (β) estimates and shows how cost varies with changes in density. This curve is constructed by holding network fixed at the sample mean value of 4,766 route-miles while allowing ton-miles and passenger-miles to vary proportionally. The curve indicates that increasing returns to density persist over a wide range of output. As we noted previously, we find increasing returns to density at every sample point, and extrapolating outside the sample, we find substantial increasing returns to density even at levels of density several times as large as the sample values.

As noted in section 1, failure to account for unobserved network effects can be expected to yield biased estimates. In general we expect the bias in returns to density to be more severe than the bias in returns to scale. To investigate this further we have reestimated Eq. (16), omitting the firm effects. The results are shown in column 3 of Table 4.1.

---

[9] Because of the fixed network, we do not provide for any increase in length of haul and trip in computing economies of density. Had we done so by including E_H and E_T in (21), RTD would be 3.0.

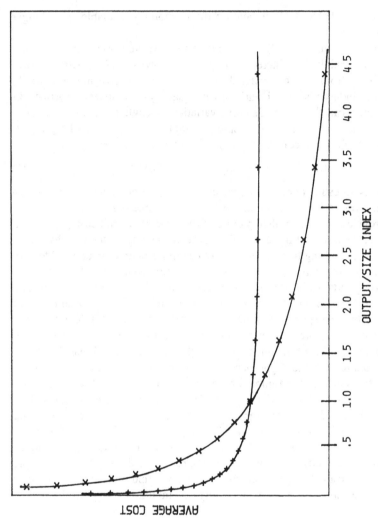

Figure 4.1. Average cost versus scale and density. + = average cost versus scale (haul and trip varied); x = average cost versus density.

Comparing columns 1 and 3 we see that the first-order output and route-miles coefficient are drastically altered by the omission of the firm effects. The column 3 estimates come much closer to $\beta + \pi$ (column 2) than to β (column 1). This is to be expected in railroad samples, where variation in the cross-section dimension dominates variation in the time-series dimension.

Because the column 3 estimates are close to the $\beta + \pi$ estimates of column 2, the returns to scale estimates based on column 3 are quite similar to corresponding estimates from column 2. But the bias resulting from use of the column 3 estimator is readily apparent in the estimate of returns to density. Column 3 yields 1.11 compared to the unbiased column 1 estimate of 1.76.

The estimates in Table 4.1 are all based on models of total cost. It can be argued that railroad firms are in disequilibrium with respect to the stock of way and structures and that a variable-cost model would be more appropriate. If so, then it is possible that our results stem from misspecification of the model. The variable-cost approach involves estimation of an equation similar to (16), except that the price of structures is replaced by the quantity of structures, and total cost is replaced by total cost less the annualized cost of structures. This was the approach taken by Caves, Christensen, and Swanson (1981) and Friedlaender and Spady (1981). In general we find that use of the variable-cost approach does not change our conclusions.[10] Under the variable-cost specifications returns to density are 1.74 at the sample mean, compared to 1.76 in the total-cost model; returns to scale are 0.96, compared to 0.98, when haul and trip are fixed. The variable-cost model was less suitable than the total cost model because of imprecise coefficients on length of haul and trip, which implied positive cost elasticities for these characteristics at the sample mean.[11]

5.   Conclusions

Theoretical results obtained by Mundlak (1978) indicate that failure to include unobserved network effects in the regression may seriously bias estimates of returns to density. Depending upon the nature of the sample, such estimates may nonetheless yield unbiased or nearly unbiased estimates of returns to scale. In Table 4.3 we display estimates of returns to scale and density from

[10] Caves, Christensen, and Swanson (1981) also found results to be largely insensitive to the difference between the total-cost and variable-cost specifications.

[11] We also tested for the possibility that technological change has caused returns to density to increase over time. Although the results showed some evidence of such an effect, its magnitude was small and its inclusion in the model did not alter the findings in any important way.

Table 4.3. *Comparison of returns to scale and density from previous studies computed at the sample means*[a]

	Returns to density	Returns to scale	
		Fixed haul and trip	Increased haul and trip
Friedlaender and Spady (1981)	1.16	.88–1.08	1.07–1.37
Caves, Christensen, and Swanson (1981)	—	1.01	1.13
Harmatuck (1979)	1.92	.93	1.02
Harris (1977)	1.72	1.03	1.17
Keeler (1974)	1.79	1.01	—
This study	1.76	.98	1.09

Note: Dash means data not available.
[a]Sources for these values are presented in Appendix 4C.

five previous studies. As might be expected on the basis of the Mundlak findings, the returns-to-scale estimates are relatively consistent, indicating constant or nearly constant returns to scale when haul and trip are fixed and some degree of increasing returns when length of haul and trip are increased. But the returns to density estimates are diverse. Friedlaender and Spady (1981) and Caves, Christensen, and Swanson (1981) gave little evidence of increasing returns to density, while the other three studies found substantial increasing returns to density. These results are consistent with Mundlak's theoretical findings, with the instability of the density estimates reflecting the differing biases in the specific estimators.

To correct for unobserved network effects we apply the estimators developed by Mundlak to a panel of rail data for the 1951–75 time period. We find returns to density at the sample mean of 1.76, which is similar to the estimates of Harmatuck (1979), Harris (1977), and Keeler (1974). However, in contrast to these studies we find no tendency for returns to density to diminish at higher levels of density. Our results show substantial increasing returns to density at every point in the sample and at density levels far above those observed in the sample. We find returns to scale that are in substantial agreement with earlier studies.

When we omit the correction for unobserved network effects from our sample, we find that returns to scale are largely unaffected, but that returns to density fall dramatically, into the range suggested by the Friedlaender and Spady (1981) and Caves, Christensen, and Swanson (1981) studies. This demonstrates the importance of using panel data and controlling for unobserved network effects in estimating returns to density for railroads.

Appendix 4A. *List of firms in sample*

Firm	Time period	Abbreviation used in Appendix 4B
Atchison, Topeka, & Santa Fe	1951–75	ATSF
Atlantic Coast Line	1951–66	ACL
Baltimore & Ohio	1951–75	BO
Boston & Maine	1951–75	BM
Burlington Northern	1970–75	BN
Chesapeake & Ohio	1951–75	CO
Chicago, Burlington, & Quincy	1951–69	CBQ
Chicago & Eastern Illinois 1[a]	1951–68	CEI1
Chicago & Eastern Illinois 2[a]	1969–75	CEI2
Chicago, Milwaukee, & St. Paul	1951–75	MILW
Chicago, Rock Island, & Pacific	1951–75	ROCK
Clinchfield	1951–75	CLN
Delaware & Hudson	1951–75	DH
Delaware, Lackawanna, & Western	1951–59	DLW
Denver, Rio Grande, & Western	1951–75	DRGW
Duluth South Shore	1951–60	DSS
Erie	1951–59	ERIE
Erie-Lackawanna	1960–75	EL
Florida East Coast	1951–75	FEC
Great Northern	1951–69	GN
Louisville & Nashville 1[a]	1951–56	LN1
Louisville & Nashville 2[a]	1957–70	LN2
Louisville & Nashville 3[a]	1971–75	LN3
Missouri-Pacific 1[a]	1951–55	MP1
Missouri-Pacific 2[a]	1956–75	MP2
Monon (Chicago, Indianapolis, & Louisville)	1951–70	MON
Nashville, Chattanooga, & St. Louis	1951–56	NCSL
New York Central	1951–67	NYC
New York, Chicago, & St. Louis	1951–63	NKP
Norfolk-Southern	1951–73	NS
Norfolk & Western 1[a]	1951–58	NW1
Norfolk & Western 2[a]	1959–63	NW2
Norfolk & Western 3[a]	1964–75	NW3
Northern Pacific	1951–69	NP
Northwestern Pacific	1957–75	NWP
Penn Central	1968–75	PC
Pennsylvania	1951–67	PRR
Reading	1951–75	RDG
Richmond, Fredricksburg & Potomac	1951–69	RFP
Seaboard Airline	1951–66	SAL
Seaboard Coast Line	1967–75	SCL
SOO Line	1961–75	SOO
Southern Pacific 1[a]	1951–60	SP1

(*continued*)

Appendix 4A. *(Continued)*

Firm	Time period	Abbreviation used in Appendix 4B
Southern Pacific 2[a]	1961–75	SP2
Spokane, Portland, & Seattle	1951–69	SPS
Texas & Pacific	1951–75	TP
Union Pacific	1951–75	UP
Virginia	1951–58	VGN
Wabash	1951–63	WAB
Western Pacific 1[a]	1951–71	WP1
Western Pacific 2[a]	1972–75	WP2

[a]These firms have more than one firm effect due to a major acquisition or sale during the years 1951–75. For instance, the Louisville & Nashville acquired the Nashville, Chattanooga, & St. Louis in 1957 and therefore has a firm effect for the period 1951–56 and a second firm effect from 1957–70. In 1971 it acquired the Chicago, Indianapolis, & Louisville and therefore has a third firm effect from 1971–75.

Appendix 4B. *Regression coefficients*

	Estimates of β, Eq. (16)	Estimates of π, Eq. (9)	Restricted estimates of β, Eq. (16) with $F = 0$
First-order terms			
Constant	19.632	.065	19.653
	(.113)[a]	(.173)	(.013)
Ton-miles	.468	.288	.718
	(.020)	(.098)	(.013)
Passenger-miles	.101	.095	.184
	(.009)	(.089)	(.010)
Length of haul	−.153	.074	−.094
	(.044)	(.132)	(.020)
Length of trip	−.086	.023	−.081
	(.016)	(.053)	(.007)
Route-miles	.404	−.338	.107
	(.110)	(.187)	(.020)
Labor price	.486	−.007	.484
	(.002)	(.012)	(.002)
Fuel price	.044	−.001	.044
	(.001)	(.003)	(.001)
Materials-capital price	.469	.008	.472
	(.003)	(.013)	(.003)

Appendix 4B. *(Continued)*

	Estimates of β, Eq. (16)	Estimates of π, Eq. (9)	Restricted estimates of β, Eq. (16) with $F = 0$
Interaction terms			
Labor price × labor price	.094	−.079	.100
	(.008)	(.073)	(.008)
Fuel price × fuel price	.007	−.014	.007
	(.001)	(.015)	(.001)
Materials-capital price × materials-capital price	.151	−.129	.160
	(.009)	(.083)	(.009)
Labor price × materials-capital price	−.119	.097	−.125
	(.008)	(.076)	(.008)
Fuel price × materials-capital price	−.032	.032	−.035
	(.002)	(.017)	(.002)
Labor price × fuel price	.025	−.018	.028
	(.002)	(.020)	(.002)
Ton miles × ton-miles	−.094	−.044	−.201
	(.034)	(.371)	(.043)
Passenger-miles × passenger-miles	.043	.014	.063
	(.005)	(.042)	(.005)
Ton-miles × passenger-miles	−.034	−.072	−.070
	(.008)	(.073)	(.009)
Length of haul × length of haul	.192	−.449	−.048
	(.143)	(.679)	(.088)
Length of trip × length of trip	−.002	.040	.011
	(.008)	(.092)	(.010)
Length of haul × length of trip	.002	−.015	.002
	(.012)	(.121)	(.015)
Length of haul × ton-miles	.036	−.315	−.110
	(.045)	(.400)	(.047)
Length of haul × passenger-miles	−.010	.010	.002
	(.015)	(.154)	(.018)
Length of trip × ton-miles	.018	.044	.031
	(.006)	(.070)	(.008)
Length of trip × passenger-miles	−.020	−.015	−.030
	(.006)	(.050)	(.005)
Route-miles × route-miles	.025	−.550	−.462
	(.113)	(.514)	(.059)
Ton-miles × labor price	−.007	.015	−.015
	(.005)	(.024)	(.005)
Ton-miles × fuel price	.005	.003	.004
	(.001)	(.006)	(.001)
Ton-miles × materials-capital price	.002	−.018	.008
	(.005)	(.027)	(.005)

(continued)

Appendix 4B. *(Continued)*

	Estimates of β, Eq. (16)	Estimates of π, Eq. (9)	Restricted estimates of β, Eq. (16) with $F = 0$
Passenger-miles × labor price	.015	−.009	.015
	(.002)	(.009)	(.002)
Passenger-miles × fuel price	.000	−.002	.000
	(.000)	(.002)	(.000)
Passenger-miles × materials-capital price	−.015	.011	−.016
	(.002)	(.010)	(.002)
Length of haul × labor price	−.014	.008	−.006
	(.007)	(.035)	(.002)
Length of haul × fuel price	.005	.000	.006
	(.002)	(.008)	(.007)
Length of haul × materials-capital price	.009	−.008	.000
	(.008)	(.038)	(.008)
Length of trip × labor price	−.003	.002	−.003
	(.001)	(.008)	(.001)
Length of trip × fuel price	.001	.000	.001
	(.000)	(.002)	(.000)
Length of trip × materials-capital price	.002	−.003	.002
	(.002)	(.009)	(.002)
Route-miles × length of haul	.008	.276	.091
	(.069)	(.416)	(.057)
Route-miles × length of trip	.022	−.029	.021
	(.009)	(.088)	(.010)
Route-miles × labor price	000	.000	.002
	(.006)	(.029)	(.006)
Route-miles × fuel price	−.006	−.001	−.006
	(.001)	(.006)	(.001)
Route-miles × materials-capital price	.006	−.006	.005
	(.006)	(.031)	(.006)
Route-miles × ton-miles	.088	.278	.339
	(.035)	(.388)	(.042)
Route-miles × passenger-miles	−.023	.048	−.005
	(.013)	(.091)	(.001)
Time trend			
Time	−.022	−.006	−.023
	(.001)	(.012)	(.001)

Appendix 4B. *(Continued)*

Firm effects	Estimates of β, Eq. (16)	Firm effects	Estimates of β, Eq. (16)	Firm effects	Estimates of β, Eq. (16)
ATSF	−.028 (.058)	EL	.120 (.156)	NWP	−.534 (.290)
ACL	−.205 (.109)	FEC	−.200 (.249)	PC	.089 (.190)
BO	.197 (.099)	GN	−.210 (.051)	PRR	.248 (.094)
BM	−.144 (.196)	LN1	−.077 (.120)	RDG	−.227 (.217)
BN	−.386 (.217)	LN2	−.072 (.099)	RFP	−1.223 (.449)
CO	.075 (.107)	LN3	−.028 (.085)	SAL	−.169 (.133)
CBQ	−.303 (.065)	MP1	−.118 (.077)	SCL	−.089 (.068)
CEI1	−.402 (.223)	MP2	−.244 (.047)	SOO	−.377 (.123)
CEI2	−.338 (.239)	MON	−.463 (.251)	SP1	.098 (.056)
MILW	−.246 (.059)	NCSL	−.286 (.215)	SP2	−.033 (.063)
ROCK	−.316 (.071)	NYC	.123 (.085)	SPS	−.311 (.218)
CLN	−.597 (.302)	NKP	.128 (.175)	TP	−.151 (.181)
DH	−.242 (.230)	NS	−.821 (.248)	UP	.000
DLW	−.182 (.227)	NW1	.107 (.176)	VGN	−.494 (.243)
DRGW	−.684 (.155)	NW2	−.063 (.160)	WAB	.011 (.166)
DSS	−.966 (.255)	NW3	.096 (.073)	WP1	−.075 (.209)
ERIE	.054 (.172)	NP	−.087 (.068)	WP2	−.095 (.197)

[a]Standard errors are in parentheses.

Appendix 4C

In Table 4.3 we reported measures of returns to scale holding average length of haul and average length of trip constant (RTS1), returns to scale allowing average length of haul and average length of trip to vary (RTS2), and returns to density for other studies. These measures were obtained either directly from the study or as a result of calculations based on the results presented in the studies.

Keeler (1983, p. 159) reports returns to density for the mean firm based on all Class I railroads in 1969. Keeler's estimate of RTS1 is reported in Keeler (1974, p. 205). Keeler reports these numbers as the percentage increase in costs associated with a 1 percent increase in the appropriate variables. We invert his results to get returns to scale and density. Keeler's study does not include average length of haul or trip, and therefore RTS2 cannot be computed.

Harris does not report returns to either density or scale in his paper. In order to compute these measures, we derived the formulas for the elasticity of cost with respect to revenue ton-miles, revenue freight tons, and miles of roads from his cost equation. These elasticities were evaluated at our mean firm. We then computed returns to density as the inverse of the sum of the cost elasticities of revenue ton-miles and revenue freight tons.[12] RTS1 was computed as the inverse of the sum of all three cost elasticities, while RTS2 was computed as the inverse of the sum of the cost elasticities of revenue ton-miles, miles of road, and one-half the cost elasticity of revenue freight tons.

Harmatuck (1979), Friedlaender and Spady (1981), and Caves, Christensen, and Swanson (1981) use translog cost functions with the variables normalized. This allows us to interpret the first-order coefficients as cost elasticities at their respective mean firms. Harmatuck includes total gross ton miles and tons of revenue and nonrevenue traffic as his outputs.[13] Using the coefficients in Table 3 of Harmatuck (1979), we compute returns to density as the inverse of the sum of first-order coefficients as ton-miles and freight tons. RTS1 is computed as the inverse of the sum of the first-order coefficients on ton-miles, freight tons, and miles of road, while RTS2 is computed as the inverse of the sum of the first-order coefficients on ton-miles, miles of road and one-half the cost elasticity of freight tons.

---

[12] Revenue ton-miles, revenue freight tons, and miles of road were the only variables in Harris's cost function. Increasing revenue ton-miles and revenue freight tons proportionately holds length of haul fixed.

[13] Harmatuck also includes a variable to account for the percentage of cars that carry metallic ore, crushed stone, gravel, and sand. Our computations assumed that this percentage remains fixed at the sample mean as output grows.

Friedlaender and Spady use a fixed-factor model and thus computation of returns to scale and density must be adjusted for the effect of the fixed factor. This is done by substituting variable cost for total cost elasticities in Eqs. (5) and (6), and multiplying Eqs. (5) and (6) by $(1 - E_K)$, where E_K is the variable-cost elasticity of the fixed factor. Friedlaender and Spady have two outputs in their cost function: ton-miles and passenger-miles. In addition, they include four technological variables: route-miles, low-density route-miles, average length of haul, and traffic mix. In our computations of returns to density, we hold all four technological factors fixed and compute Eq. (5) adjusted for the fixed factor. This procedure necessarily ignores one important component of Friedlaender and Spady's evidence on returns to density: The large and discrete decline in costs that occurs with their specification at one million gross ton-miles per route-mile. If traffic increases cause low-density route-miles to decline, then returns to density will be greater. But the increase in returns to density depends on the distribution of traffic increases across low-density and regular route-miles, and whether the traffic increases push any of the low-density lines across the 1 million gross ton-miles per route-mile threshold. There is no straightforward way to account for this peculiarity.

To compute RTS1 from the Friedlaender and Spady results, we allow route-miles to enter the computation as in Eq. (6). The results depend on how low-density route-miles change with scale changes; thus we show a range of results. If we allow low-density route-miles to remain a fixed proportion of total route-miles, then we obtain the smaller values for RTS1 (0.88). Specifying that low-density route miles do not change yields the larger value (1.08). RTS2 is computed similarly, except that one-half the first-order coefficient on length of haul is included in the computation of Eq. (6). The coefficients reported in Friedlaender and Spady (1981, pp. 231–36) served as a basis for these calculations.

RTS1 and RTS2 for Caves, Christensen, and Swanson are taken from Caves, Christensen, and Swanson (1981, p. 999). These numbers are for the year 1963.

References

Braeutigam, R. R., A. F. Daughety, and M. A. Turnquist (1984). "A Firm Specific Analysis of Economics of Density in the U.S. Railroad Industry." *Journal of Industrial Economics, 33*, no. 1, September: 3–20.

Caves, D. W., L. R. Christensen, and J. A. Swanson (1980). "Productivity in U.S. Railroads, 1951–1974," *Bell Journal of Economics, 11*, no. 1, Spring: 166–81.

(1981). "Productivity Growth, Scale Economies, and Capacity Utilization in U.S. Railroads, 1955–1974." *American Economic Review, 71*, December: 994–1002.

Caves, D. W., L. R. Christensen, J. A. Swanson, and M. W. Tretheway (1982). "Economic Performance of U.S. and Canadian Railroads: The Significance of Ownership and the Regulatory Environment." In W. T. Stanbury and Fred Thompson, eds., *Managing Public Enterprises.* New York: Praeger.

Caves, D. W., L. R. Christensen, and M. W. Tretheway (1980). "Flexible Cost Functions for Multiproduct Firms." *Review of Economics and Statistics,* August: 477–81.

Friedlaender, A. F., and R. H. Spady (1981). *Freight Transport Regulation: Equity, Efficiency, and Competition in the Rail and Trucking Industry.* Cambridge, Mass.: MIT Press.

Harmatuck, D. J. (1979). "A Policy-Sensitive Railway Cost Function." *Logistics and Transportation Review,* 15 May: 277–315.

Harris, R. G. (1979). "Economies of Traffic Density in the Rail Freight Industry." *Bell Journal of Economics,* 8, Autumn: 556–64.

Keeler, T. E. (1974). "Railroad Costs, Returns to Scale, and Excess Capacity." *Review of Economies and Statistics,* 56, May: 201–8.

——— (1983). *Railroads, Freight, and Public Policy.* Washington, D.C.: The Brookings Institution.

Mundlak, Y. (1961). "Empirical Production Functions Free of Management Bias." *The Journal of Farm Economics,* 43, no. 1, February: 44–56.

——— (1978). "On the Pooling of Time Series and Cross Section Data." *Econometrics,* 46, no. 1, January: 69–85.

Panzar, J. C., and R. D. Willig (1977). "Economies of Scale in Multi-Output Production." *Quarterly Journal of Economics,* 91, August: 481–93.

Shephard, R. W. (1953). *Cost and Production Functions.* Princeton, N.J.: Princeton University Press.

Zellner, A. (1962). "An Efficient Method of Estimating Seemingly Unrelated Regressions and Tests for Aggregation Bias." *Journal of the American Statistical Association,* 58, December: 977–92.

CHAPTER 5

Using indexed quadratic cost functions to model network technologies

RICHARD H. SPADY

The purpose of this chapter is to introduce the indexed quadratic (IQ) function and to examine its applications to empirical problems in the econometrics of production, with particular attention to the problem of modeling network technologies. The function in its most general form is a slight modification of a proposal by Baumol, Panzar, and Willig (1982) to construct cost functions as quadratic functions of outputs and to regard the resulting coefficients as concave independent homogeneous functions of input prices. Baumol et al. demonstrated that this formulation is well suited for modeling the technologies of multiple-output firms.

While the techniques developed in this chapter are applicable to a wide variety of industries characterized by network technologies – telecommunications, the postal system, most public utility systems (water, electricity) – the most obvious application is to transportation systems. A leading issue in transportation economics has been the appropriate measurement of output, since most transportation networks are sufficiently complex that an enumeration of outputs by origin–destination combination yields a very high number of ostensibly different outputs, possibly thousands. To distinguish these outputs for the statistical estimation of cost or production functions is infeasible. Moreover, it is not clear that such a treatment would be entirely desirable, since prior information concerning the nature of the relations among the outputs could not be easily incorporated in the estimation procedure; nor would the important network aspects of the technology – which induce the economies of scale and scope that are of primary interest – be perspicuous in the resulting representation.

Investigators have long recognized these problems but have generally been forced to ignore them or to handle them in an ad hoc fashion. One approach has been to aggregate outputs more carefully (say, by shipment size and length of haul) and/or to include aggregate descriptions of the network (such as the proportion of all possible nodal connections that are actually made) directly into the cost function (see for example Wang and Friedlaender, 1981 and Harmatuck, 1981). This approach has the advantage of eliminating an obvious source of bias in the estimation process and providing a useful but limited basis for addressing network issues such as the effects of reconfiguration, but it still yields, in the terminology of Winston's (1985) survey, a spatially aggregated model that cannot yield a truly satisfactory analysis of specific traffic movements; moreover, the source of network effects is obscure and the resulting estimates possibly unreliable. A second approach, taken by Jara-Diaz and Winston (1981), is to treat each origin–destination combination as a separate output in a conventional cost function, but this is feasible only for very small networks and the network aspect of the technology is unrepresented. Thus, while this approach (when feasible) provides estimates of the costs of specific traffic flows, it cannot provide a good intuition about the source of scale and scope economies, nor can it generally provide cost estimates outside the context of historically observed networks. My ambition in this chapter is to remedy the shortcomings of previous approaches while maintaining econometric tractability.

In Section 3 I adopt the following simplified view of a transportation network. Transport always occurs between two "nodes"; the path between the nodes is called a "link." Switching, as well as pickup and delivery, is handled by nodes. The total cost on the network is the sum of the costs incurred at the nodes and links; these in turn depend on the node and link activities and characteristics. More precisely, all links and all nodes have neoclassical cost functions that represent their technologies; these cost functions are of the same parametric family, in the sense that all links (nodes) have the same technology, though the description of the technology includes information specific to the link (node). For example, a railroad's links would consist of the rail line connecting two points (nodes); the characteristics of a rail link include its length, the condition of its track, and the like. In the case of an airline, the link is the air path between two airports; its characteristics are the length and (say) the probability of bad weather.

On this view, the activity of the network is the sum of its node and link activities. The point of this chapter is that one can place assumptions on the constituent node and link technologies such that one need not observe the complete list of input and output activities by location, but only a small number of statistics thereof, in order to estimate econometrically a compact yet complete description of the network's technology. The appropriate assumption is that the nodes and links can be described by IQ cost functions.

The remainder of this chapter is organized as follows. Section 1 develops a convenient interpretation of the function and suggests a restricted version (RIQ) that is more easily implemented econometrically and also embodies some intuitive notions concerning joint production. Section 2 develops a simple but remarkable aggregation property for such functions: When aggregating over production units facing identical input prices, aggregate input demand is a function only of prices and the first two moments of the joint distribution of the output and characteristic vectors of the production units.

Specifically, this means that an aggregate cost function can be written as a function of means, variances, and covariances of outputs and characteristics, and that the production-unit technology can be entirely recovered from aggregate behavior. Section 3 develops a model of network technologies in which production is spatially dispersed and products are differentiated by origins and destinations. The proposed model allows each origin–destination pair to be treated differently (for example, the model typically generates a different marginal cost for every origin–destination–product combination) without expanding the output vector unduly – the model is econometrically tractable. Section 4 shows how the model can be applied to a number of important policy issues facing regulators of network technologies; Section 5 is a summary.

1.   Indexed quadratic functions

The functional form analyzed here is a slight modification of the quadratic cost function proposed by Baumol, Panzar, and Willig (1982). In the context of production, it gives the cost of producing vector output y at factor prices p under technological conditions t; denoting (y,t) by z:

$$c = \alpha_0 h_0(p) + \sum_k \alpha_k h_k(p) z_k + \tfrac{1}{2} \sum_k \sum_m \beta_{km} \phi_{km}(p) z_k z_m. \qquad (1)$$

In Baumol et al. it is suggested that the functions $h_k(p)$ and $\phi_{km}(p)$ be considered independent functions, and it is noted that if $a_k = \alpha_k h_k(p)$ and $b_{km} = \beta_{km} \phi_{km}(p)$ are nondecreasing, linearly homogeneous, and concave in p, then (1) is a valid cost function. We can modify this approach in two successive steps.

First, to facilitate both the interpretation and econometric implementation of (1), we require that the functions $h_k(p)$ and $\phi_{km}(p)$ be valid price indexes, i.e. that they be nonnegative and be nondecreasing, linearly homogeneous, and concave in p; for convenience, they are normalized so $h_k(1) = \phi_{km}(1) = 1$, for all k and m. Thus, at fixed unit prices (1) is a simple quadratic function in the z's. A simple extension (which nonetheless may be useful in practice) is to replace z_k by some function $g_k(z_k)$, as desired. We will call (1) with the h's and ϕ's restricted only as shown an *indexed quadratic form*. Notice that since the α's and β's are unrestricted as to sign, the properties we have placed on the h's and ϕ's are not sufficient to guarantee that (1) is a globally valid cost function.

Second, to reduce the number of parameters in (1) to manageable econometric proportions, we replace $\phi_{km}(p)$ with $\phi_{km}(h_k(p),h_m(p))$, when ϕ_{km} is a price-index function of the two indexes $h_k(p)$ and $h_m(p)$. For example, a simple ϕ_{km}, which depends on k and m, is the weighted geometric mean given by $\phi_{km} = (h_k^{\delta_k} h_m^{\delta_m})^{1/(\delta_k + \delta_m)}$ with $\delta_1 = 1$ and $\delta_k > 0$ for all k; another possibility requiring no new parameters is the simple geometric mean. We will call an IQ function with this restriction on the ϕ_{km}'s a *restricted indexed quadratic* (RIQ) function.

In an RIQ function, $h_k(\mathbf{p})$ can be interpreted as the price index of inputs relevant for z_k. To see this, suppose that $z_k = 0$ for $k \neq 1$ so that (1) gives the "stand-alone" technology for the first output at $t = 0$ (which is not a substantive constraint, since, the components of t can be rescaled to have a mean of zero without loss of generality). Then marginal cost in this stand-alone technology is

$$\frac{\partial c}{\partial z_1} = h_1(\mathbf{p})[\alpha_1 + \beta_{11} z_1]. \tag{2}$$

It is apparent from (2) that a substantive effect of imposing the restrictions of the restricted indexed quadratic function is that the "nonfixed" portion of any stand-alone technology (at any fixed value of t) is homothetic; that is, aside from the inputs used in "setting-up," the input proportions of every single-product firm are independent of the scale of production.[1] Moreover, if an input is not used by a collection of single-product firms that collectively produces a particular product set, then it is not used by a multiproduct firm producing any subset of that product set. Thus, the RIQ function implies joint production never induces demand for a new input; the general form allows for this possibility.

Additional insight concerning the RIQ function can be gained by distinguishing "production costs" (costs that vary with the level of production) from "setup costs" [represented by $\alpha_0 h_0(\mathbf{p})$ in (1)] and comparing the behavior of production costs (and the corresponding input demands) for the production of $z_1, \ldots, z_k$ by k single-product firms with production by a single multioutput firm. The ith single-output's (production) cost function can be written as $c^i(z_i) = h_i(\mathbf{p})\theta_i(z_i)$, where $\theta_i(z_i) = \alpha_i z_i + \frac{1}{2}\beta_{ii} z_i^2$. The difference in production costs between completely joint and single-output production is then simply

$$C(\mathbf{z}) - \Sigma c^i(z_i) = \frac{1}{2}\sum_k \sum_{m \neq k} \beta_{km} \phi_{km}(\mathbf{p}) z_k z_m. \tag{3}$$

The corresponding difference in demand for the jth input is

$$X_j - \Sigma x_j^i = \frac{1}{2}\sum_k \sum_{m \neq k} \beta_{km} \frac{\partial \phi_{km}}{\partial p_j} z_k z_m. \tag{4}$$

---

[1] For a more careful analysis of set-up costs, see Baumol et al. (1982); there are some obvious variants of our statements above if set-up costs are made to depend on product sets; for example, are given by $\Sigma \lambda_k h_k(\mathbf{p})\delta_k + \frac{1}{2}\Sigma\Sigma\Lambda_{km} \psi(h_k, h_m)\delta_k\delta_m$, where $\delta_k = 1$ if product k is produced, and zero otherwise.

When the RIQ function is used, so that $\phi_{km}(\mathbf{p}) = \phi_{km}(h_k(\mathbf{p}), h_m(\mathbf{p}))$, (4) can be written

$$X_j = \Sigma \gamma^i x_j^i, \tag{5}$$

where

$$\gamma^i = \left\{ 1 + \frac{z_i}{\theta_i(z_i)} \left[\sum_{j \neq i} \beta_{ij} z_j \frac{\partial \phi_{ij}}{\partial h_i} \right] \right\}. \tag{6}$$

Since economies of joint production mean γ^i will typically be less than 1, (5) and (6) indicate that input vector for the joint production firm is the sum of the shrunken input vectors of the single-output firms. This is a substantive constraint when the number of inputs exceeds the number of outputs. The interpretation of (6) is aided by substituting a specific function for ϕ_{ij}; for example if $\phi_{ij} = (h_i h_j)^{\frac{1}{2}}$, then (6) becomes

$$\gamma^i = \left\{ 1 + \frac{z_i}{2\theta_i(z_i)} \left[\sum_{j \neq i} \beta_{ij} z_j \sqrt{h_j / h_i} \right] \right\}. \tag{7}$$

When $h_i(\mathbf{p})$ is high relative to the $h_j(\mathbf{p})$'s, (7) indicates that savings along the ith single-product firm's input ray are *smaller* (if, as is typical, $\beta_{ij} < 0$). This may seem somewhat paradoxical, since $h_i(\mathbf{p})$ is the price index of production for the ith product; but when $h_i(\mathbf{p})$ is high relative to $h_j(\mathbf{p})$ (recall $h_i(\mathbf{1}) \equiv h_j(\mathbf{1}) \equiv 1$), this means that prices of inputs for which the ith technology has poorer substitutes than the jth technology are relatively high; since there are no good substitutes for these goods, their optimal quantity does not fall much; and this relatively larger demand is embodied in a greater demand for the composite in which they play a relatively larger role, namely, the input vector of the ith single-product technology.

Equation (7) can be further interpreted by noting that

$$\frac{\partial C/\partial z_i - \partial c^i/\partial z_i}{h_i(\mathbf{p})} = \sum_{j \neq i} \beta_{ij} z_j \sqrt{h_j / h_i} \tag{8}$$

Denoting the marginal cost of the ith output when production is joint, $\partial C/\partial z_i$, by MC_i, and the marginal and average costs of the ith single-product technology by mc^i and ac^i, respectively, substitution of (8) into (7) yields

$$\gamma^i = \left\{ 1 + \frac{1}{2} \left[\frac{MC_i - mc^i}{ac^i} \right] \right\} \tag{9}$$

so that the ith input vector is reduced by half the reduction in marginal cost as a percentage of average cost.

The basic phenomenon generating (5) and (6) is that the factor ratios in the single-product technologies are determined entirely through the h_k's; and these h_k's are also the only vehicle through which prices enter the joint-production technology. Thus, the joint-production input ratios must be fairly simple functions of the single-product ratios.

While the RIQ function does impose a number of important restrictions on the underlying technology, it is also reasonably parsimonious in parameters. For example, if there are K z's and J inputs, there are $\frac{1}{2}(K^2 + 3K + 2)$ α's and β's (this includes α_0) and possibly as few as $(K + 1)(J - 1)$ parameters for the h's and ϕ's (this includes h_0 and assumes a different Cobb–Douglas or CES $h_k(\mathbf{p})$ for each z_k and no additional parameters for the ϕ_{km}'s). In contrast, the corresponding (homogeneous in $\mathbf{p}$) translog function has $\frac{1}{2}(K^2 + J^2 + 2JK + 5(K + J))$ parameters, or $\frac{1}{2}[J(J + 3) + 4K]$ more. Since the RIQ function has fewer parameters than the number of first and second derivatives of an arbitrary cost function, it cannot "approximate" the behavior of such a function at an arbitrary point, as the translog can. In particular, one can choose the parameters of the translog so that the resulting cost function will have at a specified point any Allen elasticities of (input) substitution one might desire. That is, there need be no functional dependencies among the Allen elasticities (at that point) other than those implied by homogeneity and concavity of the cost function in factor prices. The RIQ does not have this property. The nature and dimension of the functional dependencies depends upon the particular specifications employed for the h_k and ϕ_{km} functions and is complicated even in the simplest cases. Of course, with respect to the z's, the RIQ is fully as flexible as the translog. Thus, the RIQ is most attractive in cases where the behavior of costs in the z's is of paramount interest, or where the amount of price variation in a particular sample is insufficient to support sharp identification of the full range of price effects posited by the translog. Moreover, the RIQ handles zeroes in the z's in a natural way, while the translog cannot be used in such cases.[2] However, the decisive advantage of the IQ and RIQ in many cases resides in its aggregation properties, to which we now turn.

2.   Aggregation of indexed quadratic function

Suppose that cost function (1) is faced by n production units, with all units facing the same $\mathbf{p}$; denote the $\mathbf{z}$ and $\mathbf{c}$ of the ith production unit by z^i and c^i, and the mean $\mathbf{z}$ and c by $\bar{z}$ and $\bar{c}$. Defining $\varepsilon^i = \mathbf{z}^i - \bar{\mathbf{z}}$, Eq. (1) can be written

$$c^i = \alpha_0 h_0(\mathbf{p}) + \sum_k \alpha_k h_k(\mathbf{p})(\bar{z}_k + \varepsilon_k^i)$$

$$+ \frac{1}{2}\sum_k \sum_m \beta_{km}\phi_{km}(\mathbf{p})(\bar{z}_k + \varepsilon_k^i)(\bar{z}_m + \varepsilon_m^i), \qquad (10)$$

---

[2] Caves, Christensen, and Tretheway (1981) have suggested a remedy for this problem in the translog.

with corresponding demand of firm i for input j given by

$$x_j^i = \frac{\partial c^i}{\partial p_j} = \alpha_0 \frac{\partial h_0}{\partial p_j} = \sum_k \alpha_k \frac{\partial h_k}{\partial p_j}(\bar{z}_k + \varepsilon_k^i)$$

$$+ \tfrac{1}{2} \sum_k \sum_m \beta_{km} \frac{\partial \phi_{km}}{\partial p_j}(\bar{z}_k + \varepsilon_k^i)(\bar{z}_m + \varepsilon_k^i). \tag{11}$$

Summing (11) over the n units, one obtains the convenient expression

$$X_j = \sum x_j^i = n\left[\alpha_0 \frac{\partial h_0}{\partial p_j} + \sum_k \alpha_k \frac{\partial h_k}{\partial p_j}\bar{z}_k \right.$$

$$\left. + \tfrac{1}{2} \sum_k \sum_m \beta_{km} \frac{\partial \phi_{km}}{\partial p_j}(\bar{z}_k\bar{z}_m + \sigma_{km}) \right], \tag{12}$$

where $\sigma_{km} = (1/n)\Sigma\varepsilon_k^i\varepsilon_m^i$ can be interpreted as the covariance of z_k and z_m. Aggregation of (10) yields

$$C = \Sigma c^i = n\left[\alpha_0 h_0(\mathbf{p}) + \sum_k \alpha_k h_k(\mathbf{p})\bar{z}_k \right.$$

$$\left. + \tfrac{1}{2} \sum_k \sum_m \beta_{km} \phi_{km}(\mathbf{p})[\bar{z}_k\bar{z}_m + \sigma_{km}] \right]. \tag{13}$$

Thus, there exists an exact representation of the aggregate technology which depends only on the number of units and the means and variances of the outputs and characteristics. Aggregate input demands are given by the application of Shephard's lemma to the aggregate cost function. A convenient reexpression of (14) is

$$C = n\left[c(\bar{\mathbf{z}},\mathbf{p}) + \tfrac{1}{2} \sum_k \sum_m \beta_{km} \phi_{km}(\mathbf{p})\sigma_{km} \right], \tag{14}$$

where $c(\bar{\mathbf{z}},\mathbf{p})$ is the production unit level IQ cost function at mean $\mathbf{z}$.

From (14) it is apparent that aggregate costs differ from n times the cost of a production unit operating under "average" conditions only because $\sigma_{km} \neq 0$. This suggests that in simple networks with a small number of z's reasonable estimates can be obtained by substituting a priori estimates for σ_{km} or estimating σ_{km} parametrically. Certainly in many cases $\sigma_{km} = 0$ may be reasonably close to the truth for many pairs of z components. Notice in this regard that β_{km} and $\phi_{km}(\mathbf{p})$ appear in $c(\bar{\mathbf{z}},\mathbf{p})$ so that $\sigma_{km} \neq 0$ does not introduce any new parameters into the problem (aside from σ_{km} itself); this fact is potentially useful in analyzing cases in which strong a priori knowledge concerning likely departures of σ_{km} from 0 is available.

One assumption embodied in (14) is that activity in production unit i does not affect costs in unit j. In the context of network technologies, production units are identified with links and/or nodes of the network, so that this assumption is restrictive; however, this can be mitigated by including the congestion and so on of adjacent links or nodes among the z's. (In other contexts, such as aggregation over establishments in an industry, the independence restriction is natural.) Current econometric practice in this regard is generally even more restrictive: Costs are modeled as functions of aggregate values of the z's, a practice that is usually inconsistent with *any* well-defined disaggregate technology. Equation (14) demonstrates that under reasonably plausible conditions, one can hope to recover the underlying disaggregate technology from basically aggregate data without the introduction of so many additional parameters that econometric estimation is intractable. The aggregation property follows from the basic assumption of quadratic costs embodied in (1); additional tractability – and in many practical cases, *essential* tractability – is gained by the successively more restrictive forms represented by IQ and RIQ cost functions.

3.   Characterizing network technologies

The salient characteristics of network technologies we seek to model is that the notions of origin and destination are so important for product definition that differences in origin or destination must be explicitly represented if the nature of the underlying technology and consumer demand is to be understood. Examples of such technologies include transportation systems, most public utilities, and the postal system. In the United States, these industries have been heavily regulated, ostensibly to prevent exploitive price discrimination on the basis of origins or destinations and to take advantage of the perceived natural monopoly nature of the technology. In fact, most regulated industries have network technologies, and most network technologies are regulated. Moreover, some of these industries are also now feeling the effects of relaxed price and entry regulation, and consequent entry by firms who offer a comparatively narrow range of services.

Econometric modeling of firms in these industries has always been hampered by the formidable problems of output measurement these technologies pose. Aggregate measures of output such as passenger-miles, message-minutes, and the like are clearly inadequate not only for econometric purposes but also from a policy viewpoint, since models based on such measures cannot generally yield defensible estimates of the marginal costs of specific products, nor can they generally evaluate the feasibility of a particular combination of market structure and pricing policy. The present effort is an attempt to overcome such difficulties.

Specifically, we model networks as connected series of links (or arcs) and nodes, with vector-valued flows on the links. (Each link and each node has its own technology, the form of which is discussed subsequently.) Output, as viewed by a user of the network, is produced by an entry into the network at a node, followed by a flow along a series of connecting links, to a terminating node where the flow exits. Nodes thus perform both local gathering and distribution (which may be a costly activity performed by the node, at local post offices or truck terminals, for example), and also switching. Links only provide transport. Costs are incurred at each link and node as functions of each link or node's own activity; total "on-network costs" are obtained by summing costs over links and nodes; below, we also allow for costs not associated with any particular node or link.[3]

Figure 5.1 illustrates a simple network; circles represent nodes, lines represent links connecting them. Nodes are numbered, and if the direction of flow is important, flows from node j to node i, $j > i$, are additional components of the vector-valued flow from i to j. Thus, the flow between nodes i and j may be differentiated as to time of day, type of flow (transport by commodity type, passenger service during rush hours, and so forth) and direction of flow, for example. To simplify the exposition, we will consider only scalar flows, which might be thought of as phone connections at a given time; the extension of the model to vector-valued flows will generally be obvious.

The network of Figure 5.1 has ten possible node combinations, corresponding to ten possible connections a user of the network may wish to make; denote total user demand by the column vector $\mathbf{u}$. The actual "physical" production flows on the network are given by a five-component column vector $\mathbf{y}$. [Use the convention of labeling both user and production flows lexicographically by component so, for example, $\mathbf{y}$ consists of the flows on (1,2), (2,3), (2,4), (3,5) and (4,5), in that order. See Table 5.1.] In general, let k be the dimension of $\mathbf{u}$ and n the dimension of $\mathbf{y}$.

Suppose that there are m_l noncircular connected routes for the lth user output u_l; each route can be represented by an n-component column vector of 0's and 1's indicating which of the n physical links in the production network are utilized to produce u_l. Joining k of these column vectors together, one for each component of u, gives an $(n \times k)$ matrix representing a *basic routing*. There are $\prod_{l=1}^{k} m_l$ basic routings; any valid routing is a convex combination of these basic routings.

For a fixed routing represented by a matrix $\mathbf{T}$, $\mathbf{y} = \mathbf{Tu}$; of course, for any

---

[3] In most cases, users are indifferent to the routing used to satisfy their demand. When they are not, this affects the definition of output from the user's point of view rather than the modeling of the productive activity of the firm.

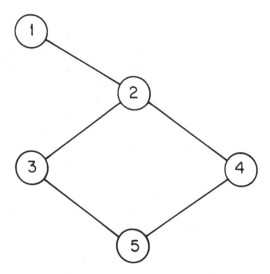

Figure 5.1. A simple network.

given **y**, any number of different **u**'s can be produced. Define the set $\mathbf{u}(\mathbf{y}|\mathbf{T}) = \{\mathbf{u}|\mathbf{y} = \mathbf{Tu} \text{ and } \mathbf{u} \geq 0\}$ as the set of (efficient) "user-output" vectors corresponding to "producer output" **y** under routing **T**; let $\mathbf{T}^{-g}$ denote the generalized inverse of **T**. Then every element of $\mathbf{u}(\mathbf{y}|\mathbf{T})$ can be expressed as $\mathbf{u} = \mathbf{T}^{-g}\mathbf{y} + (\mathbf{I} - \mathbf{T}^{-g}\mathbf{T})\mathbf{h}$ for some vector **h**, and for arbitrary **h**, $\hat{\mathbf{u}} = \mathbf{T}^{-g}\mathbf{y} + (\mathbf{I} - \mathbf{T}^{-g}\mathbf{T})\mathbf{h}$ is an element of $\mathbf{u}(\mathbf{y}|\mathbf{T})$ provided $\hat{\mathbf{u}} \geq 0$; $\mathbf{u}(\mathbf{y}|\mathbf{T})$ is convex.

Our strategy for modeling firms producing network outputs is to divide their production into on- and off-network activities; to make their off-network activities functions of aggregates of the components of u; and to note that if nodes and links each have IQ costs functions, then first and second moments of the y's and the link and node characteristics are sufficient statistics of network activity. Specifically, let $\mathbf{y}^n$ and $\mathbf{t}^n$ be the outputs and characteristics of node n, $\mathbf{y}^l$ and $\mathbf{t}^l$ be outputs and characteristics of link l; and let $g(\mathbf{u})$ be a vector of appropriate aggregates over **u**; then total costs c are

$$C = \sum_n C_N(\mathbf{y}^n, \mathbf{t}^n, \mathbf{p}) + \sum_l C_L(\mathbf{y}^l, \mathbf{t}^l, \mathbf{p}) + v(g(\mathbf{u}), g', \mathbf{p}), \qquad (15)$$

where C_N, C_L, and v are node, link, and off-network cost functions, respectively; g' represents nonnetwork outputs (and possibly other arguments).

From the analysis of Section 2, we know that if C_N and C_L are IQ cost functions; then the following completely summarize the determinants of the firm's activities: the first and second moments of the joint distributions of $(\mathbf{y}^n, \mathbf{t}^n)$ and $(\mathbf{y}^l, \mathbf{t}^l)$; **p**; $g(\mathbf{u})$; and g'. In most practical cases, the main

Table 5.1. *A basic routing for the network of Figure 5.1*

	u_1 (1,2)	u_2 (1,3)	u_3 (1,4)	u_4 (1,5)	u_5 (2,3)	u_6 (2,4)	u_7 (2,5)	u_8 (3,4)	u_9 (3,5)	u_{10} (4,5)
$y_1 = (1,2)$	1	1	1	1	0	0	0	0	0	0
$y_2 = (2,3)$	0	1	0	1	1	0	1	0	0	0
$y_3 = (2,4)$	0	0	1	0	0	1	0	0	0	0
$y_4 = (3,5)$	0	0	0	1	0	0	1	1	1	0
$y_5 = (4,5)$	0	0	0	0	0	0	0	1	0	1

difficulty will be in obtaining the moments of the $(\mathbf{y}^n, \mathbf{t}^n)$ and $(\mathbf{y}^l, \mathbf{t}^l)$ distributions; these data can be obtained only by taking a survey of the network's nodes and links. However, since sample means and variances converge to their population values rapidly, it will probably be the case that fairly good estimates can be obtained from comparatively small samples.

It is worth noting that the estimation of (15) (which would proceed after adding the corresponding input demand equations) does *not* depend on an assumption of efficient routing, but only on an assumption that production in each node or link is cost-minimizing given the flow assigned to it. Nor does it assume that the network is optimally configured. Of course, this cuts both ways: Eq. (15) does not give cost as a function of output as users view it, but as a function of output as the producer views it for the problem of *cost minimization*. Nonetheless, nearly all the leading policy problems posed by network technologies can be correctly analyzed within this framework.

4.   Analyzing the policy problems posed by network technologies

Airlines, railroads, trucks, and telecommunications are network technologies now experiencing significant regulatory reform. This section considers the extent to which the model I have outlined is capable of practically addressing a number of issues bearing on public policy towards these industries: the nature of economies of scale and scope in these industries, the determination of marginal costs, the viability of reconfigured networks, and asset valuation.

With respect to economies of scale and scope, these methods are capable of giving empirical content to a number of folk truisms. First, the multiproduct nature of the link technology enables backhaul and time-of-day type scope economies to be explicitly represented. Second, if the link and node technologies have declining ray average costs (as would seem natural, particularly in the long run), then simple notions of economies of scale can be accommodated. Third, when demands with disparate origins and destinations can be funneled along a single long link, then economies of scale in the link tech-

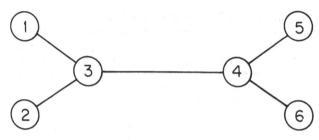

Figure 5.2.

nology translate into economies of scope defined over disparate components of the user-relevant output vector **u.**

Consider, for example, the fairly common situation illustrated in Figure 5.2: firm A serves all six nodes and new entrant B proposes to offer service between nodes 3 and 4 only; a very large proportion of A's **y** vector over (3,4) consists of user demand that B's product partially satisfies. A has been charging proportional to distance, B's proposed tariff undercuts A's; A proposes to lower rates between the inner nodes and raise them elsewhere, where it faces little or no competition. With A's cost function estimated as we have proposed, useful empirical evidence can be adduced concerning A's proposal.

In the simple network of Figure 5.2, it is easy to calculate all the economically relevant cost concepts for each **u**-output configuration, since there is only one route for each component of **u.** As the complexity of the network grows, the number of alternative routings grows rapidly; but if the firm routes efficiently, the marginal costs of all routes for a particular **u**-component are the same. Thus, the marginal (on-network) cost of a particular product can be calculated from the activity along the links and nodes of one route used to produce the product.[4] The sum of short-run on- and off-network marginal costs is the minimum nonpredatory price.

Unlike most econometric cost models, the methods proposed here actually attempt to model the network aspects of network technologies. In principle, these models ought to be better able to evaluate alternative network configura-

---

[4] The method described for calculating marginal costs assumes that routing is efficient. When the complete set of u's is available and the network configuration is known, the estimated technology can in principle be used to calculate the optimal y activity, after which it is easy to compare the cost of the optimal (y^l, t^l) and (y^n, t^n) distributions with the cost of the actual distributions. (Notice that optimal costs are not compared with actual costs, since the latter vary because of the deviation of actual inputs from optimal inputs.) Unfortunately, the optimization problem this implies (unless the C_N and C_L functions are severely restricted) is infeasible for any reasonably sized network; even heuristic algorithms are slow for complicated systems.

tions (as induced, for example, by mergers or divestitures), since they embody more of the known network structure in their formulation and estimation. Predictions from traditional aggregate models implicitly embody the assumption that future networks will be very much structurally akin to past networks, since the estimation process for such aggregate models assumes that unmeasured variations in network structure are comparatively unimportant across observations. Most often, measures of network structure do not even appear as arguments of the technology's representation. In contrast, in the models developed here, questions concerning even radically new network structures have directly calculable and specific answers (providing, of course, that they are to be built from existing or similar components).

One of the leading problems in modeling network technologies is that some elements of the capital stock are put in place at various times and embody not only the state of technology at that time, but also a decision concerning the scale (or even nature) of operation that may be difficult to change. Examples of this include the size and degree of automation of a post office or trucking terminal; the size of a telephone switching station or the transmission capacity of a communications cable; the weight (and thus carrying capacity) of railroad rails; or the size of a jet. In some cases the capacity of a link or node is in this way entirely determined; in others the "capacity" can be exceeded, but only at great additional cost.

To model this, suppose that the capital good in question has two attributes, S, the degree to which it can be substituted for other inputs, and $\bar{Q}$, its (possibly nominal) capacity.[5] For equal $\bar{Q}$, higher values of S imply lower expenditures on other inputs; that is, expenditures on variable inputs are given by the variable cost function $v(\mathbf{y},\mathbf{p}; S,\bar{Q})$, where $\mathbf{y}$ is output, and $\mathbf{p}$ the variable input prices; $v_s < 0$, $v_{\bar{Q}} < 0$. To obtain at time t a capital asset $(S,\bar{Q})$ costs $R(S,\bar{Q},t;\gamma)$ where γ is a parameter vector that in practice needs to be estimated; once the asset is in place, it cannot be modified.

Given a functional form for R, an estimate $\hat{\gamma}$ of γ, and observations on the capacity $\bar{Q}$ of a capital good, the time of installation, and its cost at that time, S can be calculated. In the models presented here, $\bar{Q}$ and S are elements of the $\mathbf{t}^n$ or $\mathbf{t}^l$ vectors, as appropriate. Thus one needs first and second moments of Q and S [and, of course, the covariance of $\bar{Q}$ and S with the other elements of the appropriate (y,t) vector.] While moments involving $\bar{Q}$ are directly calculable since $\bar{Q}$ is directly observable, values of S depend on $\hat{\gamma}$, thus moments involving S must be recalculated for every $\hat{\gamma}$ unless the R function takes a simple form, such as linear in known functions of S, $\bar{Q}$, and $\mathbf{t}$.

---

[5] For a single capital good, one might have $g(\mathbf{y}) \leq \bar{Q}$. If one wanted to dispense with a sharp capacity constraint, one might assume that for $\bar{Q}_2 > \bar{Q}_1$ and $g(\mathbf{y},\mathbf{p}) \geq G$ that $v(\mathbf{y},\mathbf{p},S,\bar{Q}_2) < v(\mathbf{y},\mathbf{p},S,\bar{Q}_1)$, with $g_y \geq 0$ and $g(\mathbf{y},\mathbf{p})$ homogeneous of degree zero in $\mathbf{p}$. For a similar neoclassical capacity model, see Panzar (1976).

Such a procedure has two important features. The first is that it explicitly recognizes that some facilities are built in anticipation of serving large demands, and that when demands are small, the fact that these facilities were expensive to construct does not imply they will be less expensive to operate than facilities that were designed to service small demands and consequently cost less to construct; the cost advantages of large-capacity facilities may become apparent only at large output levels.

The second advantage of this procedure is that since it generates estimates of the $R(S,\bar{Q},t)$ function, it generates estimates of the replacement value of a given capital asset. Moreover, given a particular network flow, one can calculate using the estimated cost function and the $R(S,\bar{Q},t)$ function, the optimal capital configuration for the network, the investment necessary to attain that configuration, and the corresponding variable costs. Variable costs under the current configuration can also be calculated. Thus, the current period loss (that is, variable costs) due to an inappropriate capitalization can be calculated. Since the current period replacement value is the economic value of the network's fixed assets only when the assets are optimally deployed, the capitalized value of the difference in variable costs should be subtracted from the current network's replacement value to arrive at its economic value.[6]

5.   Summary

This chapter has examined the indexed quadratic functional form, which is an interpretation of a suggestion of Baumol, Panzar, and Willig (1982), and introduced the restricted indexed quadratic function, which is more tractable econometrically. The RIQ cost function has some interesting properties of its own, and either function can be used in conventional multioutput production studies. Baumol et al. demonstrated the particular power and convenience of these functions in such contexts.

A further interesting property of these functions is that they aggregate nicely over production units facing identical prices. Thus, they will be useful

---

[6] I have glossed over two difficulties in this paragraph that take us beyond the scope of this paper. The first is that since investment is essentially irreversible and future demand uncertain, there is a problem in the optimal timing of lumpy investments and the discounting of future variable-cost reductions (which will not be the same as today's). The second is that "economic value" here means that value which, when assigned to an existing asset, would make a cost-minimizing producer indifferent between that asset and the best asset it could purchase given today's $R(S,\bar{Q})$ function. The economic value is the same as market value only if the future operation of the network generates exactly zero economic rents.

in the study of multiplant firms or in studies using data aggregated over establishments.

These functions are particularly attractive for modeling network technologies. Section 3 outlined a model of network technologies which not only reduced the output dimensionality of such technologies in an entirely intuitive and rigorous fashion but also is econometrically feasible even for large networks, provided the underlying technologies are well represented by RIQ cost functions. Section 4 demonstrated that these methods are in principle capable of generating answers to important policy problems at an appropriate microeconomic level. This level has hitherto been inaccessible; thus, the relatively small amount of extra information our methods require may well be worth collecting.

References

Baumol, W. J., J. C. Panzar, and R. D. Willig (1982). *Contestable Markets and the Theory of Industry Structure*. New York: Harcourt Brace Jovanovich.

Caves, D. W., L. R. Christensen, and M. W. Tretheway (1980). "Flexible Cost Functions for Multiproduct Firms." *Review of Economics and Statistics*, 62: 477–81.

Harmatuck, D. J. (1981). "A Motor Carrier Joint Cost Function: A Flexible Form with Activity Prices." *Journal of Transport Economics and Policy*, 15, no. 1, May: 135–53.

Jara-Diaz, S., and C. Winston (1981). "Multiproduct Transportation Cost Functions: Scale and Scope in Railway Operations." In Nicklaus Blattner et al., eds., *Eighth European Association for Research in Industrial Economics*, vol. 1. Basle, Switzerland: University of Basle, pp. 437–69.

Panzar, J. C. (1976). "A Neoclassical Approach to Peak-Load Pricing." *The Bell Journal of Economics*, 7: 521–30.

Wang, Judy S., and A. F. Friedlaender (1981). "Mergers, Competition and Monopoly in the Regulated Trucking Industry," Department of Economics, Working Paper no. 289, Massachusetts Institute of Technology, Cambridge, Mass.

C. Winston (1985). "Conceptual Developments in the Economics of Transportation: An Interpretive Survey." *Journal of Economic Literature*, 23, no. 1, March: 57–94.

CHAPTER 6

Joint estimation of freight transportation decisions under nonrandom sampling

DANIEL MCFADDEN, CLIFFORD WINSTON,
AND AXEL BOERSCH-SUPAN

An understanding of the determinants of the demand for intercity freight transportation has been a necessary input into economists' analysis of positive and normative issues in freight transportation such as the welfare effects of rate deregulation, the benefits of railroad mergers, and the potential demand for new freight modes.[1] The freight demand models that have been used to address these issues have focused on the determinants of the choice of freight mode but ignored other important transportation or production decisions that may be related to this choice. These decisions include the quantity of a commodity to ship (shipment size) and the frequency of shipments. Consequently, the theoretical characterization of the freight transportation decision-making process that underlies previous freight demand models is incomplete. Further, estimates of key magnitudes like market elasticities and shippers' value of time that have been derived from these models may be flawed if the mode choice is only part of a larger joint decision process.

The purpose of this chapter is to provide a theoretical characterization of the freight transportation decision-making process that enables one to analyze the mode choice decision jointly with the shipment size, shipment frequency, and production decisions. This characterization is particularly relevant for analyzing shippers' behavior in the recently deregulated freight transportation environment as it has been widely recognized that firms will make greater efforts than they have under regulation to coordinate their production and transportation decisions in order to take advantage of the variety of price and service offerings that have emerged under deregulation.

The theoretical model that is derived will be used as a basis for carrying out an exploratory empirical analysis of the joint choice of mode and shipment

---

[1] For an overview of these issues and the freight demand models that have been used to address them, see Winston (1983, 1985).

[2] In this study it is implicitly recognized that the actual decisionmaker in produce shipping activity is the receiver. When the receiver is responsible for the choice of mode, it is apropriate to treat shipment size as endogenous and develop a joint-choice model. The use of the term "shipper" throughout the chapter is only for purposes of exposition.

size. As an illustrative case, we will focus the analysis on movements of agricultural commodities. Unfortunately, the complexity of the theoretical model necessitates the use of simple approximations to attain empirical tractability. Nonetheless, the empirical results will be useful in suggesting the insights to be gained by adopting the theoretical framework presented here in addition to shedding some light on the consequences of deregulation in this market. Finally, the empirical analysis illustrates a methodology for carrying out estimations under a choice-based sample which is characterized by a nonrandom representation of mode shares stratified by commodity *and* origin and destination. This methodology may be useful in analyzing other data sets such as a choice based sample of intercity passenger travelers which contains origin–destination pairs where, for example, rail travel is oversampled.

The chapter proceeds as follows. Section 1 presents an inventory-theoretic model of freight transportation decision making. Section 2 develops an econometric model of joint discrete/continuous choice. Section 3 describes the data base and estimation of the model under nonrandom sampling. Section 4 discusses the empirical results, and Section 5 presents conclusions.

1.   An inventory-theoretic model of freight transportation decisions in the produce market

In this section we derive an inventory-theoretic model of freight transportation decision making for the produce market. Besides serving as an illustrative market for the theoretical analysis, this market will also be featured in the empirical analysis. It should be noted, however, that the model developed here can be easily modified to analyze other freight transportation markets.

The primary assumptions that we make in our characterization of the produce transportation market are as follows.

1.   Produce is harvested in a steady flow at constant marginal cost.
2.   After harvest, produce is inventoried until consumed. Inventories are reduced to zero immediately after shipments are sent out and immediately before shipments arrive.
3.   Produce is consumed in a steady flow. Revenue from delivered produce is an increasing, but concave, function of the rate of consumption. This corresponds to a downward sloping demand curve, as results for example from a monopolistically competitive market for wholesale produce at the point of delivery.
4.   For a specified mode, shippers balance freight charges from the rate taper against inventory carrying costs and losses to maximize profit.
5.   The interest rate, freight tariffs, and transit times are constant through time.

Under these assumptions, the shipper will have a steady-state shipment size, shipment interval, and mode which maximizes present value of profit.

The notation we use in the analysis is as follows.

$$
\begin{aligned}
y &= \text{rate of consumption} \\
x &= \text{rate of production} \\
t=0,\theta,2\theta &= \text{dates of shipments} \\
\tau_i &= \text{transit time for shipments, mode } i \\
r &= \text{interest rate} \\
\lambda &= \text{loss rate on inventories during shipment} \\
I(t) &= \text{inventory at origin awaiting shipment} \\
J(t) &= \text{inventory at destination awaiting consumption} \\
S &= \text{shipment size} \\
T_i(S) &= \text{freight tariff, mode } i \\
R(y) &= \text{revenue} \\
m &= \text{marginal cost}
\end{aligned}
$$

The equations and boundary conditions describing inventory fluctuations at the origin and destination can be written respectively, as[3]

$$\dot{I}(t) = x - \lambda I(t), \text{ where } I(0^+) = 0, I(\theta) = S \tag{1}$$

and

$$\dot{J}(t) = -y - \lambda J(t), \text{ where } J(\theta + \tau_i^+) = Se^{-\lambda\tau_i}$$
$$J(2\theta + \tau_i^-) = 0. \tag{2}$$

The steady-state solutions to Eqs. (1) and (2) are

$$I(t) = S(1 - e^{-\lambda t})/(1 - e^{-\lambda\theta}) \qquad 0 < t < \theta \tag{3}$$

and

$$J(t) = Se^{-\lambda\tau_i}(e^{\lambda(\tau_i + 2\theta - t)} - 1)/(e^{\lambda\theta} - 1)$$
$$\theta + \tau_i < t < 2\theta + \tau_i; \tag{4}$$

hence,

$$x = \lambda S/(1 - e^{-\lambda\theta}) \tag{5}$$

---

[3] It should be noted that this model of inventory behavior corresponds to the standard economic ordering quantity (EOQ) inventory model. As is well known, the EOQ model yields an optimal cost-minimizing ordering policy that is designed to prevent stockouts. While more complicated models of perishable produce inventories could be developed (see Nahmias, 1982), such models would not lead to any additional insights into the problem considered here.

and

$$y = \lambda S e^{-\lambda \tau_i}/(e^{\lambda \theta} - 1). \tag{6}$$

The firm's present discounted value of profit can now be written as

$$\Pi = \int_{\theta + \tau_i}^{\infty} R(y)e^{-rt}dt - \int_{0}^{\infty} mxe^{-rt}dt - \sum_{k=1}^{\infty} T_i(S)e^{-rk\theta}$$

$$= \frac{(R(y)e^{-r(\theta + \tau_i)} - mx)}{r} - \frac{T_i(S)}{e^{r\theta} - 1}. \tag{7}$$

The firm's optimization problem then consists of choosing the shipment size S, mode i, and shipping interval θ to maximize the profit (7) subject to conditions (5) and (6), which determine x and y.

Before proceeding further, it is useful to carry out some comparative statics on the model. To begin, note that if x and y are substituted into (7), Π is a function of S, θ, i. Alternatively, for any given mode, Π can be expressed as a function of (x, θ), (x, S), or (x, y). These alternative formulations identify the endogenous variables in the system, x, y, S and θ, given mode i. The exogenous variables are m, r, τ, λ, and the freight tariff, $T(S)$. The expected signs of the comparative statics effects are straightforward. Specifically, one expects that a change in any of the exogenous variables would have a negative effect on x, y and S, and a positive effect on θ.

As an illustration of how the comparative statics are carried out, let Π be expressed in terms of (S, θ). Maximization conditions are

$$\Pi_S = 0, \qquad \Pi_\theta = 0$$

$$\Pi_{SS} < 0, \qquad \Pi_{\theta\theta} < 0, \qquad \Pi_{SS}\Pi_{\theta\theta} > \Pi^2{}_{S\theta}.$$

The comparative statics matrix, obtained by totally differentiating the first order conditions and arranging terms, is thus

$$\begin{bmatrix} \Pi_{SS} & \Pi_{S\theta} \\ \Pi_{\theta S} & \Pi_{\theta\theta} \end{bmatrix} \begin{bmatrix} \partial S/\partial Z \\ \partial \theta/\partial Z \end{bmatrix} = - \begin{bmatrix} \Pi_{SZ} \\ \Pi_{\theta Z} \end{bmatrix},$$

where Z is any exogenous variable. Hence, in order to sign specific comparative statics effects one must sign

$$\frac{\partial S}{\partial Z} = (\Pi_{S\theta}\Pi_{\theta Z} - \Pi_{\theta\theta}\Pi_{SZ})/\Delta,$$

$$\frac{\partial \theta}{\partial Z} = (\Pi_{\theta S}\Pi_{SZ} - \Pi_{SS}\Pi_{\theta Z})/\Delta,$$

where

Table 6.1. *Comparative statics results*

	m	r	τ	λ	T_S	T
x^a	−	−	−	−	−	?
y^b	−	−	−	−	−	?
θ	+	+	+	+	+	?
S^a	−	−	−	?	−	−

^{a}These results hold for small values of the endogenous variable; otherwise they are ambiguous.
^{b}These results are based on the specific functional forms for the demand function and freight tariffs used below.

$$\Delta = \Pi_{SS}\Pi_{\theta\theta} - \Pi_{S\theta}^2 > 0.$$

As an example, consider the sign of $\partial S/\partial m$. Differentiating the first-order condition obtained for Π_S by θ and m yields $\Pi_{S\theta} < 0$, $\Pi_{Sm} < 0$. Similarly differentiating the first-order condition obtained for Π_θ by m yields $\Pi_{\theta m} > 0$. Hence, we obtain

$$\frac{\partial S}{\partial m} = (\overset{(-)(+)}{\Pi_{S\theta}\Pi_{\theta m}} - \overset{(-)(-)}{\Pi_{\theta\theta}\Pi_{Sm}})/\ \overset{(+)}{\Delta}\ < 0,$$

as expected.

Calculations were carried out for all of the possible comparative statics effects in our model. The grand summary of results is displayed in Table 6.1. These results provide the theoretical basis for the expected signs of some of the parameters to be estimated. In our actual empirical work, the results that pertain to S are of interest.

In order to carry the analysis further, let us posit a linear demand function $p = a - by$, so that $R(y) = ay - by^2$, and a two-part freight tariff $T_i(S) = f_i + v_iS$. Substituting these expressions and the definitions of x and y into (7) yields

$$\Pi(S,\theta;i) = \frac{e^{-r(\theta+\tau_i)}a\lambda Se^{-\lambda\tau_i}}{r(e^{\lambda\theta} - 1)} - \frac{e^{-r(\theta+\tau_i)}b\lambda^2S^2e^{-2\lambda\tau_i}}{r(e^{\lambda\theta} - 1)^2}$$

$$- \frac{m\lambda S}{1 - e^{-\lambda\theta}} - \frac{f_i}{e^{r\theta} - 1} - \frac{v_iS}{e^{r\theta} - 1}. \tag{8}$$

Considered as a function of S and $w = 1/\theta$ for a given mode, this function is zero at $S = w = 0$, nonnegative on a closed bounded set of S and w, and strictly concave in S. Hence it has a maximum in (i,S,θ), and a unique maximand in S for each (i,θ). Note that

$$\frac{\partial \Pi / \partial v_i}{\partial \Pi / \partial f_i} = S. \tag{9}$$

Define the optimized values

$$F(i,S) = \max_{\theta} \Pi (S,\theta,i) \tag{10}$$

$$G(S) = \max_{i} F(i,S) \tag{11}$$

$$H(i) = \max_{S} F(i,S) \tag{12}$$

$$J = \max_{S} F(S) = \max_{i} H(i). \tag{13}$$

These functions also depend on the background variables of the problem: r, a, b, m, λ, τ_1, τ_2, f_1, f_2, v_1, v_2. From (9) and the properties of optimized functions, the maximands satisfy

$$S = \left(\sum_i \partial J / \partial v_i \right) \Big/ \left(\sum_i \partial J / \partial f_i \right) \tag{14}$$

$$\delta = (\partial J / \partial f_i) \Big/ \left(\sum_i \partial J / \partial f_i \right)$$

$$\begin{aligned} &= 1 \text{ if alternative 1 is chosen} \\ &= 0 \text{ otherwise} \end{aligned} \tag{15}$$

$$\theta = \frac{1}{r} \ln\left(1 - 1 \Big/ \sum_i \partial J / \partial f_i \right). \tag{16}$$

Given the function J of the observed variables $(\tau_1, \tau_2, f_1, f_2, v_1, v_2)$ and unobserved variables (r,a,b,m,λ), the expressions (14)–(16) provide the basis for econometric analysis. The exact form for J is not obtainable in closed form. The next best approach would be to adopt a general functional approximation to J and to the distribution of the unobserved variables, and then use (14)–(16) to obtain the equations for estimation. However, we have found that even simple approximations consistent with the functional restrictions imposed by (15) lead to forms for S that are too special to be empirically reasonable. Therefore, we take a third approach of making direct functional approximations to the demand equations implied by (14)–(16). The gain in empirical generality from this method must be balanced against the loss of cross-equation restrictions and integrability of the fitted equations to recover the underlying profit function.

2. A statistical joint discrete/continuous choice model for the transportation mode and shipment size

The starting point for a statistical model of joint discrete/continuous choice is the profit function $J = J(r,a,b,m,\lambda,\tau_1,\tau_2,f_1,f_2,v_1,v_2)$ defined in (13). Empirically, the background variables r, a, b, λ, and m are not observed, and there are additional unobserved commodity and mode attributes, such as resistance of the produce to bruising or the quality of customer service provided by the mode. Therefore write $J = J(\tau_1,\tau_2,f_1,f_2,v_1,v_2,\mathbf{z},\boldsymbol{\varepsilon})$, where $\boldsymbol{\varepsilon}$ is a vector of unobserved variables and $\mathbf{z}$ is a vector of observed variables (discussed in Section 3) beyond those listed explicitly.

From (14), optimal shipment size satisfies

$$S = \frac{\left(\sum_i \partial J / \partial v_i \right)}{\left(\sum_i \partial J / \partial f_i \right)} \equiv S^*(\tau_1,\tau_2,f_1,f_2,v_1,v_2,\mathbf{z},\boldsymbol{\varepsilon}). \tag{17}$$

Approximate by a linear functional form

$$S^* = \underbrace{a_1\tau_1 + a_2\tau_2 + a_3f_1 + a_4f_2 + a_5v_1 + a_6v_2 + a_7z + a_8}_{w_1} + \varepsilon_1, \tag{18}$$

with the unobserved term ε_1 assumed normal with mean 0 and variance σ^2.

From (12) and (15), optimal mode choice satisfies

$$\delta = 1 \langle = \rangle F(1,S^*) - F(2,S^*) > 0,$$

$$\delta = -1 \quad \text{otherwise} \tag{19}$$

where S^* is optimal shipment size. Let $F(1,S^*) - F(2,S^*) = F_1 - F_2$ be approximated by

$$F_1 - F_2 = \underbrace{b_1(\tau_1 - \tau_2) + b_2(f_1 - f_2) + b_3(v_1 - v_2) + b_4z + b_5 + b_6S^*}_{w_2}$$

$$- \varepsilon_2, \tag{20}$$

where ε_2 is distributed normal with mean 0 and variance 1, and the correlation between ε_1 and ε_2 is defined by ρ.[4] Note that S^* from (18) enters the mode choice (19). In addition, the random disturbances in both equations are assumed to be dependent. Thus, we have specified a joint decision process of marginal shipment size and conditional mode choice.

---

[4] Because of the discrete nature of the mode choice, the variance of ε_2 can be normalized to one without loss of generality.

Before proceeding further, it is important to note that the joint probability of shipment size and mode choice $P(i,S^*)$ can always be decomposed as either $P(i) \cdot P(S^*|i)$ or $P(S^*) \cdot P(i|S^*)$. Our choice of the latter specification is because it is computationally simpler[5] and because its sequencing of decisions appears to be closer to industry practice (see U.S. Department of Transportation, 1977).

2.1.   Likelihood function

From the assumption about the distribution of ε_1, it follows that the marginal likelihood of shipment size S^* is

$$P(S^*) = \frac{1}{\sigma}\phi\left(\frac{S^* - W_1}{\sigma}\right),$$ (21)

where ϕ is the normal density.

The conditional probability of choosing mode 1 given ε_1 is

$$P(\delta = 1|S^*) = P(\varepsilon_2 \le W_2 | \varepsilon_1 = S^* - W_1)$$

$$= \Phi\left(\frac{W_2 - (S^* - W_1)\frac{\rho}{\sigma}}{\sqrt{1 - \rho^2}}\right),$$ (22)

where Φ is the cumulative normal distribution function. Thus the joint log likelihood of choosing mode 1 and shipment size S^* is

$$L = \log P(\delta,S^*) + \log P(\delta = 1|S^*) \cdot P(S^*)$$

$$= -\tfrac{1}{2}\ln 2\pi - \ln\sigma - \frac{1}{2\sigma^2}(S^* - W_1)^2$$

$$+ \ln\Phi\left[\frac{W_2 - (S^* - W_1)\frac{\rho}{\sigma}}{\sqrt{1 - \rho^2}}\right].$$ (23)

This likelihood function is parametrized by the coefficients of the shipment-size equation (18), a_1 through a_8, the coefficients of the mode-choice equation (20), b_1 through b_6, and the variance σ^2 and the correlation ρ of the disturbances. The parameters will be estimated by full-information maximum likelihood (FIML).

---

[5] Specifically, the first specification leads to a more complicated shipment-size equation that must account for the discontinuities caused by changes in mode choice resulting from changes in modal attributes. This complication leads to a less tractable empirical analysis and was thus not pursued here.

A final note on comparative statics concerns the signs of coefficients in the mode-choice model (22). This model implies that conditional on shipment size,

$$\text{sign} \frac{\partial P}{\partial y} = \text{sign} \left[\frac{\partial F(1,S)}{\partial y} - \frac{\partial F(2,S)}{\partial y} \right],$$
(24)

where y is a mode attribute. From (8), we obtain the following results:

	τ_1	v_1	f_1
P	?	–	–

The effect of τ_1 cannot be signed unambiguously due to offsetting terms of similar magnitude in (24), thus indicating a small overall effect.

3.   Data and estimation procedure

The data used in this analysis are from the Department of Transportation's 1977 study on produce transportation. The commodities include lettuce (71.9% of all shipments), tomatoes (12.4%), cabbage (1.5%), onions (.7%), oranges (5.5%), grapes (5.4%), and apples (2.2%). The variables in the data include modal attributes (freight charges, mean transit time) and shipment characteristics (commodity value, shipment size). These variables correspond to the shipment level,[6] while the sampling unit is the individual shipment. We will call this data set our main sample. In addition, data from the Department of Agriculture were obtained with rather precise aggregate shares of the modes for each commodity and origin–destination pair. We call this survey our auxiliary sample. The main data set was also used to obtain estimates of the marginal and fixed rates for rail and truck. These rates were incorporated in the shipment-size equation to avoid simultanuity bias that would occur from using the actual charges, which depend on the "block" in the rate schedule that the shipment size corresponds to, for each shipment. Marginal and fixed rates for each mode and commodity were obtained by estimating the following specification[7]

$$\text{Total charges} = \alpha_1 + \alpha_2 S + (\beta_1 + \beta_2 S) \cdot LH$$
(25)

where LH denotes the length of haul for a given movement, and calculating

---

[6] The data also included information regarding the standard deviation of transit time. Unfortunately, detailed examination of this variable indicated that it was not reliable enough to be of use in this study.

[7] This specification was used to capture the nonlinear nature of the rate schedule.

fixed rate $= \alpha_1 + \beta_1 LH,$

marginal rate $= \alpha_2 + \beta_2 LH.$

An important feature of the main sample, which influences the estimation procedure, is that it is a choice-based sample. That is, the mode shares in the main sample do not reflect the true shares as indicated in the auxiliary sample. This discrepancy is shown in Table 6A.2 of the chapter appendix. As is well known, biases that result from this sampling method can be corrected for by respecifying the likelihood function. In our analysis, we corrected for the bias by applying an idea developed by Cosslett (1981) to obtain fully efficient estimates. The estimator actually used is defined by the full-information concentrated likelihood equations (FICLE, see Hsieh, Manski, and McFadden, 1983). An additional complication in this analysis, as compared with Hsieh, Manski, and McFadden (1983), is that our sample is also stratified according to origin–destination pairs and type of produce with different mode shares associated with each origin–destination–produce (ODP) triple. The ODP triples and their mode shares are presented in Table 6A.2 in the appendix. Thus, the likelihood has to be corrected for each ODP triple.

Before we specify the resulting likelihood equations, it is useful to define the notation pertaining to the sampling weights. We denote three distinct proportions of mode choices. In the main sample, we observe a proportion μ_i^k of choice i in the kth ODP triple. The corresponding true proportion in the population is denoted by q_i^k. This proportion is unobserved. However, the auxiliary sample yields a good estimate of this proportion. We denote this estimate by $\hat{q}_i^k$. The number of shipments in each ODP triple in the main sample is given by T^k and in the auxiliary sample by m^k. Finally, we define $T = \sum_{k=1}^{K} t^k$ and $m = \sum_{k=1}^{K} m^k$ as total sample sizes for all K origin–destination triples. The relevant likelihood function, which estimates in addition to the parameters in (23) the true mode shares q_i^k can now be written as

$$L = \sum_{k=1}^{K} \sum_{n=1}^{T^K} \left[-\tfrac{1}{2}\left(\frac{S_n^* - W_{1n}}{\sigma}\right)^2 + ln\frac{\phi(\delta_n A_n)}{\psi(\delta_n, B_n, k)} \right]$$

$$+ m \sum_{k=1}^{K} \sum_{i=1}^{2} \hat{q}_i^k ln q_i^k - T ln\sqrt{2\pi}, \qquad (26)$$

where

$$A_n = \frac{W_{2n} - (S_n^* - W_{1n})\dfrac{\rho}{\sigma}}{\sqrt{1 - \rho^2}}$$

$$B_n = \frac{W_{2n} - (S_n^* - W_{1n})b_6}{\sqrt{1 - 2\rho\sigma b_6 + \sigma^2 b_6^2}}$$

$$\psi(\delta_n, B_n, k) = \sigma\left[\frac{m^k}{T} + \sum_{i=1}^{2} \frac{\left(\mu_i^k - \frac{m^k \hat{q}_i^k}{T}\right)\Phi(\alpha_i B_n)}{q_i^k}\right] q_{\delta_n}^k,$$

with $\alpha_1 = 1$ and $\alpha_2 = -1$ and all other notation is as previously defined. A technical discussion of the FICLE and alternative estimators including a description of the covariance calculation appears in Appendix 6A.

4.   Empirical results

The specification used here posits that the choice of mode (motor carrier versus rail) is a function of the attributes of the mode (freight charges, mean transit time) and the characteristics of the shipment (commodity value, shipment size), while the choice of shipment size is a function of the attributes of each available mode (marginal rate, fixed rate, mean transit time). Estimation of the model was achieved by iterative maximization of the log-likelihood given in (26) with respect to the parameters of (23) and minimization of the log-likelihood with respect to the population shares q_i^k (see Appendix 6A).

The estimation results are presented in Table 6.2. As is discussed in the appendix, the reported estimation results are based on a conservative estimate of the correct asymptotic standard errors for the coefficients. It should first be noted that the parameter estimates for the mode-choice equation and the motor carrier attributes in the shipment-size equation are reasonably reliable, while the parameter estimates for the rail attributes in the shipment-size equation are less reliable. It is worth pointing out that the lack of statistical reliability of the parameters of some of the modal attributes can be partly attributed to the fact that the sample variation of the transit times and freight charges is relatively small. That is, the mean transit time data by nature does not vary by individual shipment observation but by ODP triple, while the freight charges only vary by ODP triple because they were constructed using Eq. (25). This construction of the freight charges reduced the errors contained in the actual charges at the expense of sample variation. Clearly, the representation of a greater number of city pairs will alleviate the problem of sample variation in future work. Finally, note that the parameter estimate for the correlation parameter is fairly large although it is statistically imprecise. As such, it is somewhat unclear whether a model that assumes the errors are uncorrelated is appropriate for this analysis. It is worth noting, however, that although always estimated imprecisely, the fairly large negative correlation coefficient that was obtained was invariant to changes in specification or estimation procedure.

Table 6.2. *Parameter estimates*

Variable	Unweighted sample means	Parameter estimate
Mode-choice equation: alternatives (rail, motor carrier)		
Value of commodity ($/lb) motor carrier alternative	3.515	.1271
		(.0442)[a]
Freight charges ($1,000)	−.313	−.9979
	(mean difference between motor carrier and rail)	(.3973)
Mean transit time (days)	−4.154	−.0607
	(mean difference between motor carrier and rail)	(.4253)
Shipment size (10,000 lbs) motor carrier alternative	4.505	−1.027
		(.1215)
Mode-specific dummy motor carrier alternative		4.1079
		(2.0551)
Shipment-size equation		
Fixed rate		
Motor carrier ($1,000)	1.008	.7768
		(.8800)
Rail ($1,000)	1.246	−.1065
		(.5675)
Marginal rate		
Motor carrier ($/10 lb)	.138	4.7351
		(2.4336)
Rail ($/10 lb)	.131	1.3618
		(1.7130)
Mean transit time		
Motor carrier (days)	4.475	.9064
		(.5030)
Rail (days)	8.629	−.0384
		(.2529)
Constant		−1.1990
		(3.1250)
Correlation parameter (ρ)		−.3708
		(.4260)
Standard deviation (σ)		1.5795
		(.0626)
Number of observations: 2,904		

[a]Asymptotic standard errors are in parentheses.

Turning to the specific estimates, it can be seen that the parameter estimates for the mode-choice equation are of expected sign and of plausible magnitude, as indicated by the comparative statics results. Note that the positive sign of the mode-specific dummy indicates that, all else equal, shippers have an inherent preference for motor carrier over rail. This finding most likely reflects the utility that shippers attach to motor carriers' reliability and convenience.

Turning to the shipment-size equation, it will be recalled that the choice of shipment size is not conditional on a selected mode. Hence, the response to a change in a modal attribute reflects an adjustment in shipment size that indicates a greater likelihood of using a particular mode. Thus, as is consistent with our findings, an increase in motor carrier rates or transit time results in an increase in shipment size indicating that a shipper is more likely to use rail. Conversely, an increase in rail's fixed rate or transit time leads to a decrease in shipment size indicating that a shipper is more likely to use motor carrier. Note the comparative statics derived previously are based on a model where shipment size is conditional on the choice of a given mode and thus do not capture the mode switching discussed previously. On the other hand, it should be noted that mode switching may not occur where there are considerable economies (such as those due to discounts reflected in the rate schedule) from shipping in large quantities. This possibility is reflected in the positive sign that was obtained for rail's marginal rate.

4.1. Elasticities

Using the estimated coefficients, elasticities with respect to the joint probability of mode choice and shipment size were computed for the fixed rate, marginal rate, and mean transit time for each mode to provide greater quantitative insight into our estimation results. The elasticities and their standard errors are presented in Table 6.3. Note that these elasticities are derived as nonlinear functions involving several parameters from Table 6.2. Asymptotic standard errors were computed using a first-order Taylor's approximation. Before discussing the results, it is useful to describe what the elasticities actually capture. In this analysis a change in a particular modal attribute will have a direct effect on mode choice and an effect on shipment size, which in turn will have an effect on mode choice. As indicated before, these two effects will generally move in the same direction. For example, an increase in a motor carrier's transit time will increase shipment size. In the mode-choice equation, the effect of an increased shipment size will combine with the direct effect of an increase in motor carrier transit time to reduce the probability of using motor carrier. In essence, the elasticities reflect the impact of a change in a modal attribute on the probability of modal choice allowing the size of the

Table 6.3. *Elasticities of mode-choice probabilities*

Elasticity with respect to:	Rail	Motor carrier
Fixed rate		
Motor carrier	1.0301	−.5036
	(.3733)	(.2335)
Rail	−.3435	.1941
	(.2271)	(.1513)
Marginal rate		
Motor carrier	1.2547	−.7488
	(.2668)	(.3334)
Rail	−1.1557	.4649
	(.3354)	(.2394)
Mean transit time		
Motor carrier	3.4146	−1.6677
	(6.1475)	(5.351)
Rail	−.6919	.3069
	(5.510)	(1.211)

[a]Standard errors are in parentheses.

shipment to be adjusted in response to the change in the attribute. It should be noted that these elasticities differ from conventional mode-diversion elasticities in that, by allowing shipment sizes to vary, they do not incorporate the restriction that the total market size is fixed.

Turning to the specific results, it is interesting to note that for a given rail or motor carrier attribute, the elasticity for rail is always larger than the elasticity for motor carrier. This result is not surprising when one considers the large and somewhat captive market share already possessed by motor carriers in this market. Indeed, our finding is made possible by the fact that market size is not fixed in the analysis, thereby allowing rail to obtain or lose traffic by means in addition to mode diversion. It is also interesting to observe that despite motor carriers' large market share, improvements in its transit time can lead to a significant increase in its traffic, thus underscoring the importance of service time in this market. Finally, it appears that the largest effects on rail's traffic are attributable to changes in motor carriers' attributes, particularly transit time.[8] In essence, the dominant presence of motor carriers in this market and the importance of service time lead to responses in mode diversion and traffic generation that have significant implications for rail-

[8] An analogous result has also been found for the source of urban transit's largest patronage gains or losses (through changes in automobile's cost, see McFadden, 1974).

roads' participation in this market. It is thus quite understandable that the railroad industry's immediate strategy following the 1979 deregulation of produce transportation was to improve significantly its transit time in addition to setting rates in response to market demand. As pointed out by Moore (1983), this strategy has in the face of no significant changes in motor carrier service enabled railroads to double the amount of fruits and vegetables they carry within three years of the 1979 deregulation legislation.

5.   Concluding observations

It is hoped that this chapter has provided a fruitful starting point for the analysis of several important joint decisions in freight transportation. Specifically, we have developed an inventory-theoretic model that enables one to analyze simultaneously the determinants of mode choice, shipment size, shipment frequency, production at the shipping origin, and consumption at the shipping destination. Empirical implementation of the model indicated the statistical necessity of the joint estimation approach and illustrated a methodology and its computational features (explained in detail in the appendix) for efficiently estimating models with samples that are stratified in more than one dimension. Substantively, the empirical findings shed some light on railroads' competitive strategy in a deregulated market, and the methodology revealed that although the proposed estimators yielded similar results, all of the methods were plagued by a lack of quality data. Further work will be helpful in facilitating tractable empirical analyses that maintain greater consistency with the theoretical framework advanced here and helpful in assembling more reliable data. Such analyses will undoubtedly yield useful insights into positive aspects of freight transportation behavior in the recently deregulated environment and into normative guidelines for policies designed to enhance social welfare in the context of this environment.

Appendix 6A

The purpose of this technical appendix is twofold. First we review estimation techniques under choice-based sampling and extend these techniques to our case of a stratified sample by different mode shares; second, we compare the performance of three estimators in our application. A survey of sampling schemes and appropriate estimators can be found in Manski and McFadden (1981). The statistical properties of the three estimators we use are established for the case of uniform mode shares in Hsieh, Manski, and McFadden (1983).

Let us denote the endogenous mode by i, and the exogenous characteristics of each shipment by z. In each origin–destination produce (ODP) triple k, we observe a relative frequency f_{iz}^k of a combination of mode i and characteristic

z. Let us denote the marginal distributions of i and z by q_i^k and p_z^k, respectively. In Eq. (22), we posited a functional relation between mode choice i and the set of explanatory characteristics z up to a parameter vector, say, θ. We will call this response probability of mode i given z, $P_{iz}(\theta)$. Note that this relation is common for all ODP-triples. It follows that $f_{iz}^k = P_{iz}(\theta) p_z^k$. By Bayes' law we can express this relation as

$$f_{iz}^k = P_{iz} \cdot P_z^k = Q_{iz} q_i^k, \tag{A1}$$

where now Q_{iz} denotes the probability of characteristic z conditional on mode choice i. Our objective is to obtain estimates of θ that parameterize the structural relation $P_{iz}(\theta)$. This can be achieved by maximizing the sample likelihood over θ

$$L(\theta) = \sum_{k=1}^{K} \sum_{i=1}^{2} \sum_{z} s_{iz} \log \delta^k(i,z) P_{iz}(\theta) p_z^k, \tag{A2}$$

where $\delta_{iz} = 1$ if observation z chooses mode i, $\delta_{iz} = 0$ otherwise, and $s^k(i,z)$ is the relative probability of sampling an (i,z) combination in ODP triple k. Of course, for random sampling $s^k(i,z) \equiv 1$. However, our sample is drawn based on the observed endogenous choice i in a way that generated proportions μ_i^k rather than the true proportions q_i^k. Thus, in our case $s^k(i,z) = \mu_i^k/q_i^k$. Unfortunately, we do not observe the true p_z^k and q_i^k. However, we can treat them as additional parameters to be maximized over. Unfortunately, this is impractical in our application as we observe a large number of different characteristics z. As it turns out, the problem is considerably eased by the availability of consistent estimates of p_z^k and q_i^k derived from counts of two auxiliary samples that contain aggregate information on the characteristics or the mode choice, respectively. Thus, maximizing

$$L_{\text{FIML}}(\theta, p^k, q^k) = \sum_{k=1}^{K} \sum_{z} \sum_{i} \delta_{iz} \log \frac{P_{iz}(\theta) p_z^k}{q_i^k} + \sum_{k=1}^{K} \sum_{i} m_i^k \log q_i^k$$

$$+ \sum_{k=1}^{K} \sum_{z} m_z^k \log p_z^k \tag{A3}$$

subject to

$$q_i^k = \sum_z P_{iz}(\theta) p_z^k \text{ and } \sum_i q_i^k = 1$$

will yield asymptotically efficient estimates (note that m_i^k denotes the count of mode i in the first auxiliary sample, m_z^k the count of characteristic z in the second auxiliary sample). This full-information maximum likelihood (FIML) is the basis of all estimators in this appendix.

Cosslett (1981) shows that the p_z^k can be concentrated out of this criterion, and Hsieh, Manski, and McFadden (1983) are additionally able to concentrate out the Lagrange multipliers associated with the two constraints. The resulting concentrated Lagrangean objective is

$$L_{\text{FICLE}}(\theta, q^k) = \sum_{k=1}^{K} \sum_{i=1}^{2} \sum_{z} \delta_{iz} \log \frac{\lambda_i^k P_{iz}(\theta)}{\sum_{j=1}^{2} \lambda_j^k P_{jz}(\theta)}$$

$$+ \sum_{k=1}^{K} \sum_{i} (m_i^k - T_i^k) \log q_i^k + \sum_{k=1}^{K} \sum_{i} T_i^k \log \lambda_i^k, \qquad (A4)$$

where

$$\lambda_i^k = \frac{m^k}{T^k} + \frac{T_i^k - m_i^k}{T^k q_i^k}$$

and the sample sizes and proportions for each ODP triple k are denoted by

	Overall size	Count of mode i	Relative frequency of mode i
Main sample	T^k	T_i^k	μ_i^k
Auxiliary sample	m^k	m_i^k	$\hat{q}_i^k$

Optimal values of θ and q_i^k can be obtained by solving the first-order conditions of (A4), referred to as the full-information concentrated likelihood equations (FICLE). If $m^k \gg T^k$, a maximum of (A3) corresponds to a saddlepoint in (A4) yielding a maximum in θ but a minimum in q_i^k.

Applied to our specification (23), the criterion (A4) leads to (26). Parameter estimates are reported in Table 6.2. These estimates are consistent and asymptotically efficient. However, the search for a saddlepoint is computationally expensive and requires reliable starting values. Thus, we investigated estimators that may sacrifice some efficiency but are easier to calculate.

The first estimator is derived from the FICLE criterion (A4) by treating the auxiliary sample shares $\hat{q}_i^k$ as final estimates of the true population shares q_i^k. Then (A4) reduces to

$$L_{\text{CML}}(\theta) = \sum_{k=1}^{K} \sum_{i=1}^{2} \sum_{z} \delta_{iz} \log \frac{(\mu_i^k / \hat{q}_i^k) \cdot P_{iz}(\theta)}{\sum_{j=1}^{2} (\mu_j^k / \hat{q}_j^k) \cdot P_{iz}(\theta)}. \qquad (A5)$$

This estimator is called the "conditional maximum likelihood" (CML) because it can be interpreted as the sum of the likelihoods of response i conditional on characteristic z. Manski and McFadden (1981) prove its consistency and asymptotic normality for exact knowledge of q_i^k, Hsieh, Manski, and

McFadden (1983) extend these properties to the case where q_i^k are consistently estimated by $\hat{q}_i^k$ from the auxiliary sample.

The second estimator simply weights the observations inversely to $s^k(i,z)$, then treats the weighted sample as if it were an exogenous sample. This estimator is called the "weighted exogenous sample maximum likelihood" (WESML, Manski and Lerman, 1977):

$$L_{\text{WESML}}(\theta) = \sum_{k=1}^{K} \sum_{i=1}^{2} \sum_{z} \delta_{iz} \frac{\hat{q}_i^k}{\mu_i^k} \log P_{iz}(\theta). \qquad (A6)$$

Its consistency and asymptotic normality are proved in Manski and Lerman (1977), Manski and McFadden (1981), and Hsieh, Manski, and McFadden (1983). Note that this estimator also uses $\hat{q}_i^k$ as a consistent estimate of q_i^k. Finally, it is particularly inexpensive to compute.

Estimation results of our joint-choice model for all three estimators are presented in Table 6A.1. Note that the estimates are fairly close to each other in magnitude and reliability despite over- or undersampling ratios $s^k(i,z) = \mu_i^k / \hat{q}_i^k$ that depart considerably from one (see Table 6A.2). The calculation of the asymptotic covariance is discussed below. It should be noted that the FICLE estimator (A4) is equivalent to full-information maximum likelihood; hence its standard errors are smaller than (or equal to) than those produced by CML (A5) or WESML (A6) if evaluated at the same set of parameters. There is no global relation between CML and WESML (see Hsieh, Manski, and McFadden, 1983). In Table 6A.1, standard errors are evaluated at each estimator's optimal parameter set, thus standard errors are not strictly comparable.

Asymptotic covariance matrix

Hsieh, Manski, and McFadden (1983) establish the relevant asymptotic covariance matrix for the estimators (A4), (A5), and (A6) for the case of a uniform $s^k(i,z)$. For $k > 1$ these matrices have to be modified.

Let $\tilde{\beta} = (\tilde{q}_i^k, \tilde{\theta})$ be an estimator satisfying a first-order condition defined by the functions g and a

$$0 = \frac{1}{\sqrt{T}} \sum_{k=1}^{K} \sum_{i=1}^{2} \sum_{z} g(\tilde{\beta}, \hat{q}_i^k)$$

$$+ \sum_{k=1}^{K} \left(\frac{\sqrt{T}}{\sqrt{T^k}} \right) \sqrt{T^k} e^k a(\tilde{q}_i^k)(\hat{q}_i^k - \tilde{q}_i^k), \qquad (A7)$$

where e^k is a vector of zeroes and a 1 in the row corresponding to q_i^k in β. This second term is only present in the FICLE estimator (A4) and represents the

Table 6A.1. *Parameter estimates for alternative estimators*

Variable	WESML[a]	CML[a]	FICLE[a]
Mode-choice equation: alternative *(rail, motor carrier)*			
Value of commodity ($/lb) motor carrier alternative	.1122	.1621	.1271
	(.0581)	(.0366)	(.0442)
Freight charges ($1,000)	−.2564	−.5073	−.9979
	(.2866)	(.3481)	(.3973)
Mean transit time (days)	.0333	.0191	−.0607
	(.2043)	(.2470)	(.4253)
Shipment size (10,000 lbs) motor carrier alternative	−1.001	−1.005	−1.027
	(.1419)	(.1042)	(.1215)
Mode-specific dummy motor carrier alternative	4.5622	4.3378	4.1079
	(1.2626)	(1.1911)	(2.0551)
Shipment-size equation			
Fixed rate			
Motor carrier ($1,000)	.4893	.4258	.7768
	(.662)	(.8451)	(.8800)
Rail ($1,000)	−.3785	−.3124	−.1065
	(.3659)	(.5582)	(.5675)
Marginal rate			
Motor carrier ($/10 lb)	2.781	1.3717	4.7351
	(1.931)	(2.713)	(2.4336)
Rail ($/10 lb)	.6082	.4289	1.3618
	(.915)	(1.3299)	(1.7130)
Mean transit time			
Motor carrier (days)	1.089	.9966	.9064
	(.457)	(.488)	(.5030)
Rail (days)	−.0783	−.1155	−.0384
	(.1374)	(.1836)	(.2529)
Constant	−.780	−.2801	−1.1990
	(2.054)	(2.390)	(3.1250)
Correlation parameter (ρ)	−.2339	−.4124	−.3708
	(.0406)	(.373)	(.4260)
Standard deviation (σ)	1.5532	1.6150	1.5797
	(.0774)	(.0556)	(.0626)
Number of observations: 2,904			

[a]Standard errors are in parentheses.

Table 6A.2. *Mode choice by origin–destination–
produce triple*

| | | | Percentage motor carrier | | |
| | | | Main sample | Auxiliary sample | Ratio |
Origin	Destination	Produce			
California	Boston	Grapes	.75	.91	.824
		Lettuce	.33	.57	.579
		Tomatoes	.72	.63	1.14
Texas	Boston	Onions	.36	.40	.900
California	Cincinnati	Lettuce	.58	.85	.682
		Oranges	.46	.89	.517
Texas	Cincinnati	Cabbage	.39	.83	.470
California	Minneapolis	Lettuce	.66	.95	.695
		Oranges	.97	.98	.990
		Tomatoes	.95	.88	1.08
California	New York	Grapes	.75	.76	.987
		Lettuce	.28	.64	.438
		Oranges	.33	.29	1.14
		Tomatoes	.55	.69	.797
Washington	New York	Apples	.02	.44	.004

estimate of the estimated population shares. Assume the estimate $\hat{q}_i^k$ for the auxiliary sample is consistent and asymptotically normal with

$$\sqrt{T^k}(\hat{q}_i^k - q_i^k) \sim N(0, \sigma_k^2).$$

A Taylor's approximation of (A7) yields

$$0 = \underbrace{\frac{1}{\sqrt{T}}\sum_k \sum_i \sum_z g(\boldsymbol{\beta}, q_i^k)}_{(1)}$$

$$+ \sum_k \left(\frac{T^k}{T} \underbrace{\left[\frac{1}{T^k}\sum_i \sum_z gq_i^k + \mathbf{e}^k a \right]}_{(2)} \right)$$

$$\cdot \frac{\sqrt{T}}{\sqrt{T^k}}\sqrt{T^k}(\bar{q}_i^k - q_i^k)$$

$$+ \underbrace{\left(\frac{1}{T}\sum_k \sum_i \sum_z g_{\beta\beta} + \mathbf{e}^k \mathbf{e}^{k'} a \right)}_{(3)} \sqrt{T}(\bar{\boldsymbol{\beta}} - \boldsymbol{\beta}). \qquad (A8)$$

Assume for $T \to \infty$ $T^k/T \to$ constant. In addition, assume all the regularity conditions needed for the Hsieh, Manski, and McFadden (1983) theorem for uniform sampling rates. Then

(1) $\quad \overset{\text{a.d.}}{\to} N(0,G)$ with $\dfrac{1}{T} \sum_k \sum_i \sum_z gg' \overset{\text{p.}}{\to} G$

(2) $\quad \overset{\text{p.}}{\to} F^k$ $\qquad$ (3) $\quad \overset{\text{p.}}{\to} H.$

Thus,

$$\sqrt{T}(\tilde{\beta} - \beta) \overset{\text{a.d.}}{\to} N\left(0, H^{-1}\left(G + \sum_{k=1}^{K} \sigma_k^2 F^k F^{k'}\right) H^{-1}\right). \tag{A9}$$

We estimate this aymptotic variance by using the sample hessian for H, the sample outer product of the gradient for G, and the sample mixed derivative for F^k. According to the multinomial distribution, $\sigma_k^2 = (T/m)\, q_i^k(1 - q_i^k)$. Finally, note that the use of the sample outer product of the gradient as an estimate for G ignores the covariance reducing effect of stratification by mode choice and ODP triple. It thus yields a conservative estimate of the standard errors.

References

Cosslett, Stephen R. (1981). "Maximum Likelihood Estimator for Choice-Based Samples." *Econometrica* 49, September: 1289–1316.

Hsieh, David, Charles Manski, and Daniel McFadden (1983). "Estimation of Response Probabilities from Augmented Retrospective Observations." Working Paper, June, Massachusetts Institute of Technology, Cambridge, Mass.

Manski, Charles, and Steven Lerman (1977). "The Estimation of Choice Probabilities from Choice-Based Samples," *Econometrica*, 45, November: 1977–88.

Manski, Charles, and Daniel McFadden (1981). "Alternative Estimators and Sample Designs for Discrete Choice Analysis." In C. Manski and D. McFadden, eds., *Structural Analysis of Discrete Data with Econometric Applications*. Cambridge, Mass.: MIT Press.

McFadden, Daniel (1974). "The Measurement of Urban Travel Demand." *Journal of Public Economies*, 3, April: 303–28.

Moore, Thomas Gale (1983). "Rail and Truck Reform – The Record So Far." *Regulation*, November-December: 33–41.

Nahmias, Steven (1982). "Perishable Inventory Theory: A Review." *Operations Research*, 30, July-August: 680–708.

U.S. Department of Transportation (1977). "A Long-Term Study of Produce Transportation." December.

Winston, Clifford (1983). "The Demand for Freight Transportation: Models and Applications." *Transportation Research*, 17A, November: 419–27.

(1985). "Conceptual Developments in the Economics of Transportation: An Interpretive Survey." *Journal of Economic Literature*, 23, no. 1, March: 57–94.

Equilibrium, pricing, and market behavior

Freight network equilibrium: a review of the state of the art

TERRY L. FRIESZ AND PATRICK T. HARKER

The calculation of an equilibrium is fundamental to the positive analysis of any economic system. In this sense it is no surprise that one would wish to calculate an equilibrium among spatially separated markets connected by a freight transportation system, for that problem is evidently basic to regional and national economic forecasting. When the spatially separated markets of interest are represented as nodes of a network, the freight system infrastructure as links, together with some additional nodes to model modal or carrier junctions and transfer points, and some attempt to capture the complex hierarchy of decisions inherent in freight transportation is made, we refer to this equilibrium problem as the "freight network equilibrium problem." What is a surprise to the uninitiated is that a theoretically rigorous representation of such an equilibrium and its efficient computation can be quite difficult, and that these are, to some extent, unsolved problems. In this chapter we endeavor to make this last point clear, to review some of the recent advances that have been made and to suggest future research necessary to a complete understanding of freight network equilibrium.

At first glance the freight network equilibrium problem, as we have described it so far, seems essentially the same as the spatial price equilibrium problem discussed in the seminal words of Samuelson (1952) and Takayama and Judge (1971). However, as will become apparent, there are many aspects of decision making in the transport of freight that are not at all addressed by the conventional spatial price equilibrium model. The introduction of such considerations very much complicates the problem of finding an equilibrium and leads to models sufficiently distinct from the usual spatial price equilibrium model that a new name is warranted – hence our reference to such models as freight network equilibrium models.

We shall distinguish between two key aspects of freight equilibrium. The first is the usual concept of market clearing, which ensures that commodity supply equals commodity demand or, when working with the transportation market alone, that transportation supply equals transportation demand. The second aspect is the equilibrium among freight transportation decisionmakers, wherein no decisionmaker has an incentive to alter his strategy. As we shall see, this later aspect influences supply and demand magnitudes, but is otherwise distinct from market clearing.

The point of departure for modeling equilibrium among freight transportation decisionmakers is the dichotomous perspective on traffic equilibrium originally put forward by Wardrop (1952). Wardrop described two principles of equilibrium for transportation systems which we may summarize as follows (see Fernandez and Friesz, 1983, for a review of these):

Wardrop's first principle. Each user noncooperatively seeks to minimize his cost of transportation. A network flow pattern consistent with this principle is called a "user-optimized equilibrium." Specifically, a user-optimized equilibrium is reached when no user may lower his transportation cost through unilateral action.

Wardrop's second principle. The total cost of transportation in the system is minimized. A network flow pattern consistent with this principle is called a "system-optimized equilibrium" and requires that users cooperate fully or that a central authority controls the transportation system. Specifically, a system-optimized equilibrium is reached when the marginal total costs of transportation alternatives are equal.

The essential difficulty in applying these concepts of equilibrium to freight systems lies in the fact that freight network flow patterns are determined by the decisions of more than just users. In fact freight flow patterns, unlike urban automobile flow patterns, are determined by the transport system users *and* by owner operators. The users and owner operators are generally considered to be synonymous in the automobile case, since network infrastructure is held fixed. However, even when network infrastructure is fixed, this luxury is not possible in the freight case, since the means of transport over the network is typically owned and operated by entities distinct from those originating goods shipments; that is, the owner operators are distinct from the users.

Conventional wisdom has tended to model freight systems by assuming that the owner operators or "carriers" (defined precisely in the next section) obey Wardrop's second principle. This leaves unanswered the questions of how to model the users or "shippers" (also defined precisely in the next section) and of the interrelationship between shippers and carriers. This point is developed more fully in the next and subsequent sections. For convenience, we refer to any freight model that enforces market clearing and determines an equilibrium among any subset of relevant decisionmakers as a "freight equilibrium model." Clearly, however, many of the models discussed subsequently do not calculate a true equilibrium in the freight transportation market since the behavior of shippers and carriers is not determined simultaneously and consistently.

1.   Description of existing predictive freight network models

Descriptions of the key predictive freight network models developed since the 1960s are given in this section in order to better understand advances in the state of the art as well as the remaining shortcomings of freight network equilibrium models. Not all the models discussed in this section are *true* equilibrium models. Throughout our discussion in this and subsequent sections, shippers will be thought of as those decision-making entities desiring a particular commodity at a particular destination, and carriers as those decision-making entities that actually transport the commodities, thereby satisfying the transportation demands of shippers.

1.1.   Harvard–Brookings

Without question, the first significant multimodal predictive freight network model was that developed by Roberts (1966) and extended by Kresge and Roberts (1971). This work has become known in the literature as the Harvard–Brookings model. In this model, applied to the transport network of a developing country (Colombia), links correspond to transport routes (not the actual physical transport links) and nodes to cities or regions. The model is explicitly multimodal–including highway, rail, air, and water modes; it is also explicitly a multicommodity model. Shippers' modal choices and general routings are determined from shortest path calculations for the intermodal network, with arc impedances measured as constant unit origin-to-destination (path) perceived shipping costs; these are used in a standard Koppmans–Hitchcock transportation submodel to determine commodity-specific flows between origin–destination (OD) pairs (see, for example, Wagner, 1975, for a definition of the Koopmans–Hitchcock transportation problem). The commodity production and consumption numbers needed to specify the constraints of the Koopmans–Hitchcock trip-distribution submodel are obtained from a separate macroeconomic driver. For freight flows of highly aggregated heterogeneous commodity groups, a standard gravity submodel (see Isard, 1975, chap. 3) rather than a Hitchcock formulation was used to determined OD flows. Once the trip-distribution process is completed, flows are assigned to the intermodal network by using the same shortest paths found previously (those based on impedances that are shippers' perceived costs). The assignment of flows is completed by adding appropriate volumes to account for the necessary backhaul to secure another load; backhaul trips are assumed to be routed exactly as the forehaul trips.

1.2.   CACI

As part of the National Energy Transportation Study (NETS), CACI, Inc., developed a multicommodity, multimodal freight network model referred to as the Transportation Network Model (TNM) (CACI, 1980; Bronzini, 1980a–c). Although the model is intended for rather general application, it did not, as originally conceived, attempt to predict the freight shipment OD pattern, transportation demand being fixed in the model. The original version did, however, account for all plausible freight modes and could handle any number of commodities. There are two basic behavioral assumptions of the model:

1. Freight routing results exclusively from the decisions of shippers seeking to find minimum-cost paths.
2. The cost on a path is a linear combination of dollar cost, time, and energy use.

These assumptions ignore any role that carriers play in the routing of freight shipments. In addition, the cost measure is unusual in that it combines concerns usually limited to shippers, such as time, and to carriers, such as cost, as distinct from price. The inclusion of energy costs, normally considered by carriers as only a portion of total monetary costs, is used to assess various energy-conservation scenarios.

Although it is claimed that the model is both a multicommodity and equilibrium assignment model, no version of the model can rigorously accomplish both aims. In an early version of the model, the "multimodal network model" (MNM), multiple commodities are treated by loading the network sequentially. Since arcs are given absolute capacity constraints, the final loading may depend on the particular sequence in which the commodities are loaded. In addition, this version only approximates an equilibrium solution through an iterated capacity constraint algorithm. A more recent version of the model, the "transportation network model" (TNM), while implementing an equilibrium assignment model for shippers, uses aggregate instead of commodity-specific cost functions; it is in essence a single-commodity model. Backhauling is treated indirectly through adjustments to link delay and cost functions. The most recent version of the model employs a separate submodel to determine carrier routing behavior (Bronzini and Sherman, 1983); this carrier submodel employs fixed impedances and a shortest path algorithm.

Some tests of the model have been reported, although most use only highly aggregated data. These tests indicate an ability to replicate aggregate modal split data. Total link loadings generated by the model have been compared against historical link usage with significantly poorer results.

1.3. Peterson's model

Peterson (see Peterson and Fullerton, 1975) has proposed a predictive rail network model that employs either Wardrop's first or second principle of equilibrium assignment to model carrier decisions, although he states that the second principle (system optimization) is preferable for modeling freight systems. The model is in the form of a mathematical program whose objective function is constructed from arc delay measures that depend on aggregate flow volumes and is meant to be minimized. Presumably, these delay measures are obtained from one of the queueing models reported by Peterson and Fullerton (1975). The model assumes that transportation demand is fixed and determined exogenously. The constraints of the mathematical program are the usual flow conservation and nonnegativity constraints. The model does not explicitly treat multiple carriers or multiple commodities; backhauling is not addressed. Tests of predictive capability against known data are not available.

1.4. *Lansdowne's model*

Although the rail freight traffic assignment model developed by Lansdowne (1981) is not as general in its scope as the other models reviewed here, it is included because of its explicit attempt to treat shipper–carrier interactions in a manner that conforms to current rail industry practice. The model assumes as input a rail-specific trip matrix. It is thus a unimodal as well as a fixed-demand model. Its output is a set of rail paths that include the interline locations, where control of the freight shipment is transferred from one carrier to another. The route that a shipment follows on the rail network, including the number and location of interlining points where rail carriers transfer control of the shipments, is jointly determined by the involved shippers and carriers. The location of the interlining point may be specified by the shipper, but is more commonly specified by the originating railroad. The originating railroad, while seeking to maximize its revenue, must also offer a reasonable level of service to the shipper to attract its business. These principles can be summarized as follows:

1.   The only routes used will be those that have a minimum number of interlining points.
2.   Each carrier will use the shortest path within its subnetwork.
3.   Of the eligible routes, the one that maximizes the originating carrier's share of the revenue is selected.
4.   If there is more than one potential originating carrier, the shipment is divided among all the potential carriers according to some pre-specified rule.

Even though each interline movement creates additional expense, delay, and uncertainty for the shipment and would generally be avoided, the first assumption ignores a number of very real operating concerns. The condition and layout of the track being used and the delays caused by line-haul and intermediate yard congestion, for example, would certainly influence a carrier's routing choice. The third and fourth assumptions, like the first, appear to be reasonable operating premises because the originating carrier supplies the cars and negotiates the rates and is, therefore, in a strong bargaining position with the other railroads. Also, in regional analyses, the shippers may actually be an aggregation of many shippers, and thus it can be expected that each available railroad will originate part of the shipment. Backhauling is not addressed, and no tests of predictive capability against known data have been reported.

1.5.   Princeton's model

The Princeton railroad network model (Kornhauser et al., 1979) employs two submodels. The first, called the "intercarrier route generation model," utilizes shortest path techniques on a series of single-carrier rail networks; carrier arc costs are fixed and determined judgmentally to ensure that flow is primarily along main lines. The intracarrier routings, and thereby implicitly the fixed impedances, have been validated qualitatively through the presentation of graphic displays of routes to rail system managers who were asked whether their railroads routed in accordance with the displays. The second submodel, called the "intercarrier route generation model," is based on an intercarrier network that includes junction links between separate carriers known to interline. Very high impedances are assigned to such junction links to ensure that interlining along a path between a given OD pair does not occur with excessive frequency. Again, impedances are determined judgmentally and validation is through graphic displays that allow comparison with selected historical route information. Arc loadings predicted in the Princeton model are, however, apparently not checked against published Federal Railroad Administration (FRA) density codes. Backhauling is not addressed.

1.6.   Pennsylvania–Argonne National Laboratory model

The University of Pennsylvania (Penn) has developed a predictive freight network model called the "freight network equilibrium model" (FNEM) (see Friesz et al., 1981). This model was constructed under a research program sponsored by the U.S. Department of Energy and involved staff of Argonne National Laboratory (ANL) as well as Penn. FNEM explicitly treats the decisions of both shippers and carriers for an intermodal freight network with nonlinear cost and delay functions that vary with commodity volumes to model congestion externalities.

FNEM treats shippers and carriers sequentially as depicted in Figure 7.1. In particular, shippers are assumed to be user optimizers trying to non-cooperatively minimize the delivered price of commodities they ship, and therefore Wardrop's first principle is used to describe their behavior. The shipper submodel is an elastic transportation demand, user-optimized trip

Production Amounts, Consumption Amounts, Demand Function

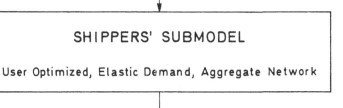

┌───┐
│   │
│   SHIPPERS' SUBMODEL   │
│   │
│   User Optimized, Elastic Demand, Aggregate Network │
│   │
└───┘

O - D Demands by Path from Production Site to Consumption Site

┌───┐
│   │
│   DECOMPOSITION ALGORITHM   │
│   │
│   Path Construction, Path Decomposition   │
│   │
└───┘

O - D Demands by Carrier

┌───┐
│   │
│   CARRIERS' SUBMODEL   │
│   │
│   System Optimized, Fixed Demand, Detailed Network │
│   │
└───┘

Arc Flows, Arc Costs, Path Flows, Path Costs

Figure 7.1. Flowchart of FNEM.

assignment model expressed as a mathematical programming problem and solvable by the usual Frank–Wolfe-type algorithms for such problems (Gartner, 1977), with diagonalization methods used to treat modal or commodity interactions (see Fernandez and Friesz, 1983). The shipper submodel employs an aggregate, perceived network including only the OD pairs, transshipment nodes, interline nodes, other key nodes, and associated links actually considered by shippers in their decision process. Solution for flows over the aggregate shippers' network at user equilibrium leads to OD demand levels by commodity, shipper, mode, or mode combinations used, and carriers used. Following a detailed bookkeeping exercise identified as the "decomposition algorithm" in Figure 7.1, one obtains carrier-specific OD demands. The carrier demands are fixed numbers and recognize that carriers control specific subnetworks of the entire intermodal network whose origin and destination nodes include interline points with other carriers. The individual carrier networks represent the full physical detail of the actual freight system. Carriers are assumed to be individual profit maximizing firms. However, since the demands for the carriers' services are fixed in this sequential modeling framework, the revenue a carrier receives is constant and, thus, profit maximization is equivalent to cost minimization. Because the carriers are viewed as sequentially reacting to the transportation demands set up by the shippers, each carrier submodel is a fixed-travel-demand, system-optimized, trip-assignment model expressed as a mathematical programming problem. Each carrier-specific mathematical program is, like each shipper submodel, solved by Frank–Wolfe-type algorithms with diagonalization methods (Gartner, 1977; Fernandez and Friesz, 1983). Individual carrier flow patterns are combined to obtain flow patterns for the entire intermodal network. Backhauling is treated through adjustments to cost and delay functions. The model replicates FRA density codes at least 50 percent better than the CACI model described previously.

In fact, extensive validation tests of FNEM have been conducted (Friesz, Gottfried, and Morlok, 1983), and the results from these tests indicate that FNEM provides a substantial improvement in predictive capability over earlier models. Section 5 will describe these tests and certain applications of FNEM in greater detail.

It is important to realize that FNEM is not limited to strictly increasing cost and delay measures such as those encountered in urban passenger applications. When nonincreasing functions are employed, the objective functions in the shippers' and carriers' submodels may fail to be convex, giving rise to multiple equilibria. When this occurs, the Frank–Wolfe algorithm is still utilized to effect an efficient solution, but care is taken to select step sizes that guarantee convergence to local optimality; in this way FNEM may be relied upon to find one of the nonunique equilibria that may occur with nonincreasing functions. Avriel (1976) provides details of the step-size selection rules that guarantee convergence of the Frank–Wolfe algorithm to a local optimum when the objective function is nonconvex.

2.   Typology of predictive freight network models

For effective comparison of the models presented in the previous section, it is useful to construct a typology of predictive freight network models. In this section, existing models are differentiated and evaluated according to the following criteria, which pertain primarily to routing and modal choice: (1) treatment of multiple modes, (2) treatment of multiple commodities, (3) sequential loading of commodities, (4) simultaneous loading of commodities, (5) treatment of congestion phenomena via nonlinear cost and delay functions, (6) inclusion of elastic transportation demand, (7) explicit treatment of shippers, (8) explicit treatment of carriers, (9) sequential solution of shipper and carrier submodels, (10) simultaneous solution of macroeconomic model and transportation network model, (11) sequential macroeconomic and network models, (12) simultaneous macroeconomic and network models, (13) solution employing nonmonotonic functions, (14) explicit treatment of backhauling, (15) explicit treatment of blocking strategies, and (16) inclusion of fleet constraints. The models described previously are evaluated in terms of these sixteen criteria in Table 7.1.

Criterion 1 recognizes that multiple modes are used to carry freight shipments. The data in Table 7.1 indicate that three of the six models address multimodal interactions whereas the remainder are unimodal (rail) models.

Criterion 2 incorporates the fact that freight transportation involves multiple commodities with distinct transportation-cost characteristics and different shipping time requirements that prevent meaningful treatment as a single commodity Criterion 3 refers to the fact that it is sometimes possible to rank commodities, assigning them individually to the network in order from highest to lowest shipment priority. Some commodity disaggregation schemes will lead, however, to commodities of identical shipment priority but with distinct unit-cost characteristics; for these commodities, a simultaneous loading procedure is required (criterion 4).

Criterion 5 recognizes the general variation of relevant costs and delays with flow volume due to congestion economies and diseconomies, and criterion 6 refers to the fact that demand for transportation will generally vary with transportation costs and delays. Two of the models incorporate elastic demand functions in the form of trip-distribution models to determine OD flow levels. The remainder of the models require fixed trip matrixes as input.

Criteria 7 and 8 address the fact that routing and modal choices in freight systems are the results of decisions of both shippers and carriers and that these

Table 7.1. *Typology of predictive freight models with respect to routing and modal-choice characteristics*

Model	Criteria[a]															
	1	2	3	4	5	6	7	8	9	10	11	12	13	14	15	16
Harvard–Brookings	Yes	Yes	Yes	Yes	No	Yes	Yes	No	NA	NA	Yes	No	No	No	No	No
CACI	Yes	Yes	Yes	No	Yes	No	Yes	No	NA	NA	Yes	No	No	No	No	No
Peterson	No	No	NA	NA	Yes	No	No	Yes	No	No	Yes	No	No	No	No	No
Lansdowne	No	Yes	Yes	No	No	No	Yes	Yes	Yes	No	Yes	No	No	No	No	No
Princeton	No	Yes	Yes	No	No	No	Yes	Yes	Yes	No	Yes	No	No	No	No	No
Penn–ANL (FNEM)	Yes	Yes	Yes	Yes	Yes	Yes	Yes	Yes	Yes	No	Yes	No	Yes	No	No	No

[a]Criteria

1. Multiple modes
2. Multiple commodities
3. Sequential loading of commodities
4. Simultaneous loading of commodities
5. Congestion

6. Elastic transportation demand
7. Explicit treatment of shippers
8. Explicit treatment of carriers
9. Sequential shipper and carrier submodels
10. Simultaneous shipper and carrier submodels
11. Sequential macroeconomic and network models

12. Simultaneous macroeconomic and network models
13. Nonmonotonic functions
14. Explicit backhauling
15. Blocking strategy
16. Fleet constraints

NA = not applicable

groups obey distinct behavioral principles that may at times have conflicting goals. Three of the six models explicitly treat shippers and multiple carriers, and of these three only the Penn–ANL model is a multimodal model. Criteria 9 and 10 refer to whether one ascertains the decisions of shippers first and then the decisions of the carriers or determines both simultaneously. Only a simultaneous determination gives a true equilibrium; otherwise there exists the possibility of further adjustments by shippers whose perceptions of freight transportation levels of service differ from those actually provided by the carriers. None of the models discussed previously determines these decisions simultaneously.

Criteria 11 and 12 recognize that virtually all reported freight network models use as input fixed supplies and demands of individual commodities obtained from a separate regional or national economic model. Generally, such economic models employ assumptions about freight transportation costs and the question naturally arises of whether the network model outputs are consistent with those costs. Iteration between the economic model and the network model in an attempt to produce consistency is, of course, a heuristic device with no rigorous convergence properties; only a simultaneous solution of the model that generates the supplies and demands of individual commodities and the network model will always result in the desired consistency.

Criterion 13 refers to the ability of a given model to treat nonmonotonic functions, particularly nonmonotonic cost functions that are expected to occur as a result of average rail operating costs that initially decline as volume increases and then begin to increase as capacity is approached (see, for example, Morlok, 1978). When nonmonotonic functions are used, multiple equilibria may exist.

Criterion 14 recognizes that a large portion of traffic is made up of empty rolling stock, empty barges, and empty trucks that contribute to costs and congestion. Freight transportation's dependence on the availability of empty rolling stock necessitates considerable attention to backhauling operations if carriers are to be able to satisfy shippers' transportation demands. Criterion 15 recognizes that rail freight flows comprise trains of varying length, made up of different types of rail cars, which are frequently "blocked" into groups bound for common or similar destinations. This blocking has a significant impact on yard delays encountered by a shipment. Criterion 16 refers to the fact that there are generally restrictions on the supply of rolling stock and vehicles that cannot be violated in the short run; as such, this criterion is intimately related to criterion 14 dealing with backhauling.

The key unresolved issues with respect to freight network models are (1) the simultaneous treatment of shipper and carrier decisions, (2) the simultaneous solution of the economic model that generates supplies and demands and the network model itself, (3) the treatment of nonmonotonic functions, particularly nonmonotonic cost functions, (4) explicit treatment of backhauling operations, (5) explicit treatment of blocking strategies, and (6) fleet constraints. In a later section we present some recent advances in the development of models addressing the first two of these unresolved issues.

3.   Simultaneity of shipper and carrier decisions

Perhaps the greatest lack of behavioral realism in the models treating both shippers and carriers is the sequential perspective on shipper and carrier decisions. Such a perspective, as Friesz and Morlok (1980) have pointed out, is not consistent with the calculation of true equilibrium flow values because it presupposes that carriers will provide commodity routings that give levels of service perfectly consistent with those levels of service perceived and anticipated by shippers. However, because the shippers' costs depend on the carriers' costs and routings, this can happen only if the shippers know beforehand the carriers' costs (or, more precisely, that portion passed through to each shipper from each carrier). But such perfect foresight is not possible because of congestion externalities that make the carriers' costs depend on routing patterns. Similarly, no carrier may establish its routes, and hence its costs, before knowing the shippers' demands. Since neither category of decisionmaker can finalize its decisions without knowing the decisions of the other category, the problem is one in which decisions by shippers and carriers must be modeled simultaneously.

It is possible to write a single mathematical program to describe simultaneous shipper–carrier decisionmaking, as Harker (1981) and Harker and Friesz (1982) have shown. This is accomplished by representing the shippers through the extended notion of Wardrop's first principle employing delivered price. The Harker–Friesz formulation, however, utilizes nonlinear, and unfortunately nonconvex, constraints patterned after Tan et al. (1979) to describe such shipper behavior. The behavior of carriers is modeled using an extended notion of Wardrop's second principle of system optimality; this perspective, when carrier networks are appropriately defined, yields a single objective function describing the carriers' operating costs that is minimized. The Tan et al. types of constraints are articulated in terms of path variables, thereby necessitating path enumeration as well as special numerical procedures to treat their nonlinear, nonconvex nature. Seemingly, these constraints may be replaced by a variational inequality, after Smith (1979) and Dafermos (1979, 1982), and the method of constraint accumulation suggested by Marcotte (1981) employed to overcome the need to enumerate paths fully and possibly to achieve some increased computational efficiency. Fisk and Boyce (1983) suggest a similar approach but represent the shippers' behavior as a nonlinear complementarity problem that appears as constraints in the carriers' extremal problem. Nonconvexity still remains in these approaches because the variational inequality or complementarity problem one employs to model Wardrop's first principle, like the constraints of Tan et al., is nonconvex.

The Harker-Friesz mathematical programming formulation, because of its innate nonconvexity, prevents investigations of the uniqueness of a shipper-carrier equilibrium; that nonconvexity also severely complicates proofs of existence of a combined equilibrium. Questions of existence and uniqueness are much more easily explored through nonlinear complementarity and pure variational inequality formulations of the problem. These questions are of theoretical interest and also affect computation in that one desires to know whether there is one equilibrium solution, more than one, or none.

Friesz, Viton, and Tobin (1985) have proposed a variational inequality formulation of the simultaneous shipper-carrier equilibrium problem that leads directly to equivalent optimization problems that may be solved quite efficiently using the usual Frank-Wolfe algorithm together with diagonalization as is done for urban network equilibrium problems. These solution methods are convergent for the simultaneous shipper-carrier equilibrium problem under appropriate conditions. Moreover, the variational inequality allows one to study the existence and uniqueness of solution of a simultaneous equilibrium. If the variational inequality is such that it admits multiple equilibria, the Frank-Wolfe diagonalization approach may be used to compute a non-unique equilibrium by utilizing appropriate step sizes, as discussed in Avriel (1976).

The variational inequality formulation of Friesz, Viton, and Tobin (1985) assumes marginal cost pricing on the carriers' part. Although this certainly is not the general case, the arguments leading to their model formulation are particularly easy to follow and are, hence, of pedagogic value, since the approach used to construct the variational inequality may be extended to other economic settings. For these reasons we go to some length in this section to present the single variational inequality for simultaneous shipper-carrier equilibrium with marginal-cost pricing.

3.1. Assumptions and notation for simultaneous shipper-carrier equilibrium

First assume that there are many shippers, each with equivalent information, who compete for limited transportation services as well as for certain homogeneous commodities needed for their individual economic activities (either production or consumption). Each shipper is assumed to be a profit-maximizing economic agent. Because of the assumed presence of many shippers, each shipper takes the supply prices (the prices at origin markets), the demand prices (the prices at the destination markets), and the effective transportation rates (which include the economic value of shipment delays as well as the actual rates that carriers charge shippers) as given when deciding upon its profit-maximizing pattern of origin–destination commodity flows. As we shall prove in the next section, this assumed profit-maximizing behavior leads to a situation wherein the shippers noncooperatively minimize the delivered price of each commodity. Because the delivered price measure reflects congestion externalities, the shippers may be viewed as the players of the noncooperative mathematical game with a Cournot–Nash equilibrium solution in quantities that is constrained by the assumptions to be made regarding the carriers' behavior.

Each freight carrier is assumed to be a profit maximizer facing an exogenous market price for its service. This assumption results in cost-minimizing behavior and marginal-cost pricing by the individual carriers. Perfect competition among freight carriers, of course, leads to both outcomes. But, interestingly, so do other assumptions about market structure, notably one in which two or more carriers produce a given transportation service (product) and cover costs. Such a configuration is termed "sustainable" by Baumol, Panzar, and Willig (1982; see especially their Proposition 11B5). The observed tendency of carriers to retain possession of a shipment and to avoid interlining with other carriers may be captured by including appropriately high penalty costs for interline movements.

Because these assumptions may be regarded as controversial, it is appropriate to discuss them in somewhat more detail. First it is generally accepted that cost functions in the rail industry exhibit economies of density; see, for example, Keeler (1983) for a review of the evidence. Under these conditions the sort of competitive equilibria discussed in this section will never obtain. That observation, however, is far from depriving them of interest, for the (loss-incurring) marginal-cost price solution, with appropriate subsidies, remains the optimal solution to which all other proposals (complete deregulation, Ramsey pricing, and so forth) should be compared. Certainly, it is unlikely that the sort of reregulation entailed by the marginal cost pricing with lump-sum payments will be enacted by Congress. Nonetheless, the criterion value of service-quality calculations based on competitive assumptions remains.

Second, it is equally well accepted that the trucking industry exhibits little or no economies of density. Marginal-cost pricing is therefore feasible, and our analysis is directly applicable to this sector of the freight transport industry. Moreover, when applied to this sector, observing that under deregulation barriers to entry will be small, our detailed analysis of freight flows over network paths will have a predictive function, as well as an evaluative one. That is, given empirical estimates of model parameters, one could compute the equilibrium situation in a contestable industry. More will be said concerning the marginal-cost pricing assumption in Section 3.4.

It is assumed that the extent of the freight network is given – in other words, that the question of optimal investment to influence network capacity does not arise. The behavior of the shippers and carriers are linked through flow-conservation constraints that, in addition to their usual role of ensuring that flow gains and losses do not occur except where intended, guarantee that carriers meet the transportation demands established by shippers. The concept of dual shipper and carrier networks put forward in Friesz and Morlok (1980), Friesz et al. (1981) and Friesz, Gottfried, and Morlok (1983) and mentioned in the discussion of FNEM in Section 1 is also used in this formulation.

That is, although each shipper has identical information about the transportation marketplace, the shippers are not generally cognizant of the entire set of routing options available; moreover these options are generally not within any shipper's purview, but rather are usually selected by the carrier originating a given shipment. For these reasons shippers are assumed to make their decisions with respect to an aggregate network representing the shippers' perceptions (all equivalent) of the freight transportation system. The set of nodes of this "perceived network" consists of all actual commodity origins and actual commodity destinations, plus interline locations (nodes at which shipments may be transferred between carriers) and transshipment locations (nodes at which shipments may be transferred between modes). Arcs of the perceived network are generally aggregations of actual arcs. Taken together, the perceived arcs represent only the very general and very restricted routing options within the control of shippers. By contrast each carrier has full routing control of some subnetwork of the actual detailed physical freight network and its behavior is modeled on such a subnetwork. The intersection of any two carrier subnetworks is taken to be empty, while the union of all carrier subnetworks is the detailed freight transportation network itself. In cases where two or more carriers share a particular transportation facility, this facility will be represented by two or more separate network elements (arcs or nodes) in the model. The effect of this assumption is merely that individual carriers control their own networks, and not that a given carrier is a local spatial monopolist. Clearly for consistency all the origins, destinations, interline locations, and transshipment locations of the shippers' network are represented in the carrier subnetworks, although generally the carrier subnetworks and, hence, the entire detailed freight network will include many more nodes to describe the junction of all physical arcs as they occur in the real world or some abstraction that will never be less detailed than the shipper's network.

The distinctions made among types of networks requires the careful use of certain terminology. In particular a true origin–destination (OD) pair differs, in general, from a carrier-specific origin–destination pair. A true OD pair consists of the actual origin and the actual final destination of some shipment. A carrier-specific OD pair consists of the node of the carrier's subnetwork at which the carrier first takes responsibility for a shipment and the node at which it relinquishes responsibility; as such, a carrier-specific OD pair may consist of one or two interlined nodes and not the true origin and/or not the true destination. The interdependency of shippers' and carriers' behavior is captured through constraints requiring that carrier OD travel demand equal the sum of shippers' flows that traverse the carrier OD pair in question.

A simple example may clarify these network distinctions. In Figure 7.2 we show a shippers' network, consisting of a single origin O and destination D; this is referred to as the true OD pair. The set of solid arcs are the arcs of the shippers' perceived network. From the shippers' point of view, this perceived network is all that matters; shipments must get from O to D with the possibility of transshipment/interline at I. In this example, shippers see two choices. But from the point of view of those who actually provide the transportation (the carriers) matters may be immeasurably more complex. Figure 7.2 also shows the assumed carriers' subnetworks, the union of which is the actual freight network. In this depiction broken lines of different types represent arcs of different subnetworks; that is, different carriers or different modes of some single carrier. It is readily apparent that the true origin and destination (on the shippers' network) are represented in the actual network as well as in the shippers' network. Further, the true OD pair may differ from a carrier-specific OD pair [see for example the carrier-specific OD pairs (O,I) and (I,D)], as the general structure previously described allows.

In the exposition that follows we employ the device of a multicopy network to simplify the notation. This concept allows us to suppress all indexes of variables and parameters, save those that identify the particular network element with which these quantities are associated and yet to treat multiple modes, multiple carriers, and multiple commodities. An example will help to clarify this concept. Consider the extremely simple network with two nodes $(1,2)$ and one arc (a) depicted in Figure 7.3a. Imagine that two commodities are transported by a single mode from node 1 to node 2. Let $\phi_a^k(f_a^1, f_a^2)$, $k = (1,2)$, denote an arbitrary measure (usually some type of cost or delay) associated with arc a where f_a^k is the flow on arc a of commodity k. This situation may be represented with more compact notation using the multicopied network of Figure 7.3b. In that figure arc α corresponds to commodity 1 movements on the actual arc a, and arc β to commodity 2; thus $\phi_\alpha(.,.)$ and $\phi_\beta(.,.)$ are the respective commodity measures on the actual arc a; similarly f_α and f_β are the respective commodity flows on the actual arc a. Consequently we can think of any multicommodity network as having arc measures $\phi_a(\mathbf{f})$, where $\mathbf{f}$ is the *full* vector of network flows, with commodity identities carried by the arc names. Quite clearly multicopy networks can be layered on top of one

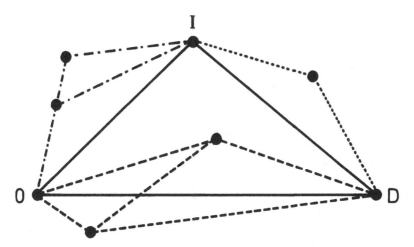

Figure 7.2. Shippers' network.

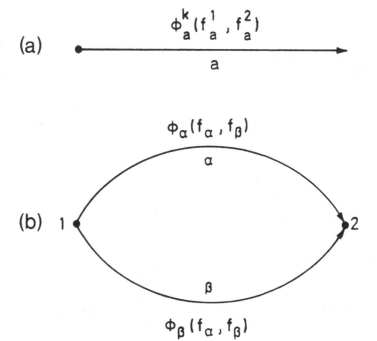

Figure 7.3. (a) and (b). Multicopy network.

another so that multiple-mode and multiple-carrier, as well as multiple-commodity considerations may be included in arc names, provided one employs nonseparable functions for each arc. It is important to reemphasize that the multicopy network concept is only a notational convenience and does not imply any separability of the network itself with respect to modes, flows, or commodities.

We turn now to a description of the setting of the shipper and carrier problem. We shall consistently use the indexes a and b to denote arcs, the indexes p and q to identify paths and w or v to denote a particular OD pair (i,j) consisting of an origin i and destination j. In light of the previous remarks we must describe two distinct networks: one pertaining to the shippers, the other to the carriers. Once this is done, we specify how the two are linked.

First, the shippers. Their network is made up of a set M of nodes and A of arcs. The shippers' graph is denoted by $G(M,A)$. Relative to G, we have the set W of OD pairs and the set P of paths. For a particular OD pair $w \in W$, we let P_w stand for the set of paths $p \in P$ connecting i and j. We shall wish to know whether a particular arc $a \in A$ is part of the path $p \in P$ between the elements of w. Consequently, we define the element δ_{ap} of the shippers' arc-path incidence matrix to be unity if $p \in P$ contains $a \in A$; and zero otherwise.

Shippers' decisions result in a vector $\mathbf{f} = (. . . ,f_a, . . .)$ of flows on arcs, with f_a the flow on arc a; similarly $\mathbf{h} = (. . . ,h_p, . . .)$ is a vector of path flows. As previously discussed, a particular arc may be congested; this congestion is modeled by an average delay function t_a on arc a. Note that in this chapter delay is measured with respect to the instantaneous traversing of an arc, and so the "average delay on arc a" is really the unit time taken to traverse arc a and *not* the excess travel time over and above some reference value. Path time is assumed to be additive in arc times; hence the delay on path p is given by $t_p = \sum_{a \in A} \delta_{ap} t_a.$

Shipper economics are described by the assumption of price-taking behavior and a demand for transportation S_w between the OD pair $w \in W$. Each S_w is assumed to be a function of the full vector of minimum delivered prices of shipments between all OD pairs. We use the notation u_w to denote the minimum delivered price between OD pair w, and $\mathbf{u}$ to denote the full vector of such delivered prices. Hence, $S_w = S_w(\mathbf{u})$. If we assume a given technology of transportation, then knowledge of transport demands is equivalent to knowledge of commodity shipments. An inverse demand function is defined for each OD pair $w \in W$ and specifies the minimum delivered price u_w of a shipment between w as a function of the full vector of transport demands; we denote the inverse demand function for OD pair w by $\theta_w(\mathbf{S})$. The commodity transported (we may speak of a single commodity because we employ a multicopy network) has a given price π_i at the origin, and the shipper faces a rate (price) of r_p per unit of the commodity shipped on its perceived path $p \in P$. In addition, all shippers have a common value ϕ of the disutility of delay for this commodity. The price π_i is assumed to be a fixed value; this might be the case if commodity production at the origin is small relative to a large national market and if transport costs are small relative to other production costs. In this case calculated network equilibria at the (given) commodity prices π_i will be in equilibrium in both the transport and commodity markets. Alternatively, one could incorporate demand and supply for the transported commodities explicitly, and introduce additional equilibrium conditions. The latter course has been pursued by Harker (1983) and Harker and Friesz (1985a–c).

The carrier structure is similarly characterized. We let K denote the set of all carriers; and the index k an individual carrier. Each carrier k has a subnetwork described by the set N_k of nodes, B_k of arcs, and V_k of OD pairs. The graph of the kth carrier is $\mathbf{H}_k\,(N_k,\,B_k)$. For the whole set K of carriers we have the sets $N = \cup_k N_k$ of nodes, $B = \cup_k B_k$ of arcs, giving rise to the carrier-system graph $\mathbf{H}(N,B)$. Letting Q denote the set of paths on $\mathbf{H}(N,B)$, we define the carriers' arc-path incidence matrix by the generic element $\Delta_{bq} = 1$ if $q \in Q$ contains $b \in B$; and zero otherwise.

Carrier decisions also result in flows: an arc flow is e_b on $b \in B$, a path flow is g_q on $q \in Q$, and the corresponding vectors of all flows are $\mathbf{e}$ for arcs and $\mathbf{g}$ for paths. The structure of the problem makes each carrier a cost minimizer. We suppose that each carrier has a path cost function that is additive in arc costs. We denote by MC_b the marginal cost of transporting additional traffic on arc b, and by additivity, $\mathrm{MC}_q = \sum_{b\in B} \Delta_{bq}\,\mathrm{MC}_b$ is the marginal cost on path q. We use the notation y_v to denote the minimum marginal carrier path cost for OD pair v, and $\mathbf{y}$ to denote the full vector of such costs.

Finally, the shippers' and carriers' networks are linked by requiring that M, the set of shipper nodes be a subset of N, the set of carrier nodes. Relative to both networks, we define the element γ_{vp} of the carrier OD/shipper path incidence matrix; $\gamma_{vp} = 1$ if shipper path $p \in P$ contains the carrier OD pair $v \in V$, and zero otherwise.

In the notation given here it is important to reiterate that, in keeping with our earlier remarks, the shippers are assumed to route themselves over a perceived network that includes all origins, destinations, interline nodes, and transshipment nodes. Furthermore, the shippers' network is a multicopied, intermodal, multicommodity network; that is, each link label identifies both a commodity and a mode. Each carrier makes routing decisions for its own detailed subnetwork; the union of all carrier subnetworks is the actual physical intercarrier network. Each subnetwork is a multicopied, intermodal, multi-commodity network, since a carrier may control more than one mode within its subnetwork (although frequently a carrier will control only a single mode) and generally moves multiple commodities.

3.2.   Mathematical characterization of simultaneous shipper–carrier equilibrium

The problem at hand is to characterize the equilibrium network flow pattern; that is, the utilized paths and flows on those paths that will be observed in equilibrium. If shippers are price takers in the final (destination) market and in the transportation factor market, and are also quality takers (where quality has a single dimension, delay), then the delivered price (DP) faced by the shippers desiring to ship commodities in the market w characterized by origin i and destination j, along path p may be expressed as

$$DP_p(\mathbf{r},\mathbf{h}) = \pi_i + r_p + \phi\, t_p(\mathbf{h}) \qquad \forall (w = (i,j) \in W, \quad p \in P_w). \tag{1}$$

Clearly (1) states that delivered price is the sum of origin price, π_i, the transportation rate on the path p of the shippers' perceived network, r_p, and the monetary value of delay experienced. Note that in (1) the path delay t_p is a function of the shippers' path flow vector $\mathbf{h}$, expressing the presence of congestion in the shippers' network. Some may consider the dependence of delays on flows, leading to congestion phenomena, to be somewhat contro-versial in the case of trucking. See, for example the exchange between Boyer (1980) on the one hand, and DeVany and Saving (1980) on the other. See, additionally, on road congestion, Keeler and Small (1977). However, conges-tion cannot be neglected in network analysis, and so it is retained here. Each shipper is assumed to maximize the profit received from moving goods among the spatially separated markets. Defining W' as the set of OD pairs under a particular shipper's control and π_j as the fixed destination price (DP), the profit function for a particular shipper can be written as

$$\sum_{w = (i,j) \in W'} \sum_{p \in P_w} [\pi_j - \pi_i - r_p - \phi t_p(\mathbf{h})] h_p$$

$$= \sum_{w = (ij) \in w'} \sum_{p \in P_w} [\pi_j - DP_p(\mathbf{r},\mathbf{h})] h_p. \tag{2}$$

At equilibrium we require that the total commodity flow on paths connecting each OD pair w equals the demand for transportation between that OD pair and that flows be nonnegative; that is,

$$S_w(\mathbf{u}) = \sum_{p \in P_w} h_p = 0 \qquad \forall (w \in W') \tag{3}$$

$$\mathbf{h} \geq 0. \tag{4}$$

Since each shipper is assumed to take transportation costs as given, the vector **u** (the vector of minimum delivered prices) is constant, and thus, so are the OD demands $S_w(\mathbf{u})$. Using (3), we can rewrite (2) as

$$\sum_{w=(i,j)\in W'} \left[\pi_j S_w - \sum_{p\in P_w} \mathrm{DP}_p(\mathbf{r},\mathbf{h})h_p \right]. \tag{5}$$

Because π_j and S_w are constant, the first term in (5) can be ignored when maximizing (5), and carrier profit maximization can be expressed as

$$\text{minimize} \sum_{w=(i,j)\in W'} \sum_{p\in P_w} \mathrm{DP}_p(\mathbf{r},\mathbf{h})h_p \tag{6}$$

subject to

$$S_w - \sum_{p\in P_w} h_p = 0 \qquad \forall(w \in W') \quad (u_w)$$

$$\mathbf{h} \ge 0,$$

where u_w is the Kuhn–Tucker multiplier for the flow conservation constraint. Taking the Kuhn–Tucker conditions for each shipper's profit-maximization problem (6), we arrive at the following set of first-order conditions:

$$[\mathrm{DP}_p(\mathbf{r},\mathbf{h}) - u_w]\, h_p = 0 \qquad \forall(w \in W', \quad p \in P_w)$$
$$\mathrm{DP}_p(\mathbf{r},\mathbf{h}) - u_w \ge 0 \qquad \forall(w \in W', \quad p \in P_w), \tag{7}$$

where u_w is the minimum delivered price for OD pair w. In words, positive shipper flow on a path p implies that the carrier-quoted delivered price for that path is the minimum price; otherwise path p has no flow. This condition is Wardrop's first principle of user optimality (Fernandez and Friesz, 1983) expressed in terms of delivered price. Thus, under the assumption of fixed commodity prices, the profit-maximizing behavior of the shippers results in the minimization of delivered price between every OD pair.

It is assumed that there is perfect competition among the freight carriers and, hence, at an equilibrium, rates are equal to marginal costs. Because a particular path will be chosen only if it adds least to total cost, and because path costs are assumed to be additive in arc costs, then in terms of the previous notation this assumption may be expressed as

$$r_p = \sum_{v\in V} \gamma_{vp} y_v \qquad \forall p \in P. \tag{8}$$

The minimum marginal costs y_v depend implicitly on the carriers' flow **g** as will be seen shortly.

Because each carrier is assumed to be a profit maximizer facing an exogenous market price, its short-run behavior is described by the minimization of operating costs. Thus, additional traffic will be carried on that path only if it adds least to total cost. If y_v is the minimum marginal cost (MC) of all paths feasible for the OD pair v, we may express this assumption as

$$(\text{MC}_q(\mathbf{g}) - y_v) \, g_q = 0 \qquad \forall (k, v \in V_k, q \in Q_v)$$
$$\text{MC}_q(\mathbf{g}) - y_v \geq 0 \qquad \forall (k, v \in V_k, q \in Q_v), \tag{9}$$

which says that, for all paths q that are feasible (in Q_v), positive commodity flow implies that costs on that path are at the minimum incremental cost; otherwise path q has no flow. Note that in (9) the marginal path cost MC_q is a function of the carriers' path flow vector $\mathbf{g}$, expressing the presence of congestion in the carriers' network. Because of the linkage between the shippers' and carriers' network, the carriers' flow conservation constraints take the form

$$\sum_{q \in Q_v} g_q - \sum_{p \in P} \gamma_{vp} h_p = 0 \qquad \forall v \in V. \tag{10}$$

In words, for each OD pair v, the sum of carrier flows g_q on the paths connecting v (the paths belonging to Q_v) must equal the sum of shippers' flows h_p that traverse v. Of course we require

$$\mathbf{g} \geq 0 \tag{11}$$

to ensure nonnegative carrier flows.

Expressions (1), (3), (4), (7)–(11) define the combined shipper–carrier equilibrium problem for freight networks. Moreover, (3), (4), (10), and (11) prompt us to define the following set of feasible solutions:

$$\Omega = \left\{ \mathbf{f}, \mathbf{e}, \mathbf{S} : \sum_{p \in P_w} h_p - S_w = 0 \qquad \forall w \in W, \right.$$

$$\sum_{q \in Q} g_q - \sum_{p \in P} \gamma_{vp} h_p = 0 \qquad \forall v \in V,$$

$$f_a - \sum_{p \in P} \delta_{ap} h_p = 0 \qquad \forall a \in A,$$

$$e_b - \sum_{q \in Q} \Delta_{bq} g_q = 0 \qquad \forall b \in B,$$

$$\left. \mathbf{h} \geq 0, \quad \mathbf{g} \geq 0 \right\}.$$

Using the foregoing notation, Friesz, Viton, and Tobin (1985) have shown that an equilibrium point of the combined shipper–carrier model is the solution of a single mathematical problem, as explained in the following theorem.

Theorem 1

A shipper-carrier flow pattern $(\mathbf{f}^*, \mathbf{e}^*, \mathbf{S}^*) \in \Omega$ is a combined shipper-carrier network equilibrium if and only if

$$\phi \sum_{a \in A} t_a(\mathbf{f}^*)(f_a - f_a^*) + \sum_{b \in B} MC_b(\mathbf{e}^*)(e_b - e_b^*)$$

$$+ \sum_{w \in W} [\pi_i - \theta_w(\mathbf{S}^*)](S_w - S_w^*) \geq 0 \qquad (12)$$

for all $(\mathbf{f}, \mathbf{e}, \mathbf{S}) \in \Omega$.

We will use the mathematical characterization (12), known as a "variational inequality," to prove the existence of a combined shipper–carrier equilibrium in the next section.

Assuming that equilibria for this problem exist, what economic properties will they have? As discussed in detail in the introduction, with price-taking behavior from all actors, an equilibrium will be first-best Pareto-optimal relative to the given infrastructure (in particular, the carriers' networks) and the given configuration of firms. In other words, the equilibrium will be a short-run phenomenon. It may or may not be a long-run competitive equilibrium, since the equilibrium here examined may result in negative economic profits for carriers if transport cost functions exhibit economies of scale or scope. Even in this eventuality, of course, the equilibrium is a valuable criterion in assessing networks, since the first-best solution to the requirement that profits be nonnegative (in other words that the industry be feasible in the sense of Baumol, Panzar, and Willig, 1982) is marginal-cost pricing with lump-sum taxation if necessary.

3.3. Existence and uniqueness of a simultaneous shipper–carrier equilibrium

In this section we give immediate proofs of the existence and uniqueness of equilibria in our model. The method of proof is based on the recognition that the equilibrium conditions stated in the last section define a "variational inequality"; we then apply available existence and uniqueness theorems for variational inequalities.

Before proceeding to the results, some general remarks on the technique used here are in order, because we believe that the applicability of the methodology, together with the efficient computational methods available makes these techniques widely useful in economic problems [for example, as an alternative to Scarf's (1973) method of calculating equilibria]. A variational inequality problem is

find $\mathbf{x} \in D$ such that
$$\mathbf{F(x)} \cdot (\bar{\mathbf{x}} - \mathbf{x}) \geq 0$$
for all $\bar{x} \in D$ \hfill (13)

where $\mathbf{x} = (x_1, \ldots, x_n)$, $\mathbf{F(x)} = [F_1(\mathbf{x}), \ldots, F_l(\mathbf{x}), \ldots, F_n(\mathbf{x})]$, and $F_i: D \subseteq R^n \to$ R with n finite. The existence and uniqueness conditions for this problem are readily characterized. For present purposes we note that two other problems may be transformed into variational inequalities. Consider first the nonlinear complementarity problem, to find $\mathbf{x}$ such that

$$\mathbf{F(x)} \cdot \mathbf{x} = 0   \mathbf{F(x)} \geq 0   \mathbf{x} \geq 0. \hfill (14)$$

This problem has immediate application to the computation of equilibria, and generalizes linear models to nonlinear formulations. The crucial result is stated for example, by Lemke (1980): The nonlinear complementary problem (14) is completely equivalent to the variational inequality (13) provided that $D = \{\mathbf{x}: \mathbf{x} \geq 0\}$. Also, consider the optimization problem

$$\text{Min } G(\mathbf{x})   \mathbf{x} \in D \hfill (15)$$

where $\nabla G(x) = \mathbf{F(x)}$, or $G(\mathbf{x}) = \oint \mathbf{F(x)} dx$, provided appropriate integrability conditions hold. It is immediate (see Rockafellar, 1980) that the necessary conditions for a local solution to (15) are given by (13), and that if G is convex, the solution is global. In other words, the solution of the variational inequality (13) is useful in the characterization and solution of a large number of problems of interest to economists.

With this excursion we now return to the main argument. In the context of the variational inequality problem (13), it is well known that if $\mathbf{F(x)}$ is continuous and D is compact (closed and bounded) and convex, then (13) has a solution. This result was first proven by Hartman and Stampacchia (1966) and is reported by Kinderlehrer and Stampacchia (1980). It is also well known that if $\mathbf{F(x)}$ is strictly monotone on D, any solution of (13) is unique. Thus, we may state the following two theorems without detailed proofs.

Theorem 2
Suppose the functions $t_a(\mathbf{f})$, $MC_b(\mathbf{e})$, and $\theta_w(\mathbf{s})$ are continuous and the shipper transportation demand functions $S_w(\mathbf{u})$ are bounded from above. Then a combined shipper–carrier freight network equilibrium exists.

Proof
The boundedness of the $S_w(\mathbf{u})$ implies $\mathbf{g}$ and $\mathbf{h}$ are bounded from above. Hence, Ω is a bounded set. By inspection Ω is closed. It is composed of linear constraints and, therefore, convex. Hence, by Theorem 3.1 on page 12 of Kinderlehrer and Stampacchia (1980) a combined shipper–carrier equilibrium exists. Q.E.D.

Theorem 3

A combined shipper–carrier freight network equilibrium exists and is unique if

i. the shipper travel delay functions $t_a(\mathbf{f})$ are continuous and strictly monotone increasing;

ii. the carrier marginal cost functions $MC_b(\mathbf{e})$ are continuous and strictly monotone increasing;

iii. the inverse shipper transportation demand functions $\theta_w(\mathbf{S})$ are continuous and strictly monotone decreasing; and

iv. the shipper transportation demand functions $S_w(\mathbf{u})$ are bounded from above.

Proof

Theorem 2 ensures existence. The strict monotonicity assumptions, by page 14 of Kinderlehrer and Stampacchia (1980), guarantee uniqueness.   Q.E.D.

It is important to recognize that in some freight environments the assumption of strict monotonicity is unrealistic. For example, Morlok (1978) describes cases for which rail travel delay is a decreasing function for low flow volume and an increasing function for higher volume, and, thus, not monotonic at all. When strict monotonicity is not maintained, it is possible that multiple equilibria will occur.

3.4.   Extensions of the simultaneous shipper–carrier model

The Friesz, Viton, and Tobin (1985) simultaneous shipper–carrier model makes the rather strong assumption that freight rates will equal marginal costs in all transportation markets. As discussed in Section 3.1, this assumption may not be unrealistic for the motor carrier industry. In analyzing the railroad, inland waterway, and deep-draft waterway systems, it may appear as if this assumption is completely unrealistic and hence useless. However, the marginal-cost pricing assumption does have merit even in these cases. First, from a pragmatic perspective, the mathematical models that are based upon the decentralization of each agents' decision are far easier to solve. In essentially all large-scale economic models the concept of marginal-cost pricing is used because it leads to a manageable fixed-point problem. When models are developed that attempt to capture the game-theoretic interactions between agents, they are typically difficult if not impossible to solve for large-scale problems. For example, the recent model by Fisk and Boyce (1983) is an attempt to formulate a Stackelberg model of freight system. The model is stated as a set of nonlinear, nonconvex mathematical programs with nonlinear, nonconvex constraints comprising the model of shippers' demand (these constraints are in the form of a nonlinear complementarity problem). This mathematical form is very similar to the model by Harker (1981) (see also Harker and Friesz, 1982). Fisk and Boyce (1983) have suggested some methods of solution, but none has been tested. In the numerical studies done on the Harker (1981) model, it was found that even small test examples were very difficult to solve and that the use of this model for large-scale problems was impossible. One may immediately say that the solution of a model is not important as long as its theoretical underpinnings are correct; this we believe is false. No one theory is completely correct, and it is the purpose of modeling to implement theory on actual data and test its correlation with reality. If a model is stated that is insoluble, it cannot be tested against data. The marginal-cost pricing assumption does lend itself readily to empirical tests. If these tests show that this assumption is very poor, then it is time to expand the theoretical framework. If these tests show that the use of this assumption replicates the empirical data fairly well, then we can have some confidence in the use of this model while at the same time we strive to expand the theory. Therefore, the logical first step in modeling freight systems is to begin with the marginal-cost pricing assumption, test its validity, and use it as a basis to develop more sophisticated models.

The second argument in favor of beginning with the marginal-cost pricing assumption is that it does provide a basis for comparison with models based upon other economic assumptions. As Heaver and Nelson (1978, pp. 128–29) write: "the model of perfect, or pure, competition is usually regarded as a standard by which a firm's pricing can be judged, even when the industry under consideration does not have firms which exhibit all of the rather stringent assumptions, that theory requires of the truly competitive firm." Friedlaender and Spady (1981, p. 75) put this argument more succinctly: "an analysis of a competitive equilibrium provides a useful benchmark with respect to the characteristics of the outcome of the competitive process." Thus, the marginal-cost pricing model does have merit in its use as a basis to judge other solutions.

The last argument is that it may not matter very much if we use marginal-cost pricing or some model of imperfect competition for commodities for which there is strong intermodal competition. In their study of midwestern agricultural goods movements, Daughety and Inaba (1981) found that there was very little difference between the rail rates in a perfectly competitive market and when the railroads acted as one firm (perfect collusion, the polar extreme of perfect competition). Thus, for some commodities the use of the perfect-competition assumption may yield essentially the same results as a more sophisticated model.

We still would like to extend the theoretical framework of the simultaneous shipper–carrier model, however, to be able to deal with imperfectly competitive markets: Harker (1983) (see also Harker and Friesz, 1985a,b) has done this through the use of a concept called a "rate function." Before

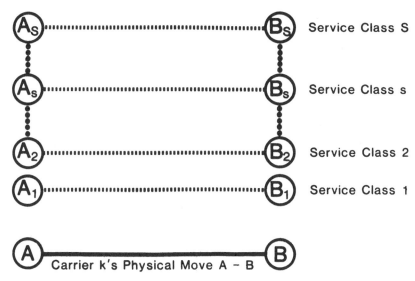

Figure 7.4. Service class network.

discussing this, however, let us first clarify one issue concerning the previous model.

At first glance, the Friesz, Viton, and Tobin model seems to assume that the only competitive factor is the freight rate. From transportation economics, however, we know that both price and level of service affect the choice of a transportation mode. One could include both a price variable and a level of service variable as part of the carrier's decision model as Fisk and Boyce (1983) have done, but their inclusion would make the model even more difficult to solve. The approach taken here is to define for each carrier OD move a set of level of service classes. In reality, there is a continuum of service classes that a carrier could offer a shipper; we are approximating this continuum by a discrete set of service classes. Figure 7.4 illustrates this concept. Each physical carrier OD pair is represented by a set of OD pairs, each having a particular service class associated with it. If carrier k supplies service between A_1 and B_1, it is actually providing this service in level of service class 1. Thus, we have expanded each carrier OD pair into a set of multiple outputs, each being represented as a particular OD pair in this extended network.

The previous discussion noted that the decentralization of each agent's decision allows one to formulate a solvable mathematical model. Harker (1983) recognized this fact when exploring the possibility of extending the simultaneous shipper–carrier model to include imperfect competition and developed the concept of a rate function. The rate function $R_\nu(\tau)$ is our a priori assumption concerning the rate a carrier will charge for service on its OD pair $v \in V$ given the vector of carrier OD flows $\tau = (\ldots,\tau_v,\ldots)$:

$$\tau_v = \sum_{q \in Q_v} g_q = \sum_{p \in P} \gamma_{vp} h_p \tag{16}$$

Under the marginal-cost pricing assumption, the rate function would equal y_v, the minimum marginal cost between OD pair v. More generally, the rate function could be used under the assumption of cost-plus pricing (rate = some markup over average cost), or pricing up to a legal limit such as those imposed by the Stagger's Act. This approach does not assume that the carrier has knowledge of the shippers' transportation demand functions as would a Cournot–Nash model of this market. Thus, this approach is not in the strictest sense a noncooperative game-theoretic model of the freight system; the rate function is an approximation of this type of model. As Harker and Friesz (1985b) discuss, this approximation retains the decentralization of each agent's decisions that is present in the marginal-cost pricing model. However, this approach has merit beyond being an approximation to a game-theoretic model. Many economists, especially those studying industrial organization, do not believe that firms behave in the manner described by the Cournot–Nash model, but in fact do price according to some simple principle such as cost-plus pricing. In reality, the firm's pricing policy most likely lies between the extremes of having perfect information concerning the demand behavior of the shippers and pricing according to some simple formula. The rate function allows one to test various pricing policies in terms of their power in replicating historical data. Thus, the rate function can be considered a method of approximating more complex game-theoretic models and a method of testing alternative pricing policies that the carriers may follow in large-scale applications.

The model of the previous section can easily be expanded to include the rate function, as the following theorem shows:

Theorem 4

A shipper–carrier flow pattern $(\mathbf{f}^*, \mathbf{e}^*, \mathbf{S}^*) \in \Omega$ is a combined shipper–carrier network equilibrium when the freight rates on each carrier OD pair are described by the rate function $R_v(\tau)$ if and only if

$$\phi \sum_{a \in A} t_a(\mathbf{f}^*)(f_a - f_a^*) = \sum_{b \in B} MC_b e^*(e_b - e_b^*)$$
$$+ \sum_{w \in W} [\pi_i - \theta_w(\mathbf{S}^*)](S_w - S_w^*)$$
$$+ \sum_{v \in V} [R_v(\tau^*) - y_v^*](\tau_v - \tau_v^*) \geq 0 \tag{17}$$

for all $(\mathbf{f},\mathbf{e},\mathbf{S}) \in \Omega$.

Proof
This proof is a special case of the proof in Theorem 3.4 of Harker (1983) or Theorem 4 of Harker and Friesz (1985b).

Harker (1983) has also shown that this model can be cast in the form of a nonlinear complementarity problem, has used this form to prove existence and uniqueness, and has developed solution algorithms for this new model; the next section will discuss these results further. The point is that through the use of this rate-function concept, we need not rely solely on the marginal-cost pricing assumption in order to apply these models to problems of realistic size.

4.   Simultaneity of macroeconomic and network models

As shown in Table 7.1, the freight models applied to date have all used exogenously determined commodity supplies and demands. These fixed freight trip productions and attractions have been forecast using various economic models that treat the freight transportation system in an aggregate fashion. Consequently, when such economic models are employed sequentially with a detailed freight network model, the question of consistency of the two models naturally arises. The legitimacy of this question was unintentionally demonstrated by the work of Charles River Associates (CRA) (1981). CRA iterated between a macroeconomic coal model (the National Coal Model) and a version of the CACI freight network model; they found this approach to be numerically unstable and nonconvergent, as well as computationally intensive.

Recent work by Friesz, Tobin, and Harker (1981), Friesz and Tobin (1981), Friesz et al. (1983), Tobin and Friesz (1983), and Friesz, Harker, and Tobin (1985) has shown that the "spatial price equilibrium problem" may be generalized to treat arbitrary networks with congestion externalities and demand and supply asymmetries. The spatial price equilibrium problem does not employ explicit transportation demand functions; instead it derives transportation demand from the production and consumption characteristics of spatially separated markets. As such, a spatial price equilibrium model can be used as a replacement for the Wardropian shipper model discussed previously; because such a model may employ elastic commodity supply and demand functions for each node, trip generation becomes endogenous and the problem of consistency we mentioned is avoided.

Gottfried (1983) has generalized the FNEM model to include trip generation by incorporating commodity supply and demand functions for each regional centroid, following the formulation of the spatial price equilibrium problem by Tobin and Friesz (1983). A demand-driven (supply functions only) version of this formulation has been programmed and applied to study

U.S. coal movements (see Tobin et al. (1983). However, this new model suffers from the same inconsistency between the shipper and carrier sub-models as is found in FNEM due to the sequential nature of FNEM.

Harker (1983) (see also Harker and Friesz 1985a,b) has recently stated a model called the "generalized spatial price equilibrium model" (GSPEM), which ties together the concepts of spatial price equilibrium and shipper–carrier equilibrium to predict simultaneously the production and consumption of goods, the shippers' routing of freight, the freight rates using the rate-function concept, and the carriers' routing of the freight traffic. We can briefly describe this model by using the notation of the previous sections and defining L to be the set of regions (actually the regional centroids) where production or consumption of goods occurs and

$$
\begin{aligned}
Q_l^S &= \text{the supply in region } \ell \in L, \\
Q_l^D &= \text{the demand in region } \ell \in L \\
\mathbf{Q}^S &= (...,Q_\ell^S,...), \\
\mathbf{Q}^D &= (...,Q_\ell^D,...), \\
\psi_\ell(\mathbf{Q}^S) &= \text{the inverse supply function for region } \ell \in L, \\
\Lambda_\ell(\mathbf{Q}^D) &= \text{the inverse demand function for region } \ell \in L.
\end{aligned}
$$

Therefore ψ_ℓ is the price a shipper would pay for the commodity at the production site ℓ and Λ_ℓ is the price for which this good could be sold in region ℓ. The conservation of flow in every region can be written as

$$
Q_\ell^D - Q_\ell^S + \sum_{w=(\ell,j)\in W} T_w - \sum_{w=(i,\ell)\in W} T_w = 0 \qquad \forall \ell \in L \quad (18)
$$

The spatial price-equilibrium concept states that if there is flow on a path between two regions, then the purchase price plus the transportation cost will equal the sale price at the destination in equilibrium. If the purchase price plus the transportation cost is less than the sale price, the shipper has an incentive to keep shipping goods until these terms equalize. If the purchase price plus the transportation cost is greater than the sale price, the shipper has no incentive to ship anything between these two regions since he would lose money in doing so; the flow on this path would thus be zero at equilibrium. To add these conditions to the simultaneous shipper–carrier model described in the previous section, let us first notice that the delivered price can be rewritten as

$$
\text{DP}_p(\mathbf{r},\mathbf{h}) = \psi_i(\mathbf{Q}^S) + r_p + \phi t_p(\mathbf{h}). \ \forall \ (w = (i,j) \in W, \ p \in P_w) \quad (19)
$$

The shipper equilibrium condition (7) is then replaced by the following:

$$
\left.
\begin{aligned}
[\text{DP}_p(\mathbf{r},\mathbf{h}) - \Lambda_j(\mathbf{Q}^D)]h_p &= 0 \quad \forall \ (w = (i,j) \in W, \ p \in P_w) \\
\text{DP}_p(\mathbf{r},\mathbf{h}) - \Lambda_j(\mathbf{Q}^D) &\geq 0 \qquad \forall \ (w = (i,j) \in W, \ p \in P_w)
\end{aligned}
\right\} \quad (20)
$$

or

$$[\psi_i(\mathbf{Q^S}) + (r_p + \phi t_p(\mathbf{h})) - \Lambda_j(\mathbf{Q^D})]h_p = 0 \ \forall \ (w = (i,j) \in W, p \in P_w)$$
$$\psi_i(\mathbf{Q^S}) + (r_p + \phi t_p(\mathbf{h})) - \Lambda_j(\mathbf{Q^D}) \geq 0. \ \Bigg\} \ (21)$$

By redefining the feasible set Ω as

$$\Omega = \{(\mathbf{Q^S}, \mathbf{Q^D}, \mathbf{f}, \mathbf{e}, \mathbf{S}):$$

$$Q_\ell^D - Q_1^S + \sum_{w=(\ell,j) \in W} T_w - \sum_{w=(i,\ell) \in W} T_w = 0 \qquad \forall \ell \in L;$$

$$\sum_{q \in Q_v} g_q - \sum_{p \in P} \gamma_{vp} h_p = 0 \qquad \forall v \in V;$$

$$f_a - \sum_{p \in P} \delta_{ap} h_p = 0 \qquad \forall a \in A;$$

$$e_b - \sum_{q \in Q} \Delta_{bq} g_q = 0 \qquad \forall b \in B;$$

$$\mathbf{Q^S} \geq 0, \quad \mathbf{Q^D} \geq 0, \quad \mathbf{h} \geq 0, \quad \mathbf{g} \geq 0\},$$

we can incorporate the spatial price–equilibrium concept into the model described in Theorem 4 as follows:

Theorem 5

The production-consumption-flow pattern

$$(\mathbf{Q}^{S*}, \mathbf{Q}^{D*}, \mathbf{f}^*, \mathbf{e}^*, \mathbf{S}^*) \in \Omega$$

is a combined spatial price-shipper-carrier equilibrium if and only if

$$\sum_{\ell \in L} \psi_\ell(\mathbf{Q}^{S*})(Q_\ell^S - Q_\ell^{S*}) = \sum_{\ell \in L} \Lambda_\ell(\mathbf{Q}^{D*})(Q_\ell^D - Q_\ell^{D*})$$

$$+ \phi \sum_{a \in A} t_a(\mathbf{f}^*)(f_a^* - f_a^*)$$

$$+ \sum_{b \in B} MC_b(\mathbf{e}^*)(e_b - e_b^*)$$

$$+ \sum_{v \in V} [R_v(\mathbf{\tau}^*) - y_v^*](\tau_v - \tau_v^*) \geq 0 \ (22)$$

for all $(\mathbf{Q^S}, \mathbf{Q^D}, \mathbf{f}, \mathbf{e}, \mathbf{S}) \in \Omega$.

Proof
See Harker (1983) or Harker and Friesz (1985b).

Harker (1983) also proves that this model can be cast in the form of a nonlinear complementarity problem. Using this formulation and the recent existence results by Smith (1984) for this class of problem, Harker (1983, pp. 66–73) proves that a combined spatial price, shipper–carrier equilibrium will exist as long as the functions are continuous; r_p, t_a and MC_b are strictly positive; and in every region there exists a price for which the supply in that region will exceed the demand in that region for any other price above this level. Thus, GSPEM is capable of using U-shaped cost curves on the carrier arcs, which is a typical case when dealing with railroad networks. The assumption of monotone marginal arc costs (which implies that the average costs are never decreasing with increasing flow) is not necessary for this model to have a solution. However, the assumption that marginal costs are strictly increasing is necessary to insure the uniqueness of an equilibrium; the use of U-shaped average-cost functions implies the existence of multiple equilibria. What can be said at this point is that GSPEM is the most complete predictive model of the freight transportation system to date; it can use realistic arc cost functions, does not rely on the marginal-cost pricing assumption, and simultaneously includes the generation of freight trips and the equilibrium behavior of the shippers and carriers.

Harker (1983) (also see Harker and Friesz, 1985c), has also developed two solution algorithms for this model. The first algorithm is for use on the nonlinear complementarity problem formulation and its convergence properties are based upon the recent work by Pang and Chan (1982). With this algorithm, any form of the rate function can be used. However, this type of algorithm requires a fair amount of computer storage and thus it is limited to problems that are not excessively large. For very large problems, Harker (1983) has developed an algorithm for the variational inequality problem (22) which is based upon the assumption of marginal-cost pricing (this algorithm is a variant of the algorithm suggested by Friesz, Viton, and Tobin, 1985). In this case $R_v = y_v$ for all $v \in V$ and thus the last summation in (22) disappears. The resulting variational inequality is then solved by a diagonalization algorithm (see, for example, Pang and Chan, 1982 or Dafermos, 1983) in which each function in (22) is made to be separable (the function depends only upon one variable, and not a vector of variables) to form a sequence of separable variational inequalities. Of course, if the functions are separable to start with, the diagonalization algorithm collapses to the solution of one variational inequality problem. This algorithm is capable of solving very large problems, as evidenced by the application of this model that will be described in the sequel. Finally, both of these algorithms are capable of dealing with nonmonotonic cost functions; Harker (1983, ch. 5) presents proofs that if these algorithms converge, they will converge to a true equilibrium solution in this case.

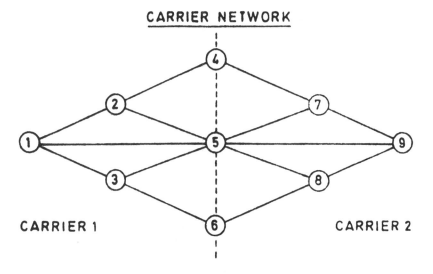

CARRIER NETWORK

CARRIER 1   CARRIER 2

SHIPPER NETWORK

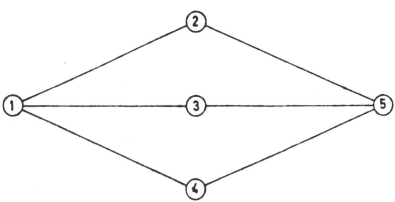

Figure 7.5. Test networks for example.

To illustrate the concepts discussed in this section, consider the networks depicted in Figure 7.5. The networks of the two carriers have been aggregated to form the shipper network as described in Section 3.1. The supply and demand function in each region is given by

Table 7.2. *Data for example*

Carrier network data

Arc b	From node	To node	XH_b	XI_b	XJ_b
1	1	2	4.0	0.1	0.01
2	1	3	3.0	0.2	0.02
3	1	5	2.0	0.2	0.03
4	2	1	1.0	0.1	0.04
5	2	4	4.0	0.1	0.01
6	2	5	3.0	0.2	0.04
7	3	1	2.0	0.2	0.03
8	3	5	1.0	0.1	0.04
9	3	6	4.0	0.1	0.01
10	4	2	3.0	0.2	0.02
11	4	7	2.0	0.2	0.03
12	5	1	1.0	0.1	0.04
13	5	2	4.0	0.1	0.01
14	5	3	3.0	0.2	0.02
15	5	7	2.0	0.2	0.03
16	5	8	1.0	0.1	0.04
17	5	9	4.0	0.1	0.01
18	6	3	3.0	0.2	0.02
19	6	8	2.0	0.2	0.03
20	7	4	1.0	0.1	0.04
21	7	5	4.0	0.1	0.01
22	7	9	3.0	0.2	0.02
23	8	5	2.0	0.2	0.03
24	8	6	1.0	0.1	0.04
25	8	9	4.0	0.1	0.01
26	9	5	3.0	0.2	0.02
27	9	7	2.0	0.2	0.03
28	9	8	1.0	0.1	0.04

Shipper network data

Arc a	From node	To node	XK_a	XL_a	XM_a
1	1	2	1.0	0.01	0.001
2	1	3	2.0	0.02	0.002
3	1	4	1.0	0.09	0.002
4	2	1	2.0	0.01	0.001
5	2	5	3.0	0.02	0.002
6	3	1	1.0	0.03	0.002
7	3	5	1.0	0.01	0.001
8	4	1	2.0	0.01	0.004
9	4	5	1.0	0.01	0.001
10	5	2	3.0	0.02	0.001
11	5	3	6.0	0.05	0.002
12	5	4	1.0	0.03	0.005

Table 7.2. (*Continued*)

Node ℓ	XA_ℓ	XB_ℓ	XC_ℓ	XE_ℓ	XF_ℓ	XG_ℓ
1	0.0	0.1	0.05	400.0	−2.0	−4.5
5	0.0	0.01	0.025	500.0	−1.0	−0.05

Note: $\phi = 1.0$, the value of time.

$$Q_\ell^S = XA_\ell + XB_\ell \pi_\ell + XC_\ell \pi_\ell^2 \quad \forall\, \ell \in L \tag{23}$$

$$Q_\ell^D = XE_\ell + XF_\ell \pi_\ell + XG_\ell \pi_\ell^2 \quad \forall\, \ell \in L \tag{24}$$

where π_ℓ is the price in region ℓ and XA_ℓ, XB_ℓ, XC_ℓ, XE_ℓ, XF_ℓ, and XG_ℓ are constants. The inverse supply and demand functions are found by numerically inverting (23) and (24). The time-delay functions on the shipper arcs are given by

$$t_a = XK_a + XL_a f_a + XM_a f_a^2 \quad \forall\, a \in A \tag{25}$$

where XK_a, XL_a, and XM_a are constants, and the marginal-cost functions for the carrier arcs are

$$MC_b = XH_b + 2.0 XI_b e_b + 1.5 XJ_b e_b^2 \quad \forall\, b \in B \tag{26}$$

where XH_b, XI_b, and XJ_b are constants. Table 7.2 lists the data for this example.

Let us first assume that $R_v = y_v$ $\forall\, v \in V$, that is, there is marginal-cost pricing on all carrier OD pairs. Table 7.3 presents the results of the model. As the reader can easily verify, all equilibrium conditions have been attained. Therefore, this small example illustrates that the solution of GSPEM does indeed yield a simultaneous solution of the spatial price–shipper–carrier equilibrium conditions. To illustrate the use of alternative rate-function specifications, let us assume that the rate for any carrier OD pair will be equal to $10 plus one half the marginal cost, or that

$$R_v = 10 + 0.5\, y_v \quad \forall\, v \in V \tag{27}$$

Thus, the rate is some fixed value plus a percentage of the marginal costs. Note that any rate specification could be used; (27) is used just for illustrative purposes. Table 7.4 presents the results of the model with this alternative rate specification. Again, all the necessary equilibrium conditions are met.

5.   Applications of FNEM and GSPEM

FNEM, the sequential shipper–carrier freight network equilibrium model described in Section 1, has been extensively tested and used in various studies of

Table 7.3. *Results of marginal-cost pricing example*

Shipper network results

Node	π_ℓ	Q_ℓ^S	Q_ℓ^D	$Q_\ell^S - Q_\ell^D$
1	27.624	40.917	1.358	39.560
5	71.908	129.990	169.550	−39.560

			Traverses			
OD $w = (i,j)$	S_w	u_w	Path p	nodes	h_p	DP_p
1,5	39.560	44.280	1	1,4,5	8.029	71.904
			2	1,3,5	21.724	71.919
			3	1,2,5	9.807	71.907
5,1	0.000	3.000	1	5,4,1	0.000	74.908

Carrier network results[a]

			Traverses			
OD $v = (i,j)$	T_v	y_v	Path q	nodes	g_p	MC_q
1,4	9.807	17.249	1	1,2,4	9.807	17.249
1,5	21.724	15.161	1	1,5	13.225	15.161
			2	1,2,5	4.362	15.161
			3	1,3,5	4.137	15.161
1,6	8.029	18.879	1	1,3,6	8.029	18.879
4,9	9.807	20.119	1	4,7,9	9.807	20.119
5,9	21.724	11.897	1	5,9	17.224	11.897
			2	5,7,9	0.062	11.897
			3	5,8,9	4.438	11.897
6,9	8.029	16.935	1	6,8,9	8.029	16.935

[a]Only those OD pairs and paths with flows are shown.

commodity movements in the United States. In terms of validation, Gottfried (1983) and Friesz, Gottfried, and Morlok (1983) report on tests conducted with three network data bases: (1) a highly detailed railway and waterway network data base of the northeastern United States with a single aggregate commodity and five rail carriers (the northeast validation), (2) a somewhat more aggregate railway network data base of the entire United States with fifteen commodities and a single aggregate rail carrier (the national rail validation), and (3) a combined railway and waterway network database of the entire United States with fifteen commodities and seventeen rail carriers (the "full" national validation). A summary of the characteristics of these validation exercises is given in Table 7.5. The network data bases used in these

Table 7.4. *Results of nonmarginal-cost pricing example*

Shipper network results

Node	π_ℓ	Q_ℓ^S	Q_ℓ^D	$Q_\ell^S - Q_\ell^D$
1	27.488	40.529	4.999	35.530
5	72.249	131.222	166.752	−35.530

			Traverses		
OD $w = (i,j)$	S_w	u_w	Path p nodes	h_p	DP_p
1,5	35.530	44.662	1 1,4,5	7.810	72.150
			2 1,3,5	18.071	72.465
			3 1,2,5	9.649	72.217
5,1	0.000	23.000	1 5,4,1	0.000	95.249

Carrier network results[a]

			Traverses		
OD $v = (i,j)$	T_v	y_v	Path q nodes	g_p	MC_q
1,4	9.649	16.211	1 1,2,4	9.649	16.211
1,5	18.071	13.355	1 1,5	11.995	13.355
			2 1,2,5	2.890	13.355
			3 1,3,5	3.186	13.356
1,6	7.810	17.493	1 1,3,6	7.819	17.493
4,9	9.649	19.637	1 4,7,9	9.649	19.637
5,9	18.071	10.369	1 5,9	14.861	10.369
			2 5,7,9	0.000	11.624
			3 5,8,9	3.210	10.371
6,9	7.810	15.827	1 6,8,9	7.810	15.827

[a]Only those OD pairs and paths with flows are shown.

validation exercises were primarily assembled from sources in the the public domain: the U.S. Federal Railroad Administration (FRA) (1980a,b), CACI (1980), Roberts and Dewees (1971), the Interstate Commerce Commission (1975, 1981), and the Transportation Systems Center (1980). In addition commercial data services were employed as required: Data Resources (1981) and Reebie and Associates (1982). Some original surveys to determine arc and modal-cost functions were conducted as described in Friesz et al. (1981) and Gottfried (1983). Transportation demand functions were of the negative exponential or entropy maximization variety suggested by Wilson (1970).

The link loadings produced by the model have been compared against the historical usage of rail links for the base year 1978. The historical usage is

Table 7.5. *Summary of FNEM validation exercises*

Characteristics	Validation name Northeast	National rail	National
Study of region	Northeast	Nation	Nation
Number of modes	2[a]	1	2[a]
Number of commodities	1	15	15
Zone definition	Transportation zone[b]	TBEA[c]	BEA[d]
Number of zones	105	129	183
Number of OD pairs	10,920	29,225	42,087
Shippers' network	FRA[e]	TSC[f]	TSC[f]
Number of shipper nodes	2,258	1,594	3,072
Number of shipper arcs	9,799	7,341	14,589
Number of rail carriers	5	1	17
Carriers' network	FRA[e]	TSC[f]	FRA[e]
Solution time (CPU minutes)[g]	35	14	86

[a]Rail and barge.
[b]There are 105 U.S. Department of Transportation (DOT) zones in the northeastern United States.
[c]Traffic BEAs or TBEAs are defined by FRA (1980b).
[d]Bureau of Economic Analysis area.
[e]FRA.
[f]Transportation Systems Center of U.S. DOT.
[g]These correspond to time on an IBM 370/3033.

derived from the density codes assigned to rail links by the FRA (1980a). The FRA density codes are given in Table 7.6. Table 7.7 exhibits the cumulative frequency distribution of the differences between the FRA historical data and the densities computed by Friesz, Gottfried, and Morlok (1983) and Gottfried (1983) in different validation exercises involving FNEM and by another recent attempt to model large scale multicommodity freight movements, the multimodal network model (MNM) (Bronzini, 1980a,b). The results presented in Table 7.6 for the MNM are the only presently available quantitative accuracy tests of a large-scale freight-network model against which to compare FNEM. As can be seen, FNEM performed substantially better than MNM. Furthermore, in the national rail and the full national validations of FNEM, the availability of commodity-specific data about OD transportation demands allows analysis of how well the OD flows predicted by FNEM conform to known data. Since previous large-scale freight-network models have tended to be based on fixed transportation demands, there are no reported predictions of this type against which to compare the model. Smith and Hutchinson (1981) recommend the three goodness-of-fit measures described in Table 7.8 for the evaluation of doubly constrained gravity-demand models

Table 7.6. *FRA density codes*

Code	Annual gross tons (millions)
1	0–1
2	1–5
3	5–10
4	10–20
5	20–30
6	>30

Table 7.7. *Differences between predicted railroad link traffic densities and FRA density codes*

Density code difference	MNM	Northeast FNEM	National rail FNEM	Full national FNEM
0	21	43	56	63
±1	55	74	76	80
±2	76	84	92	93
±3	90	92	97	97
±4	97	96	98	99
±5	99	100	100	100
±6	100	—	100	—

Table 7.8. *Definitions of goodness-of-fit statistics*

R^2 (coefficient of determination)	$1 - \dfrac{\sum_i \sum_j (T_{ij} - T_{ij}^*)^2}{\sum_i \sum_j (T_{ij} - \bar{T})^2}$
Φ (normalized)	$\sum_i \sum_j \dfrac{T_{ij}}{\hat{T}} \left\lvert \ln \dfrac{T_{ij}}{T_{ij}^*} \right\rvert$
M (normalized mean absolute error)	$\dfrac{1}{N} \sum_i \sum_j \left\lvert \dfrac{T_{ij} - T_{ij}^*}{\hat{T}} \right\rvert$

Legend: T_{ij} = observed flow from i to j.
T_{ij}^* = predicted flow from i to j.
$\bar{T}$ = mean flow of all OD pairs.
$\hat{T}$ = total flow for all OD pairs.
N = number of OD pairs.

Table 7.9. *Goodness of fit of origin–destination flows for national rail validation*

Category	R^2	Φ	M
Grain	.53	1.199	.719
Iron ore	.62	.975	.679
Coal	.53	.832	.667
Stone, sand gravel	1.00	.146	.095
Nonmetallic minerals	.85	.939	.607
Grain mill products	1.00	.322	.237
Food products	.69	.984	.641
Forest products	.44	1.029	.813
Lumber and wood products	.36	.770	.658
Pulp and paper mill products	.36	.852	.701
Chemicals	.65	.677	.566
Cement, clay, and glass	.54	.974	.777
Primary metal products	.70	.737	.571
Transportation equipment	.81	.573	.476
All other	.40	1.226	.903
Overall	.89	.916	.637
Range	.36–1.00	.146–1.226	.095–.903
Mean	.65	.822	.609

like that employed in FNEM; these are the coefficient of determination (R^2), normalized phi (ϕ), and normalized mean absolute error (M). An ideal value of R^2 is 1, while the ideal value of ϕ or M is 0. The goodness-of-fit results by commodity for the national rail and the full national validations are presented, respectively, in Tables 7.9 and 7.10, which are drawn from Friesz, Gottfried, and Morlok (1983) and Gottfried (1983).

In addition to the three applications described, FNEM has been used in a series of regional transportation studies. For example, Tobin, Jastrow, and Meleski (1983) report on the use of FNEM in assessing the impacts of power-plants converting to coal in the state of Florida. In summary, FNEM has proven itself to be a useful tool for policy analysis.

In order to illustrate the applicability of GSPEM (the simultaneous spatial price-shipper-carrier model) to realistic problems, Harker (1983) describes the application of this model to the problem of predicting domestic coal production, consumption and interregional flows. In conjunction with Argonne National Laboratory, the marginal-cost pricing version of GSPEM and its associated solution algorithm were implemented for use with the Bureau of Economic Affairs (BEA) Economic Areas and Argonne's version of the Transportation Systems Center's rail and waterway networks; Figure 7.6 illus-

Table 7.10. *Goodness of fit of origin–destination flows full national application*

Category	R^2	Φ	M
Grain	.71	.893	.582
Iron ore	.69	.884	.601
Coal	.74	.658	.553
Stone, sand gravel	.98	.228	.117
Nonmetallic minerals	.89	.825	.561
Grain mill products	.96	.339	.260
Food products	.65	.991	.666
Forest products	.55	.908	.751
Lumber and wood products	.49	.602	.581
Pulp and paper mill products	.52	.636	.596
Chemicals	.81	.490	.448
Cement, clay, and glass	.47	.992	.814
Primary metal products	.63	.801	.619
Transportation equipment	.83	.551	.449
All other	—	—	—
Overall	.91	.876	.613
Range	.47–.98	.228–.992	.117–.814
Mean	.71	.700	.543

trates the rail network. The final database used consisted of eighteen carriers, 2,577 nodes and 7,668 arcs in the carriers' network, and 960 nodes, 6,993 arcs and 1,238 origin–destination pairs in the shippers' network. Two runs of GSPEM were made. In the first run, the 1980 levels of coal exports from the ports of New Orleans, Hampton Roads, Baltimore, Philadelphia, New York, Toledo, and Mobile were taken as given and a base-year comparison of the model's results with the historical 1980 data was performed. In general, the model performed well. The total solution time for this run was 33.05 CPU minutes on an IBM 370/3033, which is very good considering the size of the problem and the amount of information which the model yields (predictions of regional prices, supplies and demands of coal, interregional coal flows and the routing of the coal traffic on the rail and water networks). In the second run, a comparative statics analysis was performed on the possibility of coal exports doubling in volume and the ports of Philadelphia, New York, and Mobile being closed to coal traffic. The results of this run when compared with the base-year results allowed analysis of the effects these events would have on the regional prices of coal, the interregional flows of coal, and the potential congestion of certain links in the transportation network. As expected, the domestic supply level rose and the domestic demand level dropped

Figure 7.6. Rail network of the U.S. Department of Transportation's Transportation Systems Center.

because of this increase in foreign demand and the upward pressure this demand places upon the regional coal prices. However, the solution of this scenario exhibited some nonintuitive results. For example some of the remaining ports where coal traffic doubled saw a *decrease* in flow from certain BEA regions, whereas one would expect flows from all BEA regions to increase with increased exports. This nonintuitive result is due to the competition among the spatially separated regions and the interrelationships between the regions which are incorporated into GSPEM. The interested reader is referred to Harker (1983) or Harker and Friesz (1985c) for a more detailed discussion of this application. The point to be made here is that this application provided proof that GSPEM is applicable to very large-scale problems and that the results of this model are far more useful than results from any of the previous freight models since it captures more of the interrelations inherent in the freight system than any other model.

6.   Conclusions

We have reviewed the key freight network equilibrium models proposed in the literature and found that several key considerations have been overlooked in the models reported heretofore. Foremost among these oversights have been (1) the simultaneous treatment of shippers and carriers, (2) the simultaneous solution of the macroeconomic model, which generates commodity supplies and demands and the network model itself, (3) explicit treatment of backhauling operations, (5) explicit treatment of blocking strategies, and (6) fleet constraints. We have seen how the first two of these issues may be resolved using single variational inequality and nonlinear complementarity formulations of the freight network equilibrium problem. We have also pointed out that nonmonotonic functions do not present any appreciable difficulty in the computation of equilibria, so long as one is content to deal with multiple equilibria. It remains an important research topic to establish what classes of nonmonotonic functions are consistent with a unique freight equilibrium and whether these functions can be used to model the economies of traffic density observed in freight transportation.

Backhauling, blocking, and fleet constraints remain essentially unaddressed; the prospects for their rigorous inclusion into a freight equilibrium model that is computationally tractable are bleak at the present owing to the fact that such considerations seem to imply the use of integer variables to model indivisibilities.

Nonetheless the results reported indicate that even a relatively simple model that includes both shippers and carriers leads to dramatic improvements in forecasting capability. This bodes well for the future of freight equilibrium models.

References

Avriel, M. (1976). *Nonlinear Programming: Analysis and Methods*. Englewood Cliffs, N.J.: Prentice-Hall.

Baumol, W. J., J. C. Panzar, and R. D. Willig (1982). *Contestable Markets and the Theory of Industry Structure*. New York: Harcourt, Brace, Jovanovich.

Boyer, K. (1980). "Queueing Analysis and Value of Service Pricing in the Trucking Industry: Comment." *American Economic Review*, 70, no. 1:174–80.

Bronzini, M. S. (1980a). "Evolution of a Multimodal Freight Transportation Network Model." Mimeo, University of Tennessee, Knoxville.

(1980b). Freight Transportation Energy Use. Report no. DOT-TSC-OST-79-1, vols. 1 and 2, U.S. Department of Transportation, Washington, D.C.

(1980c). "Evolution of a Multimodal Freight Transportation Network Model." *Proceedings of the Transportation Research Forum*, 21, no. 1:475–85.

Bronzini, M. S., and D. Sherman (1983). "The Rail-Carrier Route Choice Model." *Transportation Research*, 17A, no. 6:463–69.

CACI, Inc. (1980). Transportation Flow Analysis: The National Energy Transportation Study (NETS). 3 vols. Report nos. DOT-OST-P-10-(29-32), U.S. Department of Transportation, Washington, D.C.

Charles River Associates, Inc. (1981). An Analysis of the Interaction of the Coal and Transportation Industries in 1960. Report no. 494. Prepared for the U.S. Department of Energy, Boston.

Dafermos, S. (1979). "Traffic Equilibrium and Variational Inequalities." *Transportation Science*, 14, no. 1:42–54.

(1982). "The General Multimodal Equilibrium Problem with Elastic Demand." *Networks*, 12, no. 1:57–72.

(1983). "An Iterative Scheme for Variational Inequalities." *Mathematical Programming*, 26, no. 1:40–47.

Data Resources, Inc. (1981). DRI Coal Model. Lexington, Mass.

Daughety, A. F., and F. S. Inaba (1981). "An Analysis of Regulatory Change in the Transportation Industry." *Review of Economics and Statistics*, 53:246–55.

DeVany, A. S., and T. Saving (1980). "Queueing Analysis and Value of Service Pricing in the Trucking Industry: Reply." *American Economic Review*, 70, no. 1:181–85.

Federal Railroad Administration (1980a). Magnetic Tape of FRA Network Data Base. Washington, D.C.

(1980b). Traffic Flows 1990. Washington, D.C.

Fernandez, J. E., and T. L. Friesz (1983). "Equilibrium Predictions in Transportation Markets: The State of the Art." *Transportation Research*, 17B, no. 2:155–72.

Fisk, C. W., and D. E. Boyce (1983). Optimal Transportation Systems Planning with Integrated Supply and Demand Models. Publication no. 16, Transportation Planning Group, Department of Civil Engineering, University of Illinois at Urbana-Champaign.

Friedlaender, A. F., and R. H. Spady (1981). *Freight Transport Regulation: Equity, Efficiency and Competition in the Rail and Trucking Industries*. Cambridge, Mass.: MIT Press.

Friesz, T. L., J. Gottfried, R. E. Brooks, A. J. Zielen, R. Tobin, and S. A. Meleski (1981). The Northeast Regional Environmental Impact Study: Theory, Validation and Application of a Freight Network Equilibrium Model. Report ANL/ES-120, Argonne National Laboratory, Argonne, Ill.

Friesz, T. L., J. Gottfried, and E. K. Morlok (1983). A Sequential Shipper-Carrier Network Model for Predicting Freight Flows. Report no. CE-FNEM-1981-8-1 (rev.). Department of Civil Engineering, University of Pennsylvania, Philadelphia. Forthcoming in *Transportation Science*.

Friesz, T. L., P. T. Harker, and R. L. Tobin (1984). "Alternative Algorithms for the General Network Spatial Price Equilibrium Problem." *Journal of Regional Science*, 24(4):475–507.

Friesz, T. L., and E. K. Morlok (1980). "Recent Advances in Network Modeling and Their Implications for Freight Systems Planning." *Proceedings of the Transportation Research Forum*, 21, no. 1:513–20.

Friesz, T. L., and R. L. Tobin (1981). An Equivalent Convex Optimization Problem for Network Equilibrium with Derived Demand. Report no. CUE-FNEM-1981-8-2, Department of Civil Engineering, University of Pennsylvania, Philadelphia.

Friesz, T. L., R. L. Tobin, and P. T. Harker (1981). Variational Inequalities and Convergence of Diagonalization Methods for Derived Demand Network Equilibrium Problems. Report no. CUE-FNEM-1981-10-1, Department of Civil Engineering, University of Pennsylvania, Philadelphia.

Friesz, T. L., R. L. Tobin, T. Smith, and P. T. Harker, (1983). "A Nonlinear Complementarity Formulation and Solution Procedure for the General Derived Demand Network Equilibrium Problem." *Journal of Regional Science*, 23, no. 3:337–59.

Friesz, T. L., P. A. Viton, and R. L. Tobin (1985). "Economic and Computational Aspects of Freight Network Equilibrium Models: A Synthesis." *Journal of Regional Science*, 25, no. 1:29–49.

Gartner, N. H. (1977). "Analysis and Control of Transportation Networks." In T. Susaki and T. Yamaoka, eds., *Proceedings of the 7th International Symposium on Transportation and Traffic Theory*. Kyoto, Japan: The Institute of Systems Science Research.

Gottfried, J. A. (1983). Predictive, Network Equilibrium Model for Application to Regional and National Freight Transportation Systems. Unpublished PhD dissertation, University of Pennsylvania, Philadelphia.

Harker, P. T. (1981). A Simultaneous Freight Network Equilibrium Model with Application to the Network Design Problem. MSE thesis, University of Pennsylvania, Philadelphia.

(1983). Prediction of Intercity Freight Flows: Theory and Application of a Generalized Spatial Price Equilibrium Model. Unpublished PhD dissertation, University of Pennsylvania, Philadelphia.

Harker, P. T., and T. L. Friesz (1982). "A Simultaneous Freight Network Equilibrium Model." *Congressus Numerantium*, 36:365–402.

(1985a). "Prediction of Intercity Freight Flows, I: Theory." *Transportation Research*, 19B, no. 6.

(1985b). "Prediction of Intercity Freight Flows, II: Mathematical Formulations." *Transportation Research*, 19B, no. 6.

(1985c). "The Use of Equilibrium Network Models in Logistics Management with an Application to the U.S. Coal Industry." *Transportation Research*, 19B, no. 5.

Hartman, P., and G. Stampacchia (1966). On Some Elliptic Differential Functional Equations. *Acta Mathematica*, 115:153–88.

Heaver, T. D., and J. C. Nelson (1978). Railway Pricing Under Commercial Freedom: The Canadian Experience. Centre for Transportation Studies, Vancouver, Canada.

Interstate Commerce Commission (1975). Rail Carload Cost Scales. Statement no. 1C1-73, ICC, Washington, D.C.

(1975). Magnetic Tape of U.S. Waybill Statistics, ICC, Washington, D.C.

Isard, W. (1975). *Introduction to Regional Science*. Englewood Cliffs, N.J.: Prentice-Hall.

Keeler, T. E. (1983). *Railroads, Freight and Public Policy*. Washington, D.C.: Brookings Institution.

Keeler, T. E., and K. A. Small (1977). "Optimal Peak-Load Pricing, Investment and Service Levels on Urban Expressways." *Journal of Political Economy*, 85:1–25.

Kinderlehrer, D., and G. Stampacchia (1980). *An Introduction to Variational Inequalities and Their Applications*. New York: Academic Press.

Kornhauser, A. L., M. Hornung, Y. Harzony, and J. Lutin (1979). The Princeton Railroad Network Model: Application of Computer Graphics in the Analysis of a Changing Industry. Presented at the 1979 Harvard Graphics Conference. Transportation Program, Princeton University, Princeton, N.J.

Kresge, D. T., and P. O. Roberts (1971). *Techniques of Transport Planning: Systems Analysis and Simulation Models*. The Brookings Institution, Washington, D.C.

Lansdowne, Z. F. (1981). "Rail Freight Traffic Assignment." *Transportation Research*, 15A:183–90.

LeBlanc, L. J., E. K. Morlok, and W. P. Pierskalla (1975). "An Efficient Approach to Solving the Road Network Equilibrium Traffic Assignment Problem." *Transportation Research* 9:309–18.

Lemke, C. E. (1980). "A Survey of Complementarity Theory." In R. Cottle, et al., eds., *Variational Inequalitites and Complementarity Problems*. New York: McGraw-Hill, ch. 15.

Marcotte, P. (1981). Network Optimization with Continuous Control Parameters. Publication no. 226, Centre de Recherche sur les Transports, University of Montreal.

Morlok, E. K. (1978). *Introduction to Transportation Engineering and Planning*. New York: McGraw-Hill.

Pang, J. S., and D. Chan (1982). "Iterative Methods for Variational and Complementarity Problems." *Mathematical Programming*, 24, no. 3:284–313.

Peterson, E. R., and H. V. Fullerton, eds. (1975). The Railcar Network Models. Report no. 75-11, Canadian Institute of Guided Ground Transport. Queen's University, Kingston, Ontario.

Reebie Associates (1982). TRANSEARCH: The Data Base for Freight Transportation. Greenwich, Conn.

Roberts, P. O. (1966). Transport Planning: Models for Developing Countries. Unpublished PhD dissertation, Department of Civil Engineering, Northwestern University, Evanston, Ill.

Roberts, P. O., and D. H. Dewees (1971). *Economic Analysis for Transport Choice*. Lexington, Mass.: Lexington Books.

Rockafellar, R. T. (1980). "Lagrange Multiplers and Variational Inequalities." In R. Cottle et al., eds., *Variational Inequalities and Complementarity Problems*. New York: McGraw-Hill, ch. 20.

Samuelson, P. A. (1952). "Spatial Price Equilibrium and Linear Programming." *American Economic Review*, 42:283–303.

Scarf, H. (1973). *The Computation of Economic Equilibria*. Cowles Commission Monograph 24. New Haven, Conn.: Yale University Press.

Smith, D. P. and B. G. Hutchinson (1981). "Goodness of Fit Statistics for Trip Distribution Models," *Transportation Research*, 15A, no. 4:295–304.

Smith, M. J. (1979). "The Existence, Uniqueness and Stability of Traffic Equilibria." *Transportation Research*, 13B, no. 4:295–304.

Smith, T. E. (1984). A Solution Condition for Complementarity Problems: With an Application to Spatial Price Equilibrium. *Applied Mathematics and Computation*, 15:61–69.

Takayama, T., and G. G. Judge (1971). *Spatial and Temporal Price and Allocation Models*. New York: North Holland.

Tan, H. N., S. B. Gershwin, and M. Athans (1979). Hybrid Optimization in Urban Traffic Networks. Report DOT-TSC-RSPA-79-7, Laboratory for Information and Decision Systems, Massachusetts Institute of Technology, Cambridge, Mass.

Tobin, R. L., and T. L. Friesz, (1983). "Formulating and Solving the Network Spatial Price Equilibrium Problem with Transshipment in Terms of Arc Variables." *Journal of Regional Science*, 23, no. 2:187–98.

Tobin, R. L., J. D. Jastrow, and S. A. Meleski (1983). The Statewide Florida Coal Conversion Study: Coal Supply and Transportation Analysis. Report DOE/RG-0063, Argonne National Laboratory, Argonne, Ill.

Transportation Systems Center (TSC) (1980). Magnetic Tape of Multimodal National Freight Network Data Base. U.S. Department of Transportation, Cambridge, Mass.

Turnquist, M., and M. Daskin (1982). "Queueing Models of Classification and Connection Delay in Rail Yards." *Transportation Science*, 16, no. 2:207–30.

Wagner, H. M. (1975). *Principles of Operations Research*. Englewood Cliffs, N.J.: Prentice-Hall.

Wardrop, J. G. (1952). "Some Theoretical Aspects of Road Traffic Research." *Proceedings of the Institute of Civil Engineering*, Part II: 325–78.

Wilson, A. G. (1970). *Entropy in Urban and Regional Modelling*. London: Pion Press.

CHAPTER 8

Efficient pricing with rivalry between a railroad and a pipeline

RONALD R. BRAEUTIGAM

For many years scholars and regulators have concerned themselves with the problems of regulating industries with firms engaged in rivalry with one another. The problem goes back at least to the turn of the century with rivalry between railroads and pipelines and is particularly difficult when the rival firms both may operate with economies of scale. Yet surprisingly relatively little economic research has been done to show how such an industry should be structured and how tariffs should be set if economic resources are to be allocated efficiently.

Economist and former regulator Alfred Kahn (1970, p. 71) has described the regulatory dilemma in a number of instances, including the rivalry between or among railroads, the competition between telephone and telegraph services, and the interaction between local distributors of natural gas and electricity. As recently as 1981 he wrote that regulators need help "in devising rules that make reasonable economic sense for the regulation of competition between what appear to be natural monopolies" (p. 67).

Elsewhere I have addressed the nature of economically efficient tariffs when there exists rivalry among multiproduct firms that produce imperfectly substitutable outputs with economies of scale and operate under a viability constraint (Braeutigam, 1984). That paper provides a brief discussion of the economic research on the problem suggested by Kahn and develops a general model of the optimal pricing problem, with any number of firms producing any number of products. It is not industry specific. The present analysis takes that work as a background and applies it to the particular problem of rivalry between a railroad and a pipeline in the transport of coal.

A model of economically efficient industry structure and pricing is developed here, and I show how the choice of configuration depends on demand and cost characteristics. The chapter also investigates the nature of efficient pricing rules, develops pricing rules in terms of potentially measurable elasticities of demand and markups of price over marginal cost, and compares the rules under rivalry with economies of scale with those developed elsewhere

The author would like to thank Andrew Daughety and an anonymous reviewer for thoughtful comments on an earlier version of this chapter.

for the multiproduct monopoly (Baumol and Bradford, 1970) and for rivalry when only one of the firms operates with economies of scale (Braeutigam, 1979).

1.   The nature of the rivalry

Coal slurry pipeline operations involve the pumping of pulverized coal, suspended in a medium such as water, through a pipe (see Rieber and Soo, 1977, vol. 3 for an excellent summary of the technology). After it is mined, the coal is transported to a preparation plant, where it is finely ground and mixed with the fluid (usually water) that is used to suspend the coal particles. A water slurry mixture is typically 50 percent water and 50 percent coal by weight. The mixture may be placed in agitated storage tanks until it is ready for entry into the pipeline. Once the slurry reaches its destination, it is again placed in a storage tank until fed into a facility to remove the water. It can be separated in a number of ways, including centrifuging, filtering, or natural settling. More finely ground particles can be separated by chemical treatment. The coal is then dried and delivered to users, usually power plants.

The technology for coal slurry pipelines has been developed for some time. The first major coal slurry piepline in this country was built in 1957. It connected Cadiz, Ohio, to the East Lake Power Station of the Cleveland Illuminating Company, located on Lake Erie. The 10-inch-diameter pipeline was 108 miles long.

The potential nature of rivalry between coal slurry pipelines and railroads was evidenced even in this early case. When the pipeline was being built, rail rates were $3.47 per ton. The pipeline delivered coal at less than $3.00 per ton. The pipeline operated until 1963, when the railroad industry sought approval for new, low rates for unit train movements. The Interstate Commerce Commission allowed a rate of $1.88 per ton for unit train movements, and the pipeline did not survive at this new rate.

In recent years there have been a number of proposals for domestic coal slurry pipelines (see the Illinois Department of Energy and Natural Resources, 1982, p. 96). Modern proposals involve much higher capacity pipelines (10 million to 55 million tons moved per year for various designs), using pipelines up to 38 inches in diameter. Pipelines are most cost efficient for large volumes hauled long distances, such as 1,000 to 1,500 miles.

As this brief discussion suggests, there are a number of issues at the center of the policy debate concerning coal slurry pipelines. There is some uncertainty about whether pipelines can provide transport at a lower cost than unit trains, barges, or any other mode or combination of modes. Closely related is the issue of rates. Would coal slurry pipelines provide service at rates that divert much rail traffic? Will railroads be allowed to respond to new slurry rates with rates of their own choosing? And, if railroads lose significant traffic to pipelines, will the remaining railroad customers be left with more costly operations as the fixed costs of railroads are distributed over fewer units of output and possibly fewer services?

Over the past decade these issues have surfaced in legislative proposals designed to confer eminent domain authority for pipeline routes. Absent such authority, it will be difficult for coal slurry companies to acquire the necessary rights of way in many parts of the country. To be sure, there are other questions dealt with in the hearings on the proposed bills, including among others the availability of water, environmental impacts, and the placement of regulatory responsibility (the Federal Energy Regulatory Commission, the Interstate Commerce Commission, or some other agency). The ones of interest in this chapter are those of rates for coal services and market structure. The model of the next section addresses these questions.

2.   Model

To focus on the issues of pricing with rivalry between a railroad and a pipeline, we characterize the firms as follows. Let the pipeline provide output whose quantity (for example, ton-miles of coal or oil transported) is denoted by x^o. This output is provided at a tariff p^o. Of course, it is natural to characterize the pipeline as a single-produce firm.

In contrast to the pipeline, the railroad may provide a number of types of transport services. Let n denote the number of such services, and let the vector $(x^1, x^2, \ldots, x^n)$ denote the respective quantities of the outputs. Correspondingly let the vector $(p^1, p^2, \ldots, p^n)$ denote the tariffs at which the services are provided. Thus, service i is provided at tariff p^i, and the quantity of that service provided by the railroad is x^i.

We will assume that rivalry takes place between the two firms in the provision of services x^o and x^1. Thus, the services x^o and x^1 are regarded as imperfect substitutes for one another. The level of each service demanded will depend on what both p^o and p^1 are. Thus the demand for each can be written as

$$x^i(p^0, p^1); \qquad i = 0, 1. \tag{1}$$

Since the two services are imperfect substitutes, an increase in p^j will result in a higher quantity of service i demanded (x^i). Formally this means that

$$x^i_j > 0; \qquad i = 0,1; \quad j = 0,1; \quad i \neq j, \tag{2}$$

where the subscript in (2) denotes a partial derivative with respect to p^j; that is, $x^i_j \equiv \partial x^i / \partial p^j$. (This convention for denoting derivatives is followed throughout the chapter.)

Further properties of the transportation demands can be established by observing that transport services are inputs to the production processes of transport users, whose cost structures are concave in factor prices. Thus, transport demands are assumed to satisfy

$$x_o^o x_1^1 - x_1^o x_o^1 > 0; \tag{3}$$

and

$$x_i^i < 0, \qquad i = 0, 1, \tag{4}$$

where the latter merely denotes the usual property that each demand schedule should be downward sloping in its own price.

With respect to the demands of other railroad services, we will assume that they are independent of one another and, as usual, downward sloping. Hence the demand schedule for each can be written as

$$x^i(p^i), \qquad i \leq 2, \quad \text{with } x_i^i < 0.$$

Production costs for the pipeline will be denoted by

$$C^o(x^o, \mathbf{q}^o), \tag{5}$$

where $\mathbf{q}^o$ is a vector of factor prices. For the railroad total costs of production may be written

$$C^r(x^1, x^2, \ldots, x^n, \mathbf{q}^r), \tag{6}$$

where $\mathbf{q}^r$ is a vector of factor prices. Firms are assumed to minimize production costs given any observed levels of output. Further, factor prices remain constant in this analysis, so references to $\mathbf{q}^o$ and $\mathbf{q}^r$ are suppressed. (In this analysis we will by convention suppress arguments of functions wherever that can be done without ambiguity.) Finally, the x^i terms in (5) and (6) are themselves functions of output prices as noted previously, and firms are required to satisfy the demands as common carriers.

The profit constraints for the pipeline and the railroad can be written as in (7) and (8), respectively.

$$\pi^o = p^o x^o - C^o \geq 0; \tag{7}$$

$$\pi^r = \sum_{i=1}^{n} p^i x^i - C^r \geq 0. \tag{8}$$

One may now construct a welfare measure of the sum of consumer and producer surplus, $W(p^1, p^1, p^2, \ldots, p^n)$, written as follows:[1]

---

[1] For more on consumer surplus as a measure of welfare, see Willig (1976). For a discussion of welfare measure with interdependent markets see Braeutigam and Noll (1984).

$$W = \int_r (x^o d\bar{p}^o + x^1 d\bar{p}^1) + \sum_{i=2}^{n} \int_{p^i}^{\bar{p}^i} x^i d\bar{p}^i + \pi^o + \pi^r. \qquad (9)$$

It is assumed here that W is a function only of prices, and is therefore path independent. Thus the integrability condition

$$x_1^o = x_o^1 \qquad (10)$$

is assumed to be satisfied and allows us to choose any path r that connects (p^o, p^1) with $(\bar{p}^o, \bar{p}^1)$, where $x^i(\bar{p}^o, \bar{p}^1) = 0$ for $i = 0,1$. In other words $(\bar{p}^o, \bar{p}^1)$ are tariffs high enough to reduce quantities demanded to zero for x^o and x^1 simultaneously. Similarly, for $i \geq 2$, x^i is reduced to zero at $\bar{p}_i$.

The viable firm Ramsey optimum (VFRO) can then be formalized as in (11):

> max W
> $(p^i, \quad \forall_i)$
> subject to: $\pi^r \geq 0$
> $\pi^o \geq 0$ $\qquad (11)$

One should recognize that there are difficulties that may arise with respect to a solution to (11). These are discussed in Braeutigam (1984) and briefly reiterated here. First, suppose there are fixed costs that can be avoided if a particular output is not produced, as characterized in the treatment of long-run fixed costs in Baumol, Panzar, and Willig (1982, p. 280, definition 10A.1). If such an output becomes zero, the producing firm's profit function, and hence the welfare function would be discontinuous. A global optimum of (11) could occur at such a corner point (the welfare-maximizing industry configuration could occur when some output is not produced at all, or even when one of the firms ceases to produce).

We also observe that even if there is global continuity, W need not be globally concave. For example, if economies of scale are substantial, there may be multiple local optima, again including the possibility of an optimum when some output is zero. Of course, given continuity, concavity in W is sufficient for an optimum, and uniqueness is guaranteed if concavity is strict. Further, the first-order necessary conditions discussed below remain valid even if W is not globally concave.

3.   Possible industry configurations at a VFRO

The formal statement of the VFRO problem makes it apparent that several kinds of possible structural outcomes may be associated with socially optimal prices. It is useful at this point to enumerate them. At a VFRO it may be the case that

1. Neither firm produces any output. This may be a feasible industry structure if there are no fixed costs, or when all fixed costs are

avoidable when output becomes zero. In such a case, both revenues and costs would be zero when no output is produced, and hence (assuming $\pi^r = \pi^o = 0$) this point of operation can be feasible. The question of the optimality will be addressed below.

2. The railroad may transport products other than coal, but neither the railroad nor the pipeline transports coal.
3. The railroad transports all products, including coal, but the pipeline does not transport coal.
4. The pipeline transports coal, but not the railroad. The railroad may transport other commodities, or it may not produce at all.
5. Both the railroad and the pipeline transport coal. The railroad may transport other commodities, or it may transport only coal. Both firms earn only a normal return on investment ($\pi^r = 0$ and $\pi^o = 0$).
6. As in outcome 5, both firms transport coal, but the railroad earns a normal return ($\pi^r = 0$) and the coal slurry pipeline earns extranormal profits ($\pi^o > 0$).
7. As in outcome 5, both firms transport coal, but the pipeline earns a normal return ($\pi^o = 0$) and the railroad earns extranormal profits ($\pi^r > 0$).
8. As in outcome 5, both firms transport coal, and both firms earn extranormal profits ($\pi^o > 0$ and $\pi^r > 0$).

This is really quite a large menu of alternative outcomes that may be feasible. Fortunately we need not treat all of them in great detail in this chapter for a variety of reasons we now discuss. In reality some of the alternative possibilities, while feasible, may be less important for purposes of optimality. This is the case with the first and last alternatives, but for different reasons.

Consider alternative (1). If neither firm produces at all, observe that not only are profits zero, but, if all fixed costs are avoidable, so is the welfare measure W, as defined in equation (9). Compare this with the welfare generated under any other of the alternatives. To facilitate this, we form the Lagrangean H in the usual way for the VFRO problem of equation (11).

$$H = W + \lambda^o \pi^o + \lambda^r \pi^r, \tag{12}$$

where λ^o and λ^r are the Lagrange multipliers associated with the profit constraints $\pi^o \geqslant 0$ and $\pi^r \geqslant 0$ respectively. If prices are chosen to solve (11), λ^o and λ^r will be nonnegative. To see why outcome 1 is not likely to be an alternative of interest even if it is feasible, observe that if any outputs are positive at any feasible alternative to outcome 1, W will be positive, since total surplus in (9) will strictly exceed profits. Thus W under any alternative other than outcome 1 will strictly exceed zero, and hence be welfare superior to that outcome. This leads to our first formal observation.

Proposition 1 (optimality of the no-production alternative)
If there exists a feasible industry configuration in which some output is strictly positive ($x^i > 0$ for some i = 0, 1,...,n), then the no-production alternative ($x^i = 0$ $\forall_i$) will not be a VFRO.

This first proposition does not generally imply that coal will be moved by either firm at a VFRO, even if that is a feasible alternative. Nothing in the proposition requires that x^o or x^1 be positive at a VFRO. To find sufficient conditions under which coal will be moved by at least one firm at a VFRO, we must look further. One simple and practical sufficient condition is as follows.

Proposition 2 (sufficient condition I for coal movement at a VFRO)
If $\pi^o > 0$ for some (p^o, p^1), including a (p^o, p^1) such that $x^1 = 0$, then at a VFRO either x^o or x^1 or both are strictly positive.

This proposition says that if there exists a set of tariffs (p^o, p^1) that will allow the pipeline to move coal and remain viable, then at a VFRO coal will be moved by either the railroad, the pipeline, or both. This does not necessarily mean that the pipeline will itself move coal at a VFRO. The proposition simply states a sufficient condition that requires that at least one of the firms move coal at a VFRO.

To see why the proposition is true, let us modify the VFRO problem (11) by adding an additional constraint that the railroad haul no coal; that is, $x^1 = 0$.

The modified problem can be written as (13)

$$\begin{aligned}
&\max W \\
&(p^i, \ \forall_i), \\
&\text{subject to:} \quad \pi^r \geq 0, \\
&\qquad\qquad\quad \pi^o \geq 0, \\
&\qquad\qquad\quad x^1 = 0.
\end{aligned} \qquad (13)$$

Observe that setting $x^1 = 0$ has two effects. First it gives all of the coal business to the pipeline, a condition as favorable to the pipeline as possible. Second, it makes it possible to decompose W into two parts since there are no longer interacting demands. Thus

$$W = W^o + W^r, \qquad (14)$$

where W^o is the contribution to total surplus from pipeline operations and W^r is the contribution from railroad operations in noncoal markets. By hypothesis in Proposition 2, the feasible set of prices in (13) is nonempty. Let $\tilde{W}$ denote the level of welfare at a solution of (13). Then $\tilde{W} = W^o + W^r > 0$, since $W^o > \pi^o \geq 0$, and $W^r \geq 0$. Now let us remove the constraint $x^1 = 0$, reverting to the VFRO problem of (11), and let W^* denote a solution to this less constrained problem. Thus $W^* \geq \tilde{W}$. If $W^* > \tilde{W}$, it is because $x^1 > 0$. Thus coal is still transported by at least one of the firms.

We now develop a second sufficient condition under which coal will be moved by at least one firm at a VFRO. This one is based on an examination of whether the railroad, operating without competition from the pipeline, can transport coal without lowering its overall profit level. We focus on overall profit level for the railroad since there is no unambiguous measure of the profitability of a single service (such as coal movements) in a multiproduct firm, particularly where there are significant common costs. However, we can develop a useful measure based on whether revenues from coal movements exceed the incremental costs of coal movements. This means, of course, that in some interesting way we must specify the levels of other outputs (x^2, x^3,...,x^n) at which the incremental costs of coal movements by rail are to be calculated.

To begin, assume for the moment that there is no pipeline ($x^o = 0$). Also let the railroad haul no coal ($x^1 = 0$), and consider any vector of other railroad tariffs ($\bar{p}^2$, $\bar{p}^3$,...,$\bar{p}^n$) such that the railroad is just viable ($\pi^r = 0$). Suppose that at the corresponding vector of outputs ($\bar{x}^2$, $\bar{x}^3$,...,$\bar{x}^n$) there is the possibility of introducing coal service that does not lower the profit of the firm. This requires that there is some p^1 such that coal revenues exceed incremental costs (IC^1).

$$p^1 x^1(p^1,\bar{p}^o) - IC^1(x^1(p^1,\bar{p}^o), \bar{x}^2(\bar{p}^2), \bar{x}^3 (\bar{p}^3),..., \bar{x}^n(\bar{p}^n)) \geq 0, \quad (15)$$

where, as before, $\bar{p}^o$ is a tariff for pipeline coal movements so high that no such movements take place ($x^o = 0$). Since by hypothesis the introduction of the coal service does not lower the profitability of the railroad and since some customers now receive coal service, total welfare must be higher when the coal service is provided.

The next step in the argument is to observe that if (15) holds for all ($\bar{p}^2$, $\bar{p}^3$,...,$\bar{p}^n$) such that the firm is viable without coal transport, it must also hold in particular for the values of those tariffs which would maximize W subject to a viability constraint (this would correspond to a Ramsey optimum in which the railroad is not allowed to haul coal); let the tariffs at such an optimum be ($\hat{p}^2$, $\hat{p}^3$,...,$\hat{p}^n$). But then if there exists a p^1 such that

$$p^1 x^1(p^1, \bar{p}^o) - IC^1((x^1, \bar{p}^o), \hat{x}^2 (\hat{p}^2), \hat{x}^3(\hat{p}^3),...,\hat{x}^p(\hat{p}^n)) \geq 0, \quad (16)$$

an even higher level of total surplus can be achieved when the railroad transports coal. We can now state the following result.

Proposition 3 (sufficient condition II for coal movement at a VFRO)
Consider a Ramsey optimal set of tariffs ($\hat{p}_2$, $\hat{p}_3$,...,$\hat{p}_n$) for the railroad, with no coal movements by either the pipeline or the railroad. If the railroad can profitably introduce coal (that is, the incremental revenues equal or exceed the incremental costs of coal movements for some p^1), then either the railroad or the pipeline (or both) will transport coal at a VFRO.

One could apply this proposition by starting from a Ramsey optimum for the railroad, with no coal movements, as stated in Proposition 3. But one need not start from this point. For example, suppose one were to consider *all* of the tariffs $(p^2, p^3,...,p^n)$ at which the railroad could just break even without coal movements (call this set R), and suppose it were clear that coal movements could be undertaken at any of those tariffs without damaging profitability; then Proposition 3 applies. This follows because $(\hat{p}_2, \hat{p}_3,...,\hat{p}_n)$ lies in R.

In summary, it is perhaps worthwhile to emphasize that Propositions 2 and 3 state *sufficient* conditions under which coal movements will take place at a VFRO. These are not *necessary* conditions. There remains the possibility that the railroad should move coal at a VFRO even though the pipeline cannot do so viably at any set of tariffs (p^o, p^1), and there are not tariffs such that the revenues from railroad movements of coal equal or exceed the incremental costs of those movements. The latter could arise if the introduction of a railroad coal movement leads to a gain in consumer surplus in that market greater than the (negative) difference between revenues and incremental costs of coal movements. There also remains the possibility that coal movements are necessary to the railroad if it is to remain viable and engage in positive levels of any transport services at all; the optimality of having coal movements in this case requires no elaboration here.

4.   Characteristics of economically efficient prices

So where does this discussion leave us? In terms of the eight possible structural outcomes at a VFRO enumerated earlier, we have shown why alternative outcomes 1 and 2, in which neither firm transports coal, are not likely to be important as optimal outcomes, even when they are feasible. Alternatives 3 and 4, which involve the transport of coal by only one firm, may be economically efficient; however, we need no new economic theory of optimal pricing in these cases, since they are already treated in the literature. The case in which only the railroad transports coal corresponds to the normal case of Ramsey optimal pricing treated by Baumol and Bradford (1970). The case in which only the pipeline transports coal is even simpler since the pipeline is a single-product firm. One could still apply second-best pricing principles in this case, and, as is well known, economic efficiency with uniform pricing and certainty leads to average-cost pricing.

For these reasons the rest of this analysis focuses on the balance of the alternatives 5–8. We can further reduce the number of interesting alternatives by demonstrating that alternative 8 in which both firms transport coal and earn extranormal profits, will never be socially optimal. To demonstrate this (as well as other principles later) we write out the first-order conditions of optimality for the viable firm Ramsey optimum problem (11), here written for only those outputs that are produced at an optimum (that is, for $x^i > 0$). Let λ^o

and λ^r be the Lagrange multipliers associated respectively with the profit constraints on the pipeline and the railroad, and let H be the Lagrangean formed in the usual way.

$$H = W + \lambda^o \pi^o + \lambda^r \pi^r. \tag{17}$$

Then at a regular optimum (in which all prices are positive), the following conditions must be met.

$$\lambda^o x^o + (1 + \lambda^o)(p^o - C_o^o) x_o^o + (1 + \lambda^r)(p^1 - C_1^r)x_o^1 = 0. \tag{18}$$

$$\lambda^r x^1 + (1 + \lambda^o)(p^o - C_o^o)x_1^o + (1 + \lambda^r)(p^1 - C_1^r)x_1^1 = 0. \tag{19}$$

$$\lambda^r x^i + (1 + \lambda^r)(p^i - C_i^r)x_i^i = 0; \qquad i = 2,\dots,n. \tag{20}$$

In (18)–(20), subscripts are used to denote partial derivatives; that is, $C_o^o \equiv \partial C^o/\partial x^o$, $C_i^r \equiv \partial C^r/\partial x^i$, $x_k^i \equiv \partial x^i/\partial p^k$ ($\forall i, k$). In addition to (18)–(20), the viability constraints ($\pi^o \geq 0$ and $\pi^r \geq 0$) must also be met. Formally these necessary conditions are

$$\pi^o \geq 0, \qquad \lambda^o \pi^o = 0, \qquad \lambda^o \geq 0. \tag{21}$$

$$\pi^r \geq 0, \qquad \lambda^r \pi^r = 0, \qquad \lambda^r \geq 0. \tag{22}$$

We can now rule out alternative outcome 8 as a VFRO. Observe that if $\pi^o > 0$ and $\pi^r > 0$, then (21) and (22) require that $\lambda^o = \lambda^r = 0$. However, in that case (18)–(20) require that every price equal marginal cost. If each firm has economies of scale, then marginal-cost pricing leads to a deficit, which means that (21) and (22) would be violated. At least one of the firms must be earning normal profits, and possibly both. This principle has been stated elsewhere (Braeutigam, 1984) in a more general context, so we do not state it here as a new proposition. We do use the principle to eliminate alternative 8 from further consideration. More important, we reiterate that at a VRFO it need not be the case that both firms earn only a normal profit, contrary to the traditional regulatory wisdom that requires firms with economies of scale to earn only normal profits. In some cases it may actually be economically efficient to allow both the railroad and pipeline to transport coal and to allow one of the firms to earn extranormal profits. In short, all three remaining alternative 5–7 are possible at a VFRO.

The discussion of VFRO has already indicated that some departure of price from marginal cost is necessary at a VFRO. Can we say whether prices will exceed marginal costs in all markets? If there are zero cross elasticities of demand in coal transport ($x_o^1 = x_1^o = 0$), then (18)–(20) indicate by direct inspection that price exceeds marginal cost in all markets. [In fact, the VFRO problem (11) can be decomposed into two independent Ramsey pricing problems of the traditional kind in that unlikely case.]

However, if the two services x^1 and x^o are imperfect substitutes, an initial examination of (18)–(20) does not appear to rule out the possibility that, for example, p^1 could be less than C_1^r. However, this will not occur at an optimum. To see this we can multiply (19) by x_o^o and subtract from that resulting equation the product of (18) and x_1^o. The difference can be written as follows:

$$\lambda^r x^1 x_o^o - \lambda^o x^o x_o^1 + (x_o^o x_1^1 - x_1^o x_o^1)(1 + \lambda^r)(p^1 - C_1^r) = 0. \quad (23)$$

Taken together, conditions (20), (3), (4), and (23) require that when $\lambda^r > 0$, $(p^1 - C_1^r) > 0$. Finally, from (2) it is clear that $(P - C_i^r) > 0$ when $\lambda^r > 0$. Thus, we have proven the following.

Proposition 4 (direction of deviations of price from marginal cost)
If the profit constraint for the railroad is binding (that is, λ^r is positive), then price will exceed marginal cost in each market served by the railroad at a VFRO.

A similar proposition could be derived for the pipeline, but that need not be done since the pipeline is a single-product firm operating with economies of scale. Pricing greater than marginal cost for the pipeline is necessary if the pipeline is to be viable, whether viability means that the firm earns only normal profits or receives extranormal profits at a VFRO.

Observe that Proposition 4 applies to all markets served by the railroad. If $\lambda^r > 0$, price will exceed marginal cost in both coal transport as well as other rail transport markets served by the railroad.

There remains one other case of interest not covered by the proposition. Suppose $\lambda^r = 0$, so that the profitability constraint is not binding for the railroad at a VFRO. Will each railroad tariff exceed marginal cost in this event? Equation (20) indicates that in noncoal markets, price will equal marginal cost in this case. Further, as noted previously, if $\lambda^r = 0$, then $\lambda^o > 0$; thus by (18) $p^o - C_o^o > 0$. These observations can be summarized as follows.

Proposition 5 (pricing when railroad profitability constraint is not binding)
If the railroad profitability constraint is not binding, then the pipeline will earn a normal profit. The tariff for railroad coal transport will exceed marginal cost, but the tariffs for each other railroad service will equal marginal cost.

This proposition indicates that it would not be economically efficient for the railroad to earn extranormal profits if the pricing in any of its monopolistic markets ($i = 2,3,...,n$) differs from marginal cost. Thus, if a firm receives extranormal profits at a VFRO, it can do so with markups of price over marginal cost only in the coal market. (For an extension of this proposition to the case in which the railroad encounters rivalry in markets other than coal, see Braeutigam, 1984.)

Let us next address the case in which both firms have binding profit constraints at a VFRO. Can the rules for optimality be expressed in terms of demand elasticities and markups over marginal cost? Let M^i be the markup of p^i over marginal cost, expressed as a ratio to price. Thus

$$M^o = (p^o - C_o^o)/p^o; \tag{24}$$

and

$$M^i = (p^i - C_i^r)/p^i, \qquad i = 1,\ldots,n. \tag{25}$$

Also let price elasticity of demand for commodity i with respect to the price of j be denoted by E_j^i. One can rewrite equations (18)–(20) respectively as (26)–(28), using (10) and (25) as

$$-1 + (1 + \lambda^o)(M^o E_o^o + 1) + (1 + \lambda^r)M^1 E_1^o = 0. \tag{26}$$

$$-1 + (1 + \lambda^o) M^o E_o^1 + (1 + \lambda^r)(M^1 E_1^1 + 1) = 0. \tag{27}$$

$$-1 + (1 + \lambda^r)(M^i E_i^i + 1) = 0, \qquad i = 2,\ldots,n. \tag{28}$$

Solving for $(1 + \lambda^r)$ and then λ^r, it follows that

$$-\frac{\lambda^r}{1 + \lambda^r} = M^1 E_1^1 + M^o E_o^1 \left[\frac{1 + M^1(E_1^1 - E_1^o)}{1 + M^o(E_o^o - E_o^1)} \right]. \tag{29}$$

Also, observe from (28) that

$$-\frac{\lambda^r}{1 + \lambda^r} = M^i E_i^i, \qquad i = 2, \ldots, n.$$

Thus, we can characterize VFRO pricing rules for the case in which both firms have binding profit constraints as follows.

Proposition 6 (pricing when both firms have binding profit constraints)
If both the railroad and the pipeline earn normal profits (with binding profit constraints) at a VFRO, then
  i.   the pipeline price equals average cost,
  ii. railroad profit is normal, and
  iii. railroad and pipeline prices must satisfy

$$M^1 E_1^1 + M^o E_o^1 \left[\frac{1 + M^1(E_1^1 - E_1^o)}{1 + M^o(E_o^o - E_o^1)} \right] = M^i E_i^i, \qquad i = 2, \ldots, n. \tag{30}$$

Proposition 6 therefore specifies a modified Ramsey pricing rule for the case in which the two firms have interdependent demands for coal transport and have binding deficit constraints. To see this more clearly, consider the polar case in which the coal demands are independent. Then $E_o^1 = 0$, and the second term on the left-hand side of (30) is zero. Then (30) would reduce to the usual inverse elasticity rule, in which the extent of the markup of price over marginal cost in a market is inversely related to the own-price elasticity of demand in that market. In such a case, Proposition 6 degenerates (decouples) into two independent Ramsey pricing problems, one for each firm, which is of course the appropriate limiting case when there are no interdependencies between the firms.

The appearance of the second term on the left-hand side of (30) means that in interdependent markets some adjustment to the usual inverse elasticity rule is required. It is natural to ask whether we can say anything determinate about the direction of this adjustment when there are imperfectly substitutable coal transport demands.

In order to answer this question, we first observe that at an optimum (30) can be rewritten using (10) as

$$M^1 E_1^1 + M^o E_o^1 \left[\frac{1 + \lambda^o}{1 + \lambda^r} \right] = M^i E_i^i, \qquad i = 2, \ldots, n. \tag{31}$$

Thus the second term on the left-hand side is positive. We can now state the following.

Proposition 7 (Ramsey rule adjustments with interdependent coal demands)
If both firms operate with binding profit constraints at a VFRO, and if the coal transport demands of the railroad and pipeline are imperfect substitutes, then

$$M^1 E_1^1 < M^i E_i^i, \qquad i = 2,\ldots,n. \tag{32}$$

To illustrate Proposition 7, suppose the elasticities E_1^1 and E_i^i happen to be equal in all rail markets at a VFRO. Then the efficient percentage markup of price over marginal cost will be greater in the coal transport market of the railroad than it would be in other rail markets. If there were no rivalry in hauling coal, then (32) would be an equality instead of an inequality. Intuitively, the additional markup in a rivalrous market occurs because a given price increase with rivalry will result in a smaller loss of consumer surplus since consumers can be satisfied in other markets rather then being excluded altogether.

5.   Conclusions

This analysis has focused on a problem that both scholars and practitioners of regulation have recognized as important for many years, the economically efficient industry structure and the choice of tariffs when there is rivalry among firms with economies of scale. The development is pointed toward particular application in the rivalry between a railroad and a pipeline in the transport of coal.

It is clear from economic theory that any of a number of possible industry configurations may be consistent with an economically efficient allocation of resources and that the optimal configuration in any particular case will depend on characteristics of the costs for the railroad and the pipeline. For example, in some cases it may be optimal for both a railroad and a pipeline to haul coal in rivalrous markets; in other cases it would be economically efficient for only one of the firms to be active in coal transportation. In principle in some cases neither firm should transport coal, although in reality this is perhaps a less important possibility; nevertheless the analysis has developed sufficient conditions under which it would be economically efficient for at least one firm to move coal.

The rules for economically efficient pricing are of particular interest when in an optimal industry structure both firms transport coal. In such a case coal tariffs exceed marginal costs for both firms. At least one of the firms will earn no more than normal profits, but it is possible that one of the firms could earn extranormal profits at economically efficient prices. In order to compare the rules for economically efficient prices developed in this analysis with the rules developed elsewhere for the multiproduct monopoly, we have expressed optimal pricing rules for the railroad (the multiproduct firm) in terms of potentially measurable elasticities of demand and markups of price over marginal cost. Rivalry among firms with scale economies alters the form of the usual inverse elasticity pricing rule, so that the efficient percentage markup of price over marginal cost will be greater if a market (such as the coal transportation market) is served by rival firms.

References

Baumol, W., and D. Bradford (1970). "Optimal Departures from Marginal Cost Pricing." *American Economic Review*, 60:265–83.

Baumol, W., J. Panzar, and R. Willig (1982). *Contestable Markets and the Theory of Industry Structure*. New York: Harcourt Brace Jovanovich.

Braeutigam, R. (1979). "Optimal Pricing with Intermodal Competition." *American Economic Review*, 69:38–49.

　　(1984). "Socially Optimal Pricing with Rivalry and Economies of Scale." *The Rand Journal of Economics* 15, no. 1:124–31.

Braeutigam, R., and R. Noll (1984). "The Regulation of Surface Freight Transportation: The Welfare Aspects Revisited," *The Review of Economics and Statistics* 64, no. 1, February: 80–87.

Illinois Department of Energy and Natural Resources (1982). Analysis of Selected Problems Related to Transportation of Illinois Coal. Document 83/02, December.

Kahn, A. (1970). *The Economics of Regulation: Principles and Institutions*, vol. 1. New York: Wiley and Sons.

　　(1981). "Comment." In G. Fromm, ed., *Studies in Public Regulation*, Cambridge, Mass.: MIT Press.

Rieber, M., and S. L. Soo (1977). Comparative Coal Transportation Costs: An Economic and Engineering Analysis of Truck, Belt Rail, Barge and Coal Slurry and Pneumatic Pipelines. Center for Advanced Computation, Report 233, University of Illinois at Urbana-Champaign, August.

Willig, R. (1976). "Consumer's Surplus without Apology." *American Economic Review*, 66:589–97.

CHAPTER 9

Airline deregulation, fares, and market behavior: some empirical evidence

GREGORY D. CALL AND THEODORE E. KEELER

Since airline deregulation began in 1978, there have been many changes in fares, services, and markets. Moreover, in the relatively brief time since deregulation occurred, economists have undertaken several extensive studies of the effects of airline deregulation.[1] These studies have concerned themselves with fares, route structures, services offered between different types of cities and city pairs, entry of new firms, and other topics. Most of the economic studies of deregulation have arrived at very favorable conclusions – deregulation has, by most economists' measures, improved the functioning of airline markets.

Yet some important questions remain. Long before airline deregulation occurred, some of its strongest advocates predicted benefits from it in the form of substantial unrestricted fare reductions on high-density routes (see especially Keeler 1972, 1978, but also Jordan, 1970). While there is plenty of evidence of restricted fare cuts, the existence of such unrestricted cuts has yet to be documented in much detail. Second, there remains considerable controversy about whether the changes in fares and services occurring immediately after deregulation represent permanent or transitory changes. Third, and closely connected to the first two questions, is an issue of more general economic interest: How does the behavior of airline firms and markets during deregulation relate to the economic theory of market behavior? What, if any, existing models of oligopoly behavior can explain the behavior of airline

The authors are, respectively, graduate student in the Law and Economics Program and professor of economics, University of California, Berkeley. They wish to thank the Institute of Transportation Studies of the University of California for financial support for this research and David Parsley for research assistance. They also wish to thank the Office of Economics of the U.S. Civil Aeronautics Board for making data on market concentration and revenue yields available. Useful comments by R. Braeutigam, A. Daughety, D. Fudenberg, R. Gilbert, R. Schmalansee, and members of the Industrial Organization Seminar at the University of California, Berkeley are also acknowledged.

[1] Among these studies are Keeler and Abrahams (1981), Keeler (1981), Meyer et al., 1981, Bailey, Graham, and Kaplan (1983), and Graham, Kaplan, and Sibley (1983).

221

firms and markets during the transition to deregulation? Connected with the aforementioned issues, what might these models predict about future long-term behavior of airline markets under deregulation? And finally, based on what we have observed empirically so far, what direction might future theoretical and empirical research on the airline industry take to get a better understanding of the market behavior occurring under deregulation?

Central to several of the issues mentioned above is a theory developed in the past several years by Bailey, Baumol, Panzar, and others, an economic model labeled the "theory of contestable markets" (Bailey and Panzar, 1981; Baumol, Panzar, and Willig, 1982). If the assumptions of this model are met, then the mere threat of entry of new firms drives existing firms to charge optimal long-run prices. If this is true, then the benefits of deregulation of entry and fares should occur very shortly after deregulation occurs. If, on the other hand, the airline industry fails to meet the assumptions of the theory of contestable markets, then it might well take time and a market equilibration process before the full benefits and costs of airline deregulation are known.

The present chapter considers the issues mentioned (and some interconnected ones) about the economic effects of airline deregulation. The next section summarizes various existing theories of market behavior that offer potential explanations of the airline industry under deregulation. Furthermore, in it, we sketch out the main characteristics of a new and somewhat different model of airline pricing behavior under the threat of entry, one that we believe realistically explains airline market behavior in several ways. The second section considers in some detail the behavior of plane fares from 1977 through 1981, with emphasis on unrestricted fares on the high-density routes alleged to be so important by early advocates of airline deregulation. The third section presents some statistical models of the effects of airline deregulation on plane fares, along with some empirical tests of various theories of firm and market behavior. The final section draws conclusions regarding the issues raised here and suggests some further directions that might be pursued by way of theoretical research to explain what seems to be happening as a result of airline deregulation.

1.   Models of airline market behavior under deregulation

There exist many theories of oligopoly and competitive market behavior that are relevant to the airline industry under deregulation. One well-known theory suggests that airline markets in which market share is concentrated in the hands of fewer firms would have higher fares, all other things equal.[2] In the statistical model presented in the following section, we shall include a test of

[2] See, originally, Bain (1951). For a summary of the many studies and arguments in this literature, see Scherer (1980, ch. 9).

this and some other commonly held theories of oligopoly behavior. But the emphasis will be on one issue: the pricing behavior of firms under the threat of entry. That is because the theoretical issue now considered most controversial about the behavior of the airline industry under deregulation is the extent to which the threat of entry alone drives fares and service levels to long-run equilibrium quantities.

Before discussing the alternative models of airline market behavior under the threat of entry, it is worth making several observations about the airline industry, observations that should be useful in evaluating both theoretical models and empirical results.

First, the costs of entry into an airline city-pair market are likely to be small compared to the costs of entry into, say, heavy manufacturing. If an airline already has planes, then the costs associated with entry into a new city-pair market involve setting up operations in the cities and informing the public of the availability of flights. If the airline already serves the two cities of the city-pair market, then the only cost associated with entry is that of persuading people to use the service.

Second, the costs of many carriers are reasonably well known, available as they are from Civil Aeronautics Board records and from the trade journals.

Third, the costs of new entrants are often below those of the established firms. The established firms built in a high cost structure under regulation.

Fourth, on the demand side, existing major carriers appear to enjoy an advantage, so that consumers prefer to fly on a major carrier, all other things equal. There are several possible reasons for this. (a) Consumers are uncertain about the quality of service available on the new entrants; (b) real quality differences between the trunk carriers and the new entrants exist, such as the network route structure and perhaps the in-flight service which the major carriers offer; (c) slot restrictions at some major airports have traditionally made it more difficult for new airlines to enter some important markets, although attempts are now being made to change this policy. Finally, (d) consumers of air service can probably be divided into at least two distinct groups: personal (including vacation travel on the one hand and visiting friends and relatives on the other) and business travel. The trunks seem generally to enjoy an advantage with business travelers, since they may place more value on the trunks' network structure or face greater uncertainty flying with a new entrant. With these considerations as background, we now survey some relevant models.

1.1. Contestable markets

The theory of contestable markets extends the reach of the invisible hand. If markets are contestable – that is, if entry is free and exit is costless – then many of the theorems of perfect competition apply regardless of how many firms compete in the market. Essentially, then, the argument made by Baumol, Bailey, and others is that if markets are contestable, then prices will be at competitive levels even if there is only one firm in the industry. In a contestable market the actual entry and exit of firms should not affect prices; only the threat of entry, which persists everywhere under airline deregulation, should matter.

On the basis of casual evidence, an airline city-pair market would seem to satisfy some of the conditions of a contestable market. If, for example, a firm offers service from New York to San Francisco, then it would incur only a small cost in offering service from New York to Los Angeles as well. If a firm operated at both points on a route but not the route itself, then there would be almost no fixed costs to entering the city-pair market.

There are, however, also reasons to doubt, a priori, the validity of the contestable markets hypothesis, at least in its purest form, for the airline industry.

First, for a new entrant, establishing recognition and reputation among a significant number of customers could require significant amounts of time and money, thereby bringing in the "sunk" costs that make markets less contestable.

Second, the contestability hypothesis also relies on the assumption that hit-and-run entry is possible. In the airline industry it might be difficult for a new firm to enter a city-pair market before the established firms could reduce their prices and increase quantities. This stems in large part from the fact that entry requires advertising to inform consumers. This advertising will inform the established firms, and they will have time to react.

Consider, for example, the following scenario: (1) Southwest Airlines decides to enter the San Francisco–Los Angeles market on March 1, 1984 at fares below those currently offered. (2) In order to ensure that the planes will not fly empty, Southwest begins advertising on February 1. (3) United and Pacific Southwest Airlines (PSA), the major carriers on the route, get wind of Southwest's plans as a result of Southwest's advertising. (4) On February 15, United and PSA both announce a fare cut to Southwest's level and increase service to begin on March 1. This scenario may be more plausible than assuming Southwest will swoop in before United and PSA can react. It would therefore seem that actual entry, rather than the threat of it, could be necessary to drive fares down to some more "competitive" level in the airline industry.

Despite the theoretical problems with the contestability hypothesis, it is difficult to tell in the absence of empirical evidence how important these problems are. All economic models must to some degree stylize reality in order to work, and it is difficult to tell, a priori, how much of a stylization is too much.

Several researchers have undertaken empirical tests of the contestable markets hypothesis, as applied to the airline industry. So far the results have been mixed and somewhat ambiguous.

The first study to test this hypothesis was that of Bailey and Panzar (1981). To test this question they compare actual coach fares with the Standard Industry Fare Level, focusing their study on low-density routes of the sort served by the regional (local service) carriers. They conclude that in long-haul markets served by local service carriers, the potential entry of trunk carriers seems to make these markets contestable.

Bailey and Panzar do qualify their results, however, by saying that whether airline markets are in general perfectly contestable or not, the important point is that the low-density routes they have looked at are contestable enough that potential entry does as good a job as regulation at keeping fares down. This is a much weaker and perhaps more reasonable position than the assertion that airline markets are perfectly contestable in any absolute sense.

The results of Bailey and Panzar might, moreover, be further qualified on another count: They have looked at a rather small subsample of routes, long-haul, low-density ones. They do not claim that their results generalize beyond these routes.

Two subsequent studies, those of Graham, Kaplan, and Sibley (1983) and of Bailey, Graham, and Kaplan (1984), found some evidence against the contestability hypothesis. Their empirical tests (discussed in more detail below) found that over a cross section of city-pair airline routes higher concentration (controlling for other factors) caused higher fares. This should not happen in contestable markets, because potential entry alone should be adequate in those markets to keep fares down to costs for a given service quality. Thus, these two studies found some evidence against the contestability hypothesis. Subsequently, however, Bailey and Baumol (1984) have argued that the years of transition to deregulation cannot be used to test the contestability hypothesis, because of the dramatic shifts that deregulation caused and the resulting disequilibrium. We shall argue that, although that may be true, a properly specified model can shed more light on the contestability hypothesis even during this transition than previous studies have done.

1.2. Dynamic limit pricing

There are two sets of actors in this model, due to Gaskins (1971) and refined by several more recent studies. These actors include the dominant firm (or dominant-firm group that coordinates its prices) and a competitive fringe. The dominant firm behaves so as to maximize the present value of its profits over time, accounting for the fact that its pricing policy will affect the entry of other firms into the market. The fringe firms, the entrants, are assumed to enter as a continuous function of the price set by the dominant firm. The problem is set up as an optimal control problem, with the dominant-firm group seeking to maximize the following function:

$$\int_0^\infty (P(t) - c(t))(Q(P(t)) - x(t)))\exp(-rt)dt \tag{1}$$

subject to the constraint of the entry condition that

$$dx/dt = k(P(t) - Po), \tag{2}$$

where $P(t)$ is the price of the dominant firm at time t, c is the average cost of production (assumed to be constant) for the dominant firm; $Q(P(t))$ is the total quantity of the good sold at time t by all firms; $x(t)$ is the quantity produced by the competitive fringe; Po is the unit cost of the new entrant; r is the rate at which a firm discounts cash flows; and k is a functional relationship characterizing the speed with which new entrants enter and expand capacity.

In this model $P(t)$ is the choice variable of the dominant firm and will depend on k, so that the faster entry occurs, the lower $P(t)$ will be. To see this, consider the two extreme cases. If entry is slow and k is close to 0, the dominant firm will be able to behave like a monopolist and $P(t)$ will be consistently high. If entry is almost instantaneous, so that k is large, the market will be much like a contestable one and $P(t)$ is likely to be set at or near the competitive level.

In the airline industry the established firms usually do not enjoy a cost advantage, and therefore might behave much like declining dominant firms. In such a case the optimal strategy for the dominant firm is to set the original price between the fringe price and the dominant firm's monopoly price. The firm will earn some monopoly rents while new firms enter, but eventually the firm will lose its dominant position and either go out of business, become a member of the fringe, or (consistent with the behavior of some trunk airlines in 1984) cut its costs.

This model has considerable intuitive appeal applied to airline city-pair markets. In many markets the established firms have failed to match the fares of new entrants, a result consistent with this model. Instead of strictly matching the new entrants' fares, the established carriers have tended to reduce their fares without complete matching.

At least three a priori criticisms can be made of this model in the context of explaining airline market behavior. First, as the dominant firm shrinks, a strict application of the model does not generate rational behavior. As the dominant firm shrinks into oblivion it remains a benchmark for the fringe.

This difficulty probably stems from the second problem, namely that the model probably does not attribute enough strategic rationality to the fringe firms. In other words the fringe's behavior is dependent only on the price charged by the dominant firm at a given time, and thus the fringe does not really play a strategic game of its own. More sophisticated models of dynamic-limit pricing, developed by Milgrom and Roberts (1982), by Matthews and Mirman (1983), and by Judd and Peterson (1984) respond to this criticism of the Gaskins model in that they postulate rational behavior by the fringe. The models of Milgrom and Roberts and Matthews and Mirman, however, probably do not apply well to the airline industry in that they depend on price acting as a signal for cost. In the airline industry most rivals have an accurate idea of the others' costs. The Judd and Peterson model uses a financial constraint on the fringe to justify its limited but steady growth. This model is quite possibly realistic for the airline industry, and its implications for behavior are the same as those of the Gaskins model, so it should be considered as equivalent to the Gaskins model for purposes of empirical prediction of prices.

Closely related to the foregoing points is the third possible objection to the dynamic limit pricing model, which is that in it, the fringe does not know the costs of the dominant firm, responding only to its prices. In the airline industry, members of the competitive fringe are in a strong position to find out the dominant firms' costs.

1.3.   Game-theoretic models

The models that follow allow both the established group of firms and the entrants to behave strategically.

The Cournot oligopoly model offers one possible way of explaining airline market behavior. In a simple Cournot model, with only two periods and two firms, the firms would select respective outputs that maximized their profits assuming the output of other firms remained fixed. In this case the first period would be before the new firm entered. Therefore, firm 1, the established firm, would be the only firm in the market and would maximize its profits under the assumption that the other firm would not produce. This, of course, would put firm 1 at the standard monopoly output. In the second period the entrant, firm 2, would observe the established carrier's output in period 2 and select a level of output that maximized profits assuming firm 1 would not change its level of output. An equilibrium in period 2 would take place in which each firm's assumption that the other would not change its output was realized. A Cournot model could be expanded here in various ways, allowing the Stackelberg behavior on the part of one of the two firms, or allowing for some degree of product differentiation.

But the Cournot-based models are unappealing for the purpose of analyzing airline behavior, for several reasons. First, in airline city-pair markets, firms seem to respond much more readily to price than to quantity in their strategic behavior. Second, the nearsighted behavior that is inherent in the Cournot model is probably not descriptive of firms in the airline industry. Thus, firms would probably rather quickly catch on to each other's reaction functions after the game was played out a few times. (More sophisticated Cournot-based models are beginning to challenge this viewpoint, however; see Daughety, 1985.)

A more realistic and sophisticated alternative to the Cournot model in this context is the judo economics model of Gelman and Salop. They assume that the established carriers enjoy a lexicographic preference for their services over new entrants as follows:

$$q_1 = \begin{cases} D(p_i) \text{ if } p_1 \leq p_2 \\ 0 \text{ otherwise} \end{cases}, \tag{3}$$

$$q_2 = \begin{cases} 0 \text{ if } p_1 \leq p_2 \\ D(p_2) \text{ otherwise} \end{cases}, \tag{4}$$

where q_1 is demand for the incumbent firm and q_2 is demand for the entrant.

Given this set of preferences and the assumption that the entrant's costs are equal to or greater than the established carrier's, a Stackelberg price game without quantity limits will lead to no entry. The established firm faces two choices given a price selection by the entrant. The established firm can match the price and take all the demand, or relinquish the market. As the established firm can make money at any price the entrant might set, the established firm will always meet the entrant's price.

By opting for some limited capacity, however, the entrant can make the choice for the established firm more difficult, if the established firm cannot price-discriminate. In fact, the entrant can select some price and quantity pair such that the established firm should accommodate rather than match the entrant. By accommodating, the established firm loses a share of the market to the entrant but maintains a higher price on the seats it does sell. Just what price prevails depends on the assumption that is made regarding the rationing of the entrant's lower priced seats. If the established firm matched the price of the entrant, then the established firm would lose the profits from the higher price.

The judo economics model predicts that after entry, the entrant will have a small share of the market at some price below that of the established carrier. The main problem with the judo economics model concerns the credibility of the entrant's promise to stay small. If the incumbent firm maintains its full product advantage over the entrant, this is unlikely to be a problem, as the entrant has chosen the price and quantity pair that maximizes its profits given the incumbent firm's reaction function. It seems plausible that the demand advantage enjoyed by the established firm might erode over time as people become informed about the entrant. If the demand advantage eroded, then the promise of the entrant to stay small would not remain credible.

It should also be noted that the judo economics story is sensitive to the assumptions made about the comparative costs of the dominant firm and the new entrant. If the entrant is assumed to have lower costs, as is often the case in airline markets, then the entrant in the Stackelberg price game without quantity limits will set its price marginally below the costs of the established firm. Under these circumstances, the established firm would be priced out of the market.

To correct for this problem, Gelman and Salop suggest another direction in which their model could be expanded to allow dominant firms with higher costs to coexist with smaller, lower cost firms. That would be to allow explicitly for product differentiation, rather than simply a lexicographic preference for the dominant firm. In airline markets the importance of product differentiation likely varies among different users. For example, some business travelers may attach great importance to frequent schedules and a large, single-carrier route network, perhaps with first-class service, whereas a pleasure traveler may place little value on these comforts and conveniences.

Fudenberg and Tirole (1984), extending some ideas of Schmalensee (1983), develop a model that is useful in understanding how segmentation of the market on the demand side on the part of trunk carriers affects their strategies of pricing under the threat of entry. In this model, firm 1 in period 1 can establish a monopoly among certain customers by reaching them through advertising. In the second period, both firm 1 and firm 2 can select levels of advertising and prices simultaneously.

Each firm desires to increase its price for its monopoly customers and lower its price for its competitive customers, but the model assumes that this is not possible. The higher the degree of product differentiation, Fudenberg and Tirole find, the larger the incumbent's captured market and the smaller the incentive the incumbent has to match the entrant's price. They conclude that "the large captive market makes the incumbent a pacifist fat cat." We now sketch a way to allow some aspects of the Schmalensee–Fudenberg–Tirole model to be applied to the specific conditions of the airline industry. Following Schmalensee, Fudenberg and Tirole, we shall call this the "fat cat" model.

The application presented here produces the same result as that of Fudenberg and Tirole, namely the incumbent with a large captured market will be reluctant to match the entrant's price, at least unless the incumbent firm can discriminate completely between those customers who prefer its product and those who are indifferent between its product and that of the new entrant.

Naturally this application requires some stylized assumptions. For simplicity we assume that there exist two classes of travelers: business travelers and vacation travelers. For the vacation traveler the service provided by the new entrant is a perfect substitute for the service provided by the established carrier. The business traveler, on the other hand, is captured by the established carrier. The incumbent might well provide network service that the business traveler finds very important, or greater frequency, or better on-board service. The vacationer's demand is assumed to be more price-elastic than that of the business traveler.

In period 1, firm 1's maximization depends on whether or not the firm can price-discriminate between business travelers and tourists. In either case, firm 1 will act as if it were a monopolist. (We assume that the established firm is able to match the fare cuts of new entrants quickly; this point was made in the discussion of contestable markets.) Conditions for profit maximization are then identical to those for a discriminating or nondiscriminating monopolist; that is, marginal cost equals marginal revenue.

In period 2, we assume that firm 2 enters, so that the demand curve that firm 1 faces changes. The established firm's monopoly status is now limited to the business market. In the tourist market we assume the same lexicographic preference for the incumbent carrier assumed by Gelman and Salop.

First, consider the case in which the established firm, firm 1, can price-discriminate, and the two firms have the same cost structure. To take advantage of its strong position with the business traveler, the incumbent firm will continue to try to charge a monopoly price in that market. On the other hand it will try to "match" the fare of the new entrant not perfectly, but by adding restrictions attempting to make the fare reduction applicable only to the tourist market. Thus, the incumbent firm will not necessarily reduce its regular, unrestricted fare in response to the new entrant, but will rather reduce its restricted fares – those with advance-purchase and length-of-stay requirements, which are often capacity-controlled – as well (indeed, to facilitate such market segmentation, one carrier, Frontier, has even established a "fighting brand" airline, Frontier Horizon, with lower fares than its parent). In the business market, the established firm would continue to act like a monopolist. If each carrier knew the other's costs, the established firm could always block entry into the tourist market. As the entrant would know this, the entrant would not even attempt to enter, and price would remain at the monopoly level in the tourist segment, as well. If, however, the entrant had lower costs, then the entrant would price its fares below the established firm's competitive price and would in fact enter the tourist market and take that business away from the incumbent carrier.

A rather different situation arises when it is assumed that the incumbent carrier cannot price-discriminate. (This assumption might be rejected as unrealistic, but there is some truth to it. Fares such as the super-saver fare do not segment the market anywhere near completely. Some business travelers are able to meet super-saver restrictions, whereas some discretionary travel does not occur because the travelers cannot meet these restrictions.)

Under these assumptions, the incumbent firm will have less of an incentive to lower fares under entry. If the incumbent firm reduces its fares to match the lower fares of a new entrant, it sacrifices profits earned from business travelers. It is possible that under these circumstances, even without a cost advantage on the part of a new entrant, the new entrant will come in with a lower fare and attract a significant part of the tourist market. On the other hand, the incumbent carrier might even end up *raising* its fare as a result of the entry, because now its only market to consider will be the business market, with a less elastic demand.

The picture just sketched is a stylized one in many ways. For example, profitability evidence for incumbent carriers does not support the view that the major trunk airlines coordinate their fares and schedules well enough on routes with no low-fare entrants to earn monopoly profits. And, at some high fares on the part of the majors, most business travelers would indeed substitute low-fare carriers for majors, if they had the choice. Nevertheless, the story just told indicates clearly why major carriers might choose to match new entrants only partially, or perhaps not at all, in fare reductions.

With the exception of the contestability model, all the models discussed so far are best applied to the period of transition to a deregulated airline environment, rather than trying to provide a long-run indication of what is happening. The fat-cat model just described, for example, will cease to apply over time: as the new entrant airline becomes better established, it will be able to expand frequencies, build up its network, and become more trusted by business people as a means of travel. Thus, for example, Southwest Airlines, a low-cost carrier, is very widely used by business travelers in Texas and the southwest, and it has developed a fairly extensive route network in that part of the United States. Incumbent firms there have either had to match its fares or to abandon markets to it. One should expect that to happen in other areas as low-fare carriers become established. This suggests that perhaps some very different pricing behavior is likely to occur in the airline industry over the longer run. What will happen on that count, of course, requires some speculation. We shall make some guesses on that count later in this chapter, but first it is appropriate to consider some empirical evidence on airline pricing behavior during the transition, testing some of the hypotheses set forth in the models we have described.

2.   The behavior of air fares since deregulation

To analyze the behavior of plane fares since 1977, and to test the hypotheses described in the preceding section of this chapter, we have calculated fares for the eighty-nine largest interstate airline markets in the United States. Obviously, since deregulation, there have been many different fares on a given route, so it is necessary to do some consistent simplification of the data to make sense of them. For these purposes, to analyze the impact of deregulation on fares for high-density routes, we have collected three different data series annually for the 1977–81 period.[3]

They are, first, the highest regular, unrestricted coach fare, used by major trunk carriers on direct or nonstop flights, involving no discounts (this variable we have named COACH).

Second, we found the lowest unrestricted fare widely available on trunk airline flights (this variable we have named MAJOR). Though these are available on all flights, they are sometimes capacity-controlled, but sometimes they are not, especially when they are made to match the fare reductions of new entrants with lower fares (more about that later).

Third, we calculated the lowest unrestricted fare available daily on any nonstop or one-stop flight (this variable we have named CHEAP). Often this fare is charged by a newly certificated carrier, or a formerly intrastate carrier expanding to new markets.

Because of the effects of changing costs, it is necessary to correct these fare estimates over time. To do so, we have divided each fare estimate by the Standard Industry Fare Level (SIFL), which was previously used by the Civil Aeronautics Board to set the regulated (unrestricted) coach fare. This not only standardizes the results for cost changes, but it also gives some measure of how the fare in question compares with what the regulated fare would have been at a given time. It is worth noting, however, that between 1974 and 1976, the CAB reduced the regulated coach fare by about 20 percent, in response to the criticism that coach fares were too high and were cross subsidizing first class. It may be, as well, that the CAB reduced coach fares in this way to forestall pressure for deregulation. In any event, for most of the years of regulated plane fares, especially during the 1960s and 1970s, the regulated coach fare would have stood not at the SIFL, but rather at about 1.25 times that level.[4]

Table 9.1 presents summary evidence on means and standard deviations for all these fares for the sample of eighty-nine city pairs, for each of the years from 1977 through 1981. Table 9.2 lists the city pairs in our sample.

Based on these figures, it should be quite evident that on almost every route, unrestricted discount fares have fallen since deregulation. This goes not only for CHEAP, the fare charged by the lowest fare carrier, but also for MAJOR, the lowest fare widely available on trunk carriers.

---

[3] Sources are as listed in Table 9.1. A data appendix, summarizing all the fare data given in Table 1 for each of the eighty-nine city pairs in the sample, is available on request from the us.

[4] For a description of the Domestic Passenger Fare Investigation, see Douglas and Miller (1974, chap. 4).

Table 9.1. *Summary evidence on plane fares for eighty-nine city pairs*

Year and fare type	Mean	Standard deviation
1977		
COACH	1.0288	.0837
MAJOR	1.0133	.0943
CHEAP	1.0115	.0926
1978		
COACH	.9847	.0626
MAJOR	.9327	.1484
CHEAP	.9255	.1354
1979		
COACH	1.0640	.088
MAJOR	.9943	.1428
CHEAP	.8936	.226
1980		
COACH	1.2372	.1040
MAJOR	.8881	.3007
CHEAP	.8132	.3002
YIELD	.8530	.1936
1981		
COACH	1.2703	.1106
MAJOR	.8830	.3099
CHEAP	.7540	.2626

Source: COACH, MAJOR, and CHEAP come from the *Official Airline Guide,* North American Edition, and *The Official North American Passenger Tariff,* various years. YIELD data were kindly provided by the Office of Economics of the U.S. Civil Aeronautics Board.

It is worth noting that the fare cuts discussed here are all based on unrestricted fares. Obviously, given the wide range of restricted fares available, the typical passenger is likely to have paid less than the fares shown here. For one year, 1980, we have estimates of revenue yields for each city pair, a measure of the actual fare paid rather than the unrestricted fare. Table 9.1 summarizes evidence for this variable and indicates that the fare paid was in many cases below even the numbers we have cited.

As regards the highest unrestricted coach fares charged by the trunk airlines, it would first appear that they rose under deregulation, and in the strictest sense, they did. But on this count it is worth remembering that for all but the last two years or so of airline regulation, regulated coach fares were in fact set at about 1.25 times the SIFL. It appears that with the advent of

Table 9.2. *List of city pairs in sample*

Observation number and city pair	Observation number and city pair
1. Atlanta–Chicago	46. Detroit–New York
2. Atlanta–Miami	47. Detroit–Tampa
3. Atlanta–New York	48. Detroit–Washington
4. Atlanta–Tampa	49. Fort Lauderdale–New York
5. Atlanta–Washington	50. Fort Lauderdale–Philadelphia
6. Boston–Chicago	51. Honolulu–Los Angeles
7. Boston–Fort Lauderdale	52. Honolulu–San Francisco
8. Boston–Los Angeles	53. Houston–Los Angeles
9. Boston–Miami	54. Houston–New Orleans
10. Boston–New York	55. Houston–New York
11. Boston–Philadelphia	56. Indianapolis–New York
12. Boston–San Francisco	57. Las Vegas–Los Angeles
13. Boston–Washington	58. Las Vegas–New York
14. Buffalo–New York	59. Los Angeles–Miami
15. Charlotte–New York	60. Los Angeles–Minneapolis
16. Chicago–Cincinnati	61. Los Angeles–New York
17. Chicago–Cleveland	62. Los Angeles–Philadelphia
18. Chicago–Dallas	63. Los Angeles–Phoenix
19. Chicago–Denver	64. Los Angeles–Portland
20. Chicago–Detroit	65. Los Angeles–Salt Lake City
21. Chicago–Fort Lauderdale	66. Los Angeles–St. Louis
22. Chicago–Houston	67. Los Angeles–Seattle
23. Chicago–Kansas City	68. Los Angeles–Washington
24. Chicago–Las Vegas	69. Miami–New York
25. Chicago–Los Angeles	70. Miami–Philadelphia
26. Chicago–Miami	71. Miami–New York
27. Chicago–Minneapolis	72. Minneapolis–New York
28. Chicago–New York	73. New Orleans–New York
29. Chicago–Orlando	74. New York–Newfolk
30. Chicago–Philadelphia	75. New York–Orlando
31. Chicago–Phoenix	76. New York–Pittsburgh
32. Chicago–Pittsburgh	77. New York–Raleigh
33. Chicago–St. Louis	78. New York–Rochester
34. Chicago–San Francisco	79. New York–St. Louis
35. Chicago–Tampa	80. New York–San Francisco
36. Chicago–Washington	81. New York–Syracuse
37. Cincinnati–New York	82. New York–Washington
38. Cleveland–New York	83. New York–West Palm Beach
39. Columbus–New York	84. Philadelphia–Pittsburgh
40. Dallas–Los Angeles	85. Portland–San Francisco
41. Dallas–New York	86. Portland–Seattle
42. Denver–Los Angeles	87. San Francisco–Seattle
43. Denver–New York	88. San Francisco–Washington
44. Denver–San Francisco	89. Seattle–Spokane
45. Detroit–Los Angeles	

deregulation, trunk carriers took the opportunity to raise their highest fares back to the levels persisting before 1974 under CAB regulation. But there is plenty of evidence that very few people paid these fares. This is confirmed not only by the evidence presented here on unrestricted discount fares and revenue yields, but also by the fact that in 1981, only 25 percent of all U.S. air travelers traveled at full coach fare (that is, the variable labeled COACH in Table 9.1), compared with 62 percent in 1977.

It would thus seem safe to say that by and large, deregulation has resulted in lower plane fares on higher density routes. But the evidence presented in this section also indicates that fare levels vary widely from route to route. The question then is what has caused fares to fall more on some routes than on others.

3.   A statistical model

Three previous studies have attempted to explain statistically the behavior of plane fares since deregulation. The first, that of Keeler and Abrahams (1981) uses relatively early, 1977 data on the behavior of unrestricted plane fares in the top ninety markets. Although their data did not reflect anywhere near the full effects of deregulation, they nevertheless found a significant relation between fares charged, concentration, and entry. Thus, concentrated markets (measured with Herfindahl statistics) tended to have higher fares than unconcentrated markets. And entry of a new firm on a given route also caused fares to fall.

Two subsequent studies, those of Graham, Kaplan, and Sibley (1983) and Bailey, Graham, and Kaplan (1984) are very similar in terms of specification, outlook, and data used, as well as having two coauthors in common. For the present discussion, we shall emphasize the second study of the two, because it seems to represent a refinement and improvement of the first. This study requires fairly detailed discussion here, because many of the issues of specification and estimation which it deals with are relevant to the present study, as well.

Bailey, Graham, and Kaplan's model, estimated over a large cross section of city pairs, is based on two equations: a price equation (derived in turn from a combination of a cost equation and a markup equation based on market structure) and a demand equation.

The price equation is specified to include the following variables:

$$P = P(\text{DIST, PAX, TS, NEWC, SLOTS, HERF, HUB}), \qquad (5)$$

where P is the average revenue per mile earned by all carriers on the route; DIST is the distance between the cities, PAX is the annual flow of passengers on the route; TS is a measure of the service quality which passengers most desire on the route (proxied by income and a set of dummies for vacation routes); NEWC is a dummy equal to one if there is a newly certificated airline on the route, and zero otherwise; SLOTS is a set of dummy variables equal to one if one of the cities in the pair is a slot-restricted airport; HERF is a Herfindahl statistic, measuring concentration on the route; and HUB is a set of dummy variables reflecting structural differences of large hubs (all routes out of the Atlanta hub have an Atlanta hub value of 1; all that do not have a value of zero; similarly, all routes out of Dallas have a Dallas hub value of 1, and a Dallas value of zero otherwise; there is thus a hub dummy variable for each hub).

The demand equation was specified as follows:

$$PAX = F(P, DIST, INC, POP, TS), \tag{6}$$

where INC is income for travelers in a market, POP is the product of the populations served in the markets, and the other variables are as in the previous equation.

Bailey, Graham, and Kaplan estimated these equations simultaneously, with PAX an endogenous variable, and alternatively with HERF as endogenous and exogenous variables. They argue that results based on treating HERF as exogenous are the more meaningful ones, both because a test for exogeneity (of the sort proposed by Hausman, 1978) indicated that it should be so treated, and because collinearity between HERF and PAX rendered their estimates with HERF treated as endogenous to be of doubtful accuracy.

Their results treating HERF as exogenous gave significant evidence of a positive relation between concentration and fares, controlling for other variables, giving some reason to question the contestability hypothesis. They note that based on their point estimates, a move from a monopoly (HERF = 1) to a relatively competitive market (HERF = 0.25) would reduce fares by only 11 percent, so that the concentration variable is both significant and of some (though not extremely large) quantitative importance in their equations.

As a motivation for specification of our model, several comments about the model of Bailey, Graham, and Kaplan are appropriate.

First, why not include in the price equation a variable reflecting the entry of trunk carriers on to new routes? Bailey, Graham, and Kaplan indeed find that newly certificated entrants have a very strong and significant negative effect on fares. But they argue that this is not a refutation of contestability because the new carriers are not large enough to represent an important threat. However, a variable reflecting the entry of trunk carriers would represent a very fair and direct test of the contestability hypothesis: If trunk air fares are lower where a trunk carrier enters, that is strong evidence against the contestability hypothesis.

Second, as we have argued, revenue yield is not the only relevant measure of plane fares. Especially to test some of the oligopoly theories we previously mentioned, it is useful to test the effects of market structure on some other relevant measures, discussed below.

Third, the HUB variable used by Bailey, Graham, and Kaplan is not only difficult to justify theoretically, but use of it is likely to cause a serious downward bias in the coefficients of the concentration and entry variables. The following example should explain why. The Atlanta hub is strongly dominated by Delta Airlines, and, to some degree, Eastern. All other airlines there are weak, so the Herfindahl statistic for most routes out of Atlanta is likely to be quite high, and many potential entrants are also reluctant to take on Delta and Eastern at that hub. Not surprisingly, fares out of Atlanta tend to be high. One of Bailey, Graham, and Kaplan's hub dummies is a variable equal to one for routes touching Atlanta and zero otherwise. Its coefficient is likely to be positive, and it is likely to "soak up" some of the variation in fares that should rightly be explained by the high concentration and lack of entry into the Atlanta hub. Thus, inclusion of the hub dummy will bias the coefficients of the Herfindahl statistics and the entry barriers, and bias them in the direction of making them look smaller. (And of course, over time, one would expect other airlines to overcome these barriers to some degree, expanding into Atlanta and lowering fares there, an effect that inclusion of the hub dummy ignores and will fail to predict.)

Third, based on the preceding argument, there is a strong a priori reason for treating concentration as an exogenous variable in addition to the empirical test for exogeneity mentioned previously. That is that during the first several years of deregulation, established carriers are likely to keep much of their market shares, even with some fare cutting by new entrants. This means that for these years, it is reasonable to treat concentration as relatively exogenous and not jointly determined with fares. It also means that Bailey, Graham, and Kaplan were correct in treating their NEWC variable (for entry of new carriers) as exogenous, despite the argument that new entry might be endogenous, occurring where fares are highest. As the case of the Atlanta hub indicates, higher fares do not necessarily guarantee the most rapid new entry (a reason to be skeptical of the dynamic-limit pricing model).

To test the hypotheses discussed earlier in this chapter, and to get a clearer sense as to what has happened to various categories of plane fares as a result of airline deregulation, we present a somewhat different model from those of previous papers, along with tests on a wider variety of plane fares as data.

First, regarding plane fares, we have tested our model on four alternative measures, all of which have been defined in the previous section. Thus, COACH is the highest standard coach fare, the highest one available on most nonstop flights. MAJOR is the lowest unrestricted fare available (albeit perhaps with capacity controls) during the daytime on any trunk carrier. Next down the line, CHEAP is the lowest unrestricted fare available on any carrier.

Often, such a fare may be charged only by a new entrant or a formerly intrastate carrier. Finally, the variable AVFARE is the average revenue yield over all carriers.

Using these four different measures of plane fare, we have estimated the following equation to analyze the determinants of these fares.

$$\text{FARE/SIFL} = A1 + A2\ \text{HERF} + A3\ \text{DIST} + A4\ \text{ED} +$$
$$A5\ \text{WB\%} + A6\ \text{TR} + A7\ \text{NTR} + A8\ \text{SLOT} \tag{7}$$

In this equation, HERF is the Herfindahl index for nonstop flights for the city-pair market in the sample for the fourth quarter of 1980.[5] The Herfindahl index measures market concentration. The contestability hypothesis suggests that this variable should have no effect on fare charged. However, under the context of the dynamic limit pricing model, concentration may be positive in its effect on fares (signifying that a dominant firm group can price more monopolistically with higher concentration, at least until entry occurs on a sufficiently large scale).

DIST measures the distance between the cities in a specific city-pair market.[6] The expected sign of this variable is negative. There are two reasons to believe that the sign will be negative, most importantly because it is believed by many that the SIFL index tends to overstate costs on long-haul routes.

ED is a measure of the elasticity of demand for city-pair markets, as estimated by Michael Abrahams (1980).[7] Demand elasticity can measure two intertwined effects. First, if fares rise with a lower demand elasticity, all other things equal, it indicates that firms price to take advantage of market power, so that the market does not appear to be contestable. Second, a low demand elasticity may measure a preference on the part of travelers for high service quality rather than low prices. Under this interpretation, a high fare charged where demand elasticities are low is consistent with competitive market behavior. Because these elasticities are structural coefficients from a simultaneous equations model, they can reasonably be treated as exogenous.

WB% measures the percentage of total flights that are widebodies.[8] It has been hypothesized that on those routes well suited to widebodies, fare wars are more likely, because of excess capacity of widebodies dating from day of regulation.

---

[5] The Herfindahl statistics were kindly provided by the Office of Economics of the U.S. Civil Aeronautics Board. They reflect market shares of all traffic on nonstop and one-stop flights in relevant city pairs.

[6] This variable was taken from the *Official Airline Guide*, North American Edition.

[7] In some cases, Abrahams found price coefficients of the wrong sign and insignificant. In that case, we assume a demand elasticity of 0.

[8] These data were calculated from the *Official Airline Guide*, North American Edition.

TR represents entry by trunks and former local service carriers. It takes a value of 1 if an established airline has entered the market since deregulation and 0 otherwise.[9] This is a key variable in determining the validity of the contestable market theory. If markets are contestable the actual entry of new firms (especially ones with the same costs as existing firms) should have no effect on price. A significant negative sign for this variable would thus be inconsistent with the contestable markets theory but consistent with the declining dominant firm theory of pricing and the fat-cat theory.

NTR is the entry variable for nontrunks. As with TR this is a key variable for testing the theory of contestable markets. In addition NTR is a key variable for testing the judo economics theory. If the Gelman–Salop model describes these markets accurately, then entry by nontrunks should have little effect on unrestricted fares of trunk carriers, COACH and MAJOR. Furthermore, if the "differentiated-product" model we developed is correct, entry by nontrunks should also have little effect on unrestricted trunk fares.

SLOT is a dummy variable, set at the value 1 if there are slot restrictions (and there were even before the controllers' strike of 1981) on a dominant airport in at least one of the cities of the city pair and 0 otherwise. Cities with airports having such restrictions include New York, Washington, and Chicago (though it is worth noting that all these cities have at least one airport not controlled by these slot restrictions). This variable controls for the fact that in these three cities, the most desirable airports from a location (or connection) point of view have a scarcity of capacity to accommodate planes. We should therefore expect flights using these airports to charge a premium fare. Because there are satellite airports in all these cities, we should not expect it to affect the lowest fares available. And this variable might or might not affect the highest unrestricted fares, given the already high levels of these prices. But one would expect fewer low or discount fares to be available from the capacity-constrained airports, so that at very least this variable should cause revenue yields overall to be higher for city pairs including these cities.

In a comparison of the above equation with the price equation of Bailey, Graham, and Kaplan, several important differences stand out. Our equation is somewhat akin to their "structure" equation, rather than their price equation, in that it is based on a markup over trunk costs (SIFL), rather than fare itself. This should not substantively affect the comparison, except that distance is much less likely to have an effect (it will do so only if the SIFL distance taper is inaccurate).

Also, we have not included a density coefficient. That is because we have restricted our sample to the eighty-nine densest routes, using sample selection

---

[9] This was determined by the changes in carriers serving each city pair between 1977 and 1980, as observed in the *Official Airline Guide*, North American Edition.

to control for this variable rather than inclusion in the equation (indeed, when it was included, it was not generally significant, and its sign shifted around, whereas it was negative and significant even in the ordinary-least-squares specification of Bailey, Graham, and Kaplan). The effects of deregulation on many variables could differ with density – indeed, as argued by Keeler (1972), the effects of deregulation on high-density routes could be quite different from its effects on low-density routes. Exclusion of the density variable has an added advantage of being the only variable that could reasonably be treated as endogenous in the Bailey, Graham, and Kaplan model. All the variables in the equation to be estimated here can be reasonably treated as exogenous (or, more accurately, unlikely to be correlated with the error term; see the discussion of the concentration and entry variables earlier), so that ordinary least squares over a cross section should yield consistent estimates of the coefficient.

Equations were thus run, using ordinary least squares, for each of the fare measures mentioned above, for the year 1980 (data for 1981 and 1982 are likely to be contaminated by the effects of the air traffic controllers' strike), using a cross section of high-density city pairs.

The results of these regressions are shown in Table 9.3. We consider each variable in turn. The distance variable is consistently negative, suggesting that the SIFL indeed seems to overstate costs on long hauls relative to short hauls.

The Herfindahl statistic is consistently positive, indicating that at least during the transition to long-run equilibrium, firms in more concentrated markets indeed manage to coordinate fares more effectively. And, except in the case of the MAJOR variable, the standard errors on the Herfindahl coefficient are low enough to suggest some degree of significance for the coefficients. As in the case of the results of Bailey, Graham, and Kaplan, these results would also seem to go against the contestability hypothesis. In terms of the magnitude of the Herfindahl coefficient, our results are in some ways very much like those of Bailey, Graham, and Kaplan. For example, if we use the Herfindahl coefficient along with the revenue yield variable for fare (as they did), we find that a shift from a monopoly to four equal-sized firms ($H = 0.25$) would reduce the fare (divided by the SIFL) by $0.75 \times 0.142 = 0.105$. Since the fare for a monopolist is likely to be above the SIFL, it follows that the reduction occurring from a shift to four firms will be below 10.5 percent, compared with the 11 percent estimate of Bailey, Graham, and Kaplan.

Of course, a shift from a monopolist to four firms will have effects through the entry variables in our specifications, as well as through the Herfindahl statistic. And for the most part, entry variables display the expected sign and are significant.

Specifically, our results show that the entry of a trunk into a new market should, on the average, reduce the lowest unrestricted trunk fare by 23 per-

Table 9.3. *Regression results*

Independent variable	Dependent variable and coefficient[a]			
	COACH	MAJOR	CHEAP	YIELD
R squared	.441	.459	.435	.607
Constant	1.1981	.9802	.7574	.9271
	(.0403)	(.1196)	(.1222)	(.0561)
Distance (thousands miles)	−.0005	−.3370	−.1142	−.1355
	(.0231)	(.6866)	(.0716)	(.0322)
Herfindahl	.1241	.2052	.4992	.1417
	(.0615)	(.1826)	(.1866)	(.0857)
Trunk entry	.0087	−.2271	−.1472	−.0750
	(.0185)	(.0549)	(.0561)	(.0258)
Nontrunk entry	.0159	−.1761	−.3150	−.0056
	(.0190)	(.0564)	(.0577)	(.0265)
Demand elasticity	−.2776	−.3231	−.3147	−.1512
	(.0437)	(.1299)	(.1327)	(.0609)
Slot restriction	.0199	.0462	.0378	.0723
	(.0200)	(.0593)	(.0606)	(.0278)
Widebody percentage (WB%)	.1980	.1980	.4833	.1072
	(.1507)	(.1506)	(.1540)	(.0707)

[a]Standard errors are in parentheses.

centage points of the SIFL, and should reduce revenue yield by 7.5 percentage points of the SIFL. This provides further evidence against the contestability hypothesis. One could possibly argue that the effect of the entry of new carriers on trunk fares does not represent a good test of the contestability hypothesis, because the new carriers may have lower costs. But if the contestability hypothesis were correct, entry of carriers with identical costs and product characteristics should not affect fares.

On the other hand the highest coach fare seems unresponsive to entry or to many other variables. It would seem that that fare is a relatively well-coordinated "list price" used by the trunks, responsive mainly to concentration and to market demand elasticity (the strong significance of the demand-elasticity variable would seem to suggest that the trunks do a good job of coordinating these prices at profit-maximizing levels; the problem is, of course, that the marketplace will not too frequently let the carriers charge them). It is also possible that a lower demand elasticity may pick up a preference for a higher quality of service, and the full coach fare may be charged to passengers preferring this.

On the other hand the lowest unrestricted fare charged by trunk carriers, labeled MAJOR, is highly responsive to market conditions. The carriers seem to reduce that fare in response to the behavior of both other trunks and low-fare carriers. This suggests that the trunk carriers do not always believe that they have enough market power to ignore their low-fare competitors, so dominant-firm and product-differentiation models apply here only if firms reduce this fare on a seat-restricted basis and price-discriminate in that manner.

The variable reflecting the lowest unrestricted fare offered by any carrier, including new airlines, is responsive to both trunk entry and nontrunk entry, but, predictably, it is slightly more responsive to nontrunk entry. This is consistent with the idea that it is the new airlines (and former intrastate ones) that have been most aggressive in reducing unrestricted fares.

Of the entry variables, the revenue-yield variable, AVFARE, is most responsive to trunk entry. This is again consistent with the hypothesis that trunks are more likely to cut fares on a restricted basis when they compete aggressively, whereas low-fare carriers cut unrestricted fares.

The demand-elasticity variable is negative and significant in all the equations, though not so much so in the last three as in the first. This suggests, as expected, that fare variables reflecting the true competitive state of the market will include less price discrimination than those fares representing what the dominant-form group tries to get when it controls a market. In fact, it is quite possible that the values of the demand-elasticity variables in the last three equations represent not price discrimination, but a natural response of the market to provide a price-service-quality combination in line with the quality preferences of a given market (thus, a market with a high demand elasticity is more likely to prefer low prices with lower frequencies and more crowded flights than a market with low demand elasticities).

The slot restriction variable behaved as predicted. It is consistently positive, but it is significant only in the revenue yield equation. Lowest unrestricted fares seem unaffected by these restrictions, because they apply either to uncrowded airports or times the main airports are less crowded. On the other hand the revenue yield responds to this variable, probably because the trunk carriers sell fewer seats at discount fares from the restricted airports, reflecting the land rents that these airports command.

The widebody variable did not perform as expected. Very likely it is not exogenous to the equation. For example, it is quite possible that the trunk carriers use widebodies on many of their more profitable routes, using them as a device for service-quality competition with other trunks, rather than engaging in fare competition (after all, the widebodies were originally bought as service-competition weapons on the long-haul, high-density routes, where regulation originally kept fares especially high relative to costs). If this variable were to be treated as endogenous (contrary to the widebody hypothesis initially posited), it would make sense to exclude it. Doing so had a negligible effect on any coefficient save in some cases the distance coefficient (the distance variable is, not surprisingly, correlated with the widebody variable).

4. Implications

What are we to make of these results? What do they imply about the main issues raised at the beginning of this chapter, namely the hypothesis that plane fares should fall on an unrestricted basis (at least gradually) on high-density routes? What do they imply about the various theories of market behavior advanced earlier in this chapter, particularly the contestable markets hypothesis?

First, the evidence strongly supports the hypothesis that unrestricted fares have fallen on high-density routes, and that the fall has not been immediate, but gradual, occurring with the entry of new and existing firms on to new routes. The implication of this is that it would have been a serious mistake to try to draw long-run implications from airline pricing behavior in the first years after airline deregulation. The benefits of airline deregulation in the form of low, unrestricted fares has not been fast in coming, but they have been sure and steady.

To those who have studied the airline industry for any length of time, these results cannot be too surprising. The first experience with "deregulated" airline markets was with the California intrastate markets in the late 1950s and early 1960s (see Jordan, 1970). For a number of years, the major intrastate carrier, Pacific Southwest Airlines (PSA) occupied a tiny part of the market. Even after it got competitive aircraft in 1958 (Lockheed Electra turboprops), it occupied a small part of the market until around 1963 when it got jet aircraft. Furthermore, with limited capacity, it charged a fare below that of most of its trunk competitors, who felt little need to match its fares as long as its market share was low. By 1963, however, its market share had grown so much that it was the largest carrier in the Los Angeles–San Francisco market, and it acquired jet aircraft totally competitive with the trunk carriers. At that time the trunk carriers matched its fares.

In the story of the California markets, the reader should by now recognize the story of the declining dominant-firm group in the behavior of the trunk carriers. They did not initially match the fares of the intrastate carriers, and by the time they did, the intrastate carriers were an important component of the market. Meanwhile, the trunk carriers earned more profit as they lost market share.

In the aggregate, the trunk carriers have behaved in the same way all over the United States since airline deregulation. They have charged relatively high coach fares, matching competitors oftentimes only if the competitors enter on a large scale. As a result, the trunks have lost market share to smaller airlines.

The market share of the trunk carriers in the U.S. market in fact fell from 87 percent in 1978 to 80 percent in 1981 (see Bailey, Graham, and Kaplan, 1984).

Thus, just as it would have made no sense to assume that the structure and fare level of California intrastate routes represented long-run results in 1959 or 1962, so it would be equally a mistake to try to infer that the deregulated interstate routes represented long-run equilibria in the late 1970s and early 1980s.

What do these results imply for the contestable markets hypothesis as applied to the airline industry? Based on the empirical evidence from transition years presented here, they would seem to provide evidence against it. Our evidence is consistent with that of Graham, Kaplan, and Sibley and of Bailey, Graham, and Kaplan, in that we have found that higher concentration in an airline market seems to cause higher fares, all other things equal, and the order of magnitude of our coefficients is the same as theirs. This is inconsistent with the contestability hypothesis. But our results are stronger than those of other studies, in that they show that the entry of trunk carriers on to new routes has a negative and significant effect on fares. This effect is strong for both restricted and unrestricted fares, but it is especially strong for unrestricted fares.

Bailey and Baumol (1984) have argued that because contestability represents a long-run concept, it cannot be expected to apply for at least the first several years during the transition to a deregulated equilibrium. Low-cost carriers simply do not have the capacity or the market reputation to be able to expand enough to be a realistic price threat to the trunks, and as a result, the trunks will not price to preempt the new carriers.[10] Undoubtedly, there is much truth to this argument, and potential entry may play a greater role in determining plane fares in the long run than in the first few years of deregulation. Nevertheless, our results cast some doubt on the contestability hypothesis for the airline industry (at least in its purest form), even for the long run. Given that most trunk carriers have roughly the same costs, and that their capacity is seemingly adequate for rapid entry into new routes, if the contestability hypothesis were correct, the entry of trunk carriers on to new routes would not affect trunk fares. Our statistical evidence goes against that hypoth-

---

[10] Bailey and Baumol (1984) thus argue that with a displacement of equilibrium as large as airline deregulation, entry lags are an important deterrent to the functioning of contestability. The theoretical argument that entry lags could prevent the contestability model from working was first made by Reynolds and Schwartz (1983). It is worth noting, though, that Bailey and Baumol argue against Reynolds and Schwartz in the same 1984 article that entry lags are in fact not an important deterrent to the functioning of the contestability model, that only sunk costs really matter. So their stand on this is somewhat ambiguous.

esis. We shall speculate more at the end of this chapter about the future structure of the airline industry under deregulation and the likely validity of Bailey and Baumol's predictions, but first it is appropriate to discuss the implications of our results for other theories of oligopoly behavior.

Of the various theoretical models discussed earlier, we found that an extension of the Fudenberg–Tirole fat-cat model seemed to best fit the circumstances of the airline industry in transition. It assumes that a major airline enjoys some advantage in product differentiation over new entrants, especially for certain groups of travelers, such as business travelers. It suggests the hypothesis that a large airline with this advantage will generally not match the lower fares of new entrants completely. If possible, it will match those cuts on a discriminatory basis. Thus, if the new carrier caters mainly to vacation travelers, it will impose advance-purchase and minimum-stay requirements on its lower fares. It might also limit the number of seats available at the lower fare. To the extent that the established carrier cannot discriminate perfectly, it will be content simply not matching the fare cut for some passengers and letting the business go to new entrants, preferring instead to reap the benefits of its product differentiation in the form of high fares for the passengers who stay with it.

Although our empirical evidence may be somewhat mixed in its support of the fat-cat theory, it nevertheless supports that theory. The evidence indicates that to a significant extent, the large airlines do match new entrants, both trunk and nontrunk, when they enter with lower fares. However, even when they are not restricted through advance-purchase or length-of-stay requirements, such lower fares are more often than not capacity-controlled. Thus, last-minute travelers on trunk airlines are often still left with very high unrestricted coach fares, and, as we have seen, these seem quite unresponsive to new entrants, while being very responsive to perceived market demand elasticity. This seems quite consistent with the fat-cat behavior hypothesized earlier in this chapter.

But in analyzing pricing behavior in the deregulated airline industry, it is important to distinguish long-term trends from short-term aberrations. By whatever means it is happening in the short run, over the longer run the low-cost airlines are expanding to new markets, and fares are falling on an unrestricted basis wherever the new airlines go. And as the low-cost carriers have expanded, they have gained sufficient acceptance on the part of travelers that the older airlines have had to match their fares (consider the cases of Southwest Airlines in Texas and Aircal and PSA in California). This is not to say that there is no place for a high-quality airline offering better service at higher fares. Indeed, some low-cost carriers, including Air One, Regent Air, New York Air, and Midway Metrolink, have recently used their cost advantage to provide better service than the trunks without charging higher fares. The point is simply that as time goes on, and as new firms enter and expand, the major carriers are likely to lose their market superiority, and whatever monopoly power they were able to exercise in charging fares will disappear. This, in turn, would suggest that over the longer pull, oligopoly models may give way to models of competition (or possibly monopolistic competition) in explaining air fares and service. Firms will simply not have any discretionary power over fares as some seem to have now, and passengers who want the benefits of low unrestricted fares without too many frills will be able to get them, at least on the higher density routes. (As those of us who advocated airline deregulation some years before it happened noted, regulated fares on low-density routes may have been too low. It is less than obvious that deregulation will bring lower unrestricted fares to low-density routes. Few people have argued that it would.)

The validity of the contestability hypothesis in the long run for the airline industry is dependent on the extent to which potential entry is adequate to keep fares and service qualities at or near optimal levels. There is already some evidence that potential entry will play an important role in setting those fares (Bailey and Panzar, 1981). And there are some routes with very low plane fares which are nevertheless monopolistic (these are mainly short-haul routes in Texas served by Southwest). Moreover, even before the concept of contestability was current, proponents of air deregulation believed that potential entry could be important in keeping fares down on monopolistic routes (see, for example, Keeler, 1978, p. 112; contestability theory does, of course, afford a clearer understanding of how potential entry might affect prices).

If this "competitive" long-run scenario for the airline industry is correct, it is likely that potential entry (whether precisely consistent with the contestability hypothesis or not) will play a more important role in setting fares than it does now. For now, however, the airline industry (on high-density routes) seems to be one of fat-cat oligopolists pursued by lean and hungry new entrants (or even hungrier new entrants risen from the ashes of bankrupt trunks).

References

Abrahams, M. B. (1980). Estimating the Demand for Air Travel: A Simultaneous Equations Approach. Unpublished PhD Thesis, University of California, Berkeley.

Bailey, E. E. and W. J. Baumol (1984). "Deregulation and the Theory of Contestable Markets." *Yale Journal on Regulation,* 1, no. 2:111–37.

Bailey, E. E., D. R. Graham, and D. P. Kaplan (1984). *Deregulating the Airlines: An Economic Analysis.* Cambridge, Mass.: MIT Press.

Bailey, E. E., and J. Panzar (1981). "The Contestability of Airline Markets during the Transition to Deregulation." *Law and Contemporary Problems,* 44:177–95.

Bain, Joe S. (1951). "Relation of Profit Rate to Industrial Concentration: American Manufacturing, 1936–1940." *Quarterly Journal of Economics,* 65:293–324.

Daughety, Andrew (1985). "Reconsidering Cournot: The Cournot Equilibrium Is Consistent." *Rand Journal of Economics,* forthcoming.

Douglas, G. W., and J. C. Miller III (1974). *Economic Regulation of Domestic Air Transport: Theory and Policy.* Washingt, D.C.: The Brookings Institution.

Fudenberg, Drew, and Jean Tirole (1984). "The Fat-Cat Effect, The Puppy-Dog Ploy, and the Lean and Hungry Look." *American Economic Review,* 74:361–66.

Gaskins, Darius W. (1971). "Dynamic Limit Pricing: Optimal Pricing under the Threat of Entry." *Journal of Economic Theory,* 3:306–22.

Gelman, J. R., and S. C. Salop (1983). "Judo Economics: Capacity Limitation and Coupon Competition." *The Bell Journal of Economics,* 14, no. 2, Autumn: 315–25.

Graham, David R., Daniel P. Kaplan, and David S. Sibley (1983). "Efficiency and Competition in the Airline Industry." *The Bell Journal of Economics,* 14:118–38.

Hausman, J. A. (1978). "Specification Tests in Econometrics." *Econometrica,* 46:1251–71.

Jordan, William (1970). *Airline Regulation in America.* Baltimore: The Johns Hopkins University Press.

Judd, Kenneth, and Bruce Peterson (1984). "Dynamic Limit Pricing and Internal Finance." Working Paper no. 603S, Center for Mathematical Studies in Economics and Management Science, Northwestern University, Evanston, Ill.

Keeler, Theodore E. (1972). "Airline Regulation and Market Performance." *The Bell Journal of Economics,* 3:399–424.

  (1978). "Domestic Trunk Airline Regulation: An Economic Evaluation," In U.S. Senate, Committee on Governmental Affairs, *Study on Federal Regulation,* appendix to vol. 6, *A Framework for Regulation.* Washington, D.C.: U.S. Government Printing Office, pp. 75–162.

  (1981). "The Revolution in Airline Regulation." In L. Weiss and M. Klass, eds, *Case Studies in Regulation: Revolution and Reform.* Boston: Little, Brown, pp. 53–85.

Keeler, Theodore E., and Michael Abrahams. "Market Structure, Pricing, and Service Quality in the Airline Industry under Deregulation." In Werner Sichel and Thomas Gies, eds., *Applications of Economic Principles in Public Utility Industries.* Ann Arbor: Division of Research, Graduate School of Business Administration, University of Michigan, pp. 103–20.

Matthews, Steven A., and Leonard J. Mirman (1983). "Equilibrium Limit Pricing: The Effects of Private Information and Stochastic Demand." *Econometrica,* 51:981–996.

Meyer, John R., Clinton V. Oster, Jr., Ivor P. Morgan, Benjamin A. Berman, and Diana L. Strassman (1981). *Airline Deregulation: The Early Experience.* Boston: Auburn House.

Milgrom, Paul, and John Roberts (1982). "Predation, Reputation, and Entry Deterrence," *Journal of Economic Theory,* 27:280–312.

Reynolds, R., and M. Schwartz (1983). "Contestable Markets: An Uprising in the Theory of Industry Structure: Comment." *American Economic Review,* 73:488–90.

Scherer, Frederick M. (1980). *Industrial Market Structure and Economic Performance.* 2nd ed. Boston: Houghton Mifflin.

Schmalensee, Richard (1983). "Advertising and Entry Deterrence," *Journal of Political Economy,* 91:636–53.

Index

Pages in *italics* indicate page for bibliographic reference at the end of the first chapter making the reference. **Boldface** page references indicate that the item appears on that page in a table or figure.

Abrahams, M. B., 238, *246*
airline deregulation
  air fare behavior, 231–**233**, 235
  discussion, 221–223
  test of contestable markets model, 237–243
Allen, W. B., 15, *22*
American Petroleum Institute, 92, *94*
Avriel, M., 169, 173, *203*

Bailey, E. E. and W. J. Baumol, 225, 244, *246*
Bailey, E. E., D. R. Graham, and D. F. Kaplan, 221, 225, 244, *246*
  discussion of analysis, 235–237, 239–240
Bailey, E. E. and J. C. Panzar, 222, 225, 246, *246*
Bain, J. S., 222, *246*
Barton, A., 73, *94*
Baumol, W. J. and D. F. Bradford, 18–19, *22*, 208, 215
Baumol, W. J., J. C. Panzar, and R. D. Willig, 8, *23*, 79–80, 121, 123–124, 134, 174, 183, 211, 222
Baumol, W. J. and H. D. Vinod, 15, *23*
Berndt, E. and D. O. Wood, 56, *63*
Borts, G., 9, *23*
Boyer, K. D., 15–**16**, *23*, 180, *203*
Braeutigam, R. R., 4, 19, 22, *23*, 207–208, 216–217, *220*
Braeutigam, R. R., A. F. Daughety, and M. A. Turnquist, 9, **10**, *23*, 99
Braeutigam, R. R. and R. G. Noll, 18, *23*, 210
Bronzini, M. S., 163, 198, *203*
Bronzini, M. S. and D. Sherman, 164, *203*

carrier output
  flow, 5–7, 121–123, 129–134, 179–183, 188–189
  aggregate, 7–8, 91, 99–101
  passenger-miles, 8, 104
  ton-miles, 7–8, 38–39, 71, 91, 104
  market paths, 5–8, 13, 15
  product mix, 6–8, 38, 71, 79–80
  service characteristics, 6–9, **10–12**, 13–15, **16–17**, 130–134, 180, **187**–189
CACI Inc., 163–164, 168, **170**, 189, 197, *203*
Call, G. D. and T. E. Keeler, 18, *22*
Caves, D. W., L. R. Christensen, and J. A. Swanson, **10**, *23*, 31, 97–98, 100, 104, 111–**112**, 118, 119
Caves, D. W., L. R. Christensen, J. A. Swanson, and M. W. Tretheway, 104, *120*
Caves, D. W., L. R. Christensen, and M. W. Tretheway, 105, *120*, 126
Caves, D. W., L. R. Christensen, M. W. Tretheway, and R. J. Windle, 8, **11**, 19
characterizations of carrier technology, 4–9, 19–21, 30–36, 66–73, 99–102
economies (*see also* cost elasticities)
  density, 8, 20, 79, 84–85, 97–99, 100, 102, **107**, 108–**112**
  scale/size, 8, 20, 51–53, **54–55**, 97–99, 101–102, **107**, 108–**112**, 117–119, 131
  scope, 8, 79–80, 131
  factor demand elasticities, 56, **57–59**, 60, 80–**81**, 82, 88–**89**
  homotheticity, 15, Í9, **44**–45, 60, 82–83, 124
  structure, 4–9, 39–40, **41**, **44**–45, 69, 82–83, **84**–85, 99–102, 111–**112**, 128–131
  substitution elasticities, 53, 55–56, **57**–**58**, 59, 80–**81**, 82, 88–**89**, 126
  subtechnologies, 85–90
  technical change, 19, 45–60, **61–62**, 65
Charles River Associates Inc., 189, *203*
choice-based sampling, 21, 138, 146–147, 151–157

Christensen, L. and W. Greene, 72, *94*
Christensen, L., D. Jorgenson and L. Lau, 69, *94*
coal slurry pipelines, 208–209, 219–220
  rivalry with railroads, 208–209
Coslett, S. R., 146, 152, *157*
cost elasticities (*see also* characterization of carrier technology)
  average length of haul, 19–20, 48–**49**, 50–51, **76, 78,** 80, *107*
  average length of trip, **107**
  average load, 19–20, 48–**49,** 50–51, **76, 78,** 80
  average size of shipment, 19–20, 48–**49,** 50–51, **76, 78,** 80
  insurance, 19–20, 48–**49,** 50–51, **76, 78,** 79–80
  network, 8, 20, 100–101, 108–109
  output, 8, 20, 51–**53, 53–55,** 79, 106–**107,** 108–111
  percent LTL, 48–**49,** 50–51
  prices, 44, 71, 91–92
    capital (and materials), 55–**57, 58–59,** 80–**81, 88–89,** **107**
    equipment, 55–**57, 58–59**
    fuel, 55–**57, 58–59,** 79–**81, 88–89, 107**
    labor, 55–**57, 58–59,** 79–**81, 88–89, 107**
    purchased transportation, 55–**57, 58–59,** 80–**81, 88–89,** 92–**93**
  route-miles, **107**
  time, 32–33, 46–**47, 61–62**
cost functions
  general carrier cost model, 7–8, 179–180
  general shipper cost model, 13–15
  delivered price model, 178–179
  motor carrier, **11–12,** 30–36, **42–43,** 66–73, **74–76,** 78
  railroad, **10–11,** 101–102, 105, **107, 114–117**
  use of duality properties, 7, 14, 56, 67–69, 80–81, 82–**83,** 84–85, 99–101, 127–128
Cowing, T. and R. Stevenson, 30, *63*

Dafermos, S., 172, 192, *203–204*
Das, C., 15, *23*
data descriptions/sources
  carriers, **10–12,** 196–202
    airlines, 231–237
    motor carriers, 36–39, 71–72, 90–94
    railroads, 104–105, **113–114**
  shippers, **16–17,** 145–146, 196–202
Data Resources, Inc., 197, *204*
Daughety, A. F., 15, *23,* 68, *94,* 228, *247*
Daughety, A. F. and F. S. Inaba, 15, **16,** 18, *23,* 186

Daughety, A. F., F. D. Nelson, and W. R. Vigdor, 8, 9, **12,** 19–20
Daughety, A. F., M. A. Turnquist, and S. L. Griesbach, 9, **11,** *23*
DeVany, A. S. and T. Saving, 180, *204*
Dobesh, L. J., 66, *94*
Douglas, G. and J. Miller, 18, *23,* 232
Dupuit, J., 18, *23*

economies of scale
  (*see* characterizations of carrier technology, cost elasticities)
Ellet, C. (Jr.), 3, 18, *23*

Färe, R. and J. Logan, 68, *94*
Federal Railroad Administration, 197–**199**
Fernandez, J. E. and T. L. Friesz, 162, 168, 181, *204*
firm-specific effects, 37, **54–55, 61–62,** 70–72, **76–78, 81,** 84–85, **89,** 98–99, 101–105
Fisk, C. W. and D. E. Boyce, 172, 185–187, *204*
freight network equilibrium model (FNEM), 166–**167,** 168–169, **170,** 171, 175
  example of use, 196–200
Friedlaender, A. F., 3, *23*
Friedlaender, A. F. and S. S. Bruce, 8, 9, **12,** 19
Friedlaender, A. F. and R. H. Spady, **10–11,** 15, **17–18,** *23,* 36–37, 44, 56, 65, 70, 83, 97–98, 103, 111–**112,** *118–119,* 186
Friedlaender, A. F., R. H. Spady, and S. J. Wang Chiang, **11,** *23,* 65
Friedlaender, A. F. and S. J. Wang Chiang, 29, 31, *63*
Friesz, T. L., J. Gottfried, and E. K. Morlok, 168, 175, 196, 198, 200, *204*
Friesz, T. L., J. Gottfried, R. E. Brooks, A. J. Zielen, R. Tobin, and S. A. Vleleski, 166, 175, 189, 197, *204*
Friesz, T. L. and P. T. Harker, 18, 21–22
Friesz, T. L., P. T. Harker, and R. L. Tobin, 189, *204*
Friesz, T. L. and E. K. Morlok, 172, 175, *204*
Friesz, T. L. and R. L. Tobin, 189, *204*
Friesz, T. L., R. L. Tobin, and P. T. Harker, 18, *24,* 189, *204*
Friesz, T. L., P. A. Viton, and R. L. Tobin, 173, 182, 185, 187, 192, *204*
Fudenberg, D. and J. Tirole, 22, *24,* 229–231, 245

Gaskins, D. W., 225–227, *247*
Gartner, N. H., 168, *204*

Gelman, J. R. and S. C. Salop, 228–229, *247*
generalized spatial price equilibrium model (GSPEM)
  examples of use, 193–196, 200–202
  formulation, 190–192
Gottfried, J. A., 189, 196–198, 200, *204*
Graham, D. R., D. P. Kaplan and D. S. Sibley (*see also* Bailey, Graham and Kaplan), 18, *24*, 221, 225, 235, 244
Grilliches, Z., **10**, *24*

Hanoch, G., 82, *95*
Harary, F., 5, *24*
Harker, P. T., 18, *24*, 172, 179, 186–187, 189–192, 200, 202, *204–205*
Harker, P. T. and T. L. Friesz, 172–173, 179, 186, 188–192, 202, *205*
Harmatuck, D. J., **10, 12**, *24*, 29, 38, *63*, 65, 97–98, 103, **112**, *118*, 121
Harris, R. G., 8, **10**, *24*, 97–98, 103, **112**, 118
Hartman, P. and G. Stampacchia, 184, *205*
Hasenkamp, G., 9, *24*
Hausman, J. A., 236, *247*
Heaver, T. D. and J. C. Nelson, 186, *205*
Hedonic cost model, **11–12**, 37, 66, 69–70, **83**
Hotelling, H., 18, *24*
Hsieh, D., C. Manski, and D. McFadden, 146, 151–155, 157, *157*

Illinois Department of Energy and National Resources, 208, *220*
indexed quadratic function
  aggregation properties, 21, 126–128, 130–131
  restricted (RIQ), 21, 123–126
Interstate Commerce Commission, 197, *205*
Isard, W., 163, *205*

Jara-Diaz, S., 9, *24*
Jara-Diaz, S. and C. Winston, 9–**10**, *24*, 122
Jordan, W., 221, 243, *247*
Joskow, P. L. and R. C. Noll, 68, *95*
Judd, K. and B. Peterson, 227, *247*
Judge, G., W. Griffiths, R. Hill, and T.-C. Lee, 73, *95*

Kahn, A., 207, *220*
Keeler, T. E., 8, **10**, 18, *24*, 97–98, 103, **112**, 118, *119*, 174, 221, 240, 246–*247*
Keeler, T. E. and M. Abrahams, 221, 235, *247*
Keeler, T. E. and K. A. Small, 180, *205*

Keenan, J., 69, *95*
Kinderlehrer, D. and G. Stampacchia, 184–185, *205*
Klein, L., 9, *24*
Koenker, R., **11**, *24*, 29
Kornhauser, A. L., M. Hornung, Y. Harzony, and J. Lutin (Princeton Model), 166, **170**, *205*
Kresge, D. T. and P. O. Roberts, 163, *205*

LaMond, A. M., *95*
Lansdowne, Z. F., 165, **170**, *205*
Leamer, E., 84, *95*
Lemke, C. E., 184, *205*
Levin, R. C., 15–**16**, 18–19, *24*
Locklin, D. P., 3, *24*

McFadden, D. F., 7, 14, *24*, 67, 69, 82, 99, 150, *157*
McFadden, D., C. Winston, and A. Boersch-Supan, 15, **17**–18, 21
Manski, C. and S. Lerman, 154, *157*
Manski, C. and D. McFadden, 151, 153–154, *157*
Marcotte, P., 172, *205*
market models, 18–19
  contestable markets
    discussion, 223–225, 243–246
    previous test in airline markets, 225, 235–237
  Cournot, 227–228
  dominant firm model, 225–227
  fat-cat effect, 229–231, 245–246
  game theoretic, 227–231
  judo economics, 228–229
  limit-pricing, 225–227
  Stackelberg, 227
Matthews, S. A. and L. J. Mirman, 227, *247*
maximum likelihood
  asymptotic covariance matrix for estimator, conditional (CML), 153–154, 156–157
  full information concentrated (FICLE), 146–147, 153–154, **155**
  iterated Zellner's method as asymptotically ML, 73, 106
  weighted exogenous sample (WESML), 154–**155**
Meyer, J. R., C. V. Oster, Jr., I. P. Morgan, B. A. Berman, and D. L. Strassman, 221, *247*
Milgrom, P. and J. Roberts, 227, *247*
Moore, T. G., 68, 79, *95*, 151, *157*
Morlok, E. K., 171, 185, *205*
Mundlak, Y., 37, *63*, 98–99, 101–102, 111–112, *120*

Nahmias, S., 139, *157*
networks, 4–**17**, 66–67, 129–131
   attributes, **10–12, 16–17**, 67, 71–72, 80
   effect on technological structure, **83**–85
   as operating characteristics (*see* produc-
      tivity measurement)
   equilibrium models (*see* predictive freight
      network models)
   multicopy, 176–**177**, 178
   nodes and arcs, 4–6, 9, 13–14, 66–67,
      129
   origin and destination pairs, 5–6, 13,
      128–129, 146–147, 151–153, 175–
      176
   paths, 4–9, 13, 129–131
   perceived, 175–176
   representation, 4–7, 13, 20–21, 67, 70–
      72, 100–101, 105, 129–131
   shipper-carrier equilibrium problem simul-
      taneous, 171–189
   size
      length of haul, 71
      route miles, 101, 105, 108–112
   technologies, 4–5, 67, 69, 82–85, 128–
      131
   unobserved network effects, 98, 101–102,
      104–105, 109–112
   variational inequality formulations, 173,
      183–185

Oum, T. H., 15, **17**–18, *24*

Panzar, J. C., 133, *135*
Panzar, J. C. and R. D. Willig, 100, *120*
Pang, J. S. and D. Chan, 192, *205*
Pegrum, D. F., 3, *24*
Peltzman, S., 4, *24*
Peterson, E. R. and H. V. Fullerton, 164–
   165, **170**, *205*
predictive freight network models
   discussion, 162–169
   typology, 169–**170**, 171–172
pricing
   deviations from marginal cost, 18–19,
      207–208, 217, 220
   first best, 18
   second best (Ramsey), 19, 207–208
   optimal rules with intermodal competition
      binding profit constraints, 218–219
      interdependent demands, 219
   viable firm Ramsey optimum (VFRO)
      characterizations, 213–219
      definition, 211
      industry configurations, 211–212

productivity measurement, 19, 30–36
   input effect, 32–36, 40–41, 53, 55–**57**
   operating characteristics effect (*see also*
      networks, attributes), 32–36, 40–41,
      48–**49**, 50–51
   output effect, 32–36, 40–41, 51–**55**
   pure productivity effect, 36, 46–48

Ramsey, F., 18, *24*
Reebie Associates, 197, *205*
Reynolds, R. and M. Schwartz, 244, *247*
Rieber, M. and S. L. Soo, 208, *220*
Roberts, P. O., 163, *205*
Roberts, P. O. and D. H. Dewees, 197, *206*
Rockafeller, R. T., 184, *206*

Samuelson, P. A., 161, *206*
Scarf, H., 183, *206*
Scherer, F. M., 222, *247*
Schmalensee, R., 22, *25*, 229, *247*
Shephard, R. W., 7, *25*, 82, 106, *120*
shipper demand
   delivered price model, 178–179
   derived demand, 13–15
      conditional, 14
      unconditional, 15, 138–142
   elasticities of mode choice probabilities,
      149–151
      rates, **150**
      time, **150**
   inventory models, 138–142
   joint probability of size and mode choice,
      143–144
   modal characteristics, 13–14, 138–139,
      141, 147–**148**, 149, **187–189**
   mode choice, 143–144, **148**–149, **155–
      156**
   network aspects, 9, 13, **170**, 175–**177**,
      178–179
   quantal choice models, 15–18
   shipper characteristics, 9, 13, 138–139,
      141, 147–**148**, 149
   shipment size, 139–**141**, 142–145, **148,
      155**
   shipping interval, 139–**141**, 142
Smith, M. J., 172, *206*
Smith, T. Z., 192, *206*
Smith and Hutchinson, 198, *206*
Spady, R. H., 21
Spady, R. H. and A. F. Friedlaender, **11**,
   25, 65–66, 70, 79, 83
Stevenson, R., 30–31, *63*
   basic model for decomposing tech-
      nological growth, 31–33

time-augmented model, 33–37
  estimated cost model, **42–43**
  test of augmented model, 40–**41**
Stigler, G., 4, *25*

Takayama, T. and G. G. Judge, 161, *206*
Tan, H. N., S. B. Gerschwin, and M.
  Athans, 172–173, *206*
Tobin, R. L. and T. L. Friesz, 189, *206*
Tobin, R. L., J. D. Jastrow, and S. A.
  Meleski, 190, 200, *206*
Townsend, H., 15–**16**, *25*
transcendental logarithmic function (translog)
  expanded (cubic and quartic), 19, 31, 33–
    35, **42–43,** 69–70, 72, **74–76, 78**
  generalized (Box-Cox), 105–106
Transportation Systems Center, 197, *206*
Trapani, J. M. and C. V. Olson, 18, *25*
Trincs Incorporated, 90, *95*

Uzawa, H., 56, *63*
United States Department of Transportation,
  144–145, *157*

Wagner, H. M., 163, *206*
Wang Chiang, S. J., 39, *63*
Wang Chiang, S. J. and A. F. Friedlaender,
  9, **12,** *25,* 29, 38, *63,* 65, 121
Wardrop, J. G., 162, *206*
Wardrop's principles, 162, 164, 166, 172,
  181
Willig, R., 210, *220*
Wilson, A. G., 197, *206*
Winston, C., 3, 15, **17,** 19, *25,* 122, 137
Wyckoff, D. D. and D. Maister, 39, *63*

Zellner, A., 73, 106, *120*